Data Science for Effective Healthcare Systems

Data Science for Effective Healthcare Systems has a prime focus on the importance of data science in the healthcare domain. Various applications of data science in the healthcare domain have been studied to find possible solutions. In this period of the COVID-19 pandemic, data science and allied areas play a vital role in dealing with various aspects of healthcare. Image processing, detection and prevention from the COVID-19 virus, drug discovery, early prediction, and prevention of diseases are some thrust areas where data science has proven to be indispensable.

Key Features

The book offers comprehensive coverage of the most essential topics, including:

- Big Data Analytics, Applications and Challenges in Healthcare
- Descriptive, Predictive and Prescriptive Analytics in Healthcare
- Artificial Intelligence, Machine Learning, Deep Learning and IoT in Healthcare
- Data Science in Covid-19, Diabetes, Coronary Heart Diseases, Breast Cancer, and Brain Tumor

The aim of this book is to provide the future scope of these technologies in the healthcare domain. This book will surely benefit research scholars, persons associated with healthcare, faculty, research organizations, and students to get insights into these emerging technologies in the healthcare domain.

Chapman and Hall/CRC Internet of Things: Data-Centric Intelligent Computing, Informatics, and Communication

The role of adaptation, machine learning, computational Intelligence, and data analytics in the field of IoT Systems is becoming increasingly essential and intertwined. The capability of an intelligent system is growing depending on various self-decision-making algorithms in IoT Devices. IoT-based smart systems generate a large amount of data that cannot be processed by traditional data processing algorithms and applications. Hence, this book series involves different computational methods incorporated within the system with the help of Analytics Reasoning, learning methods, Artificial intelligence, and Sense-making in Big Data, which is most concerned in IoT-enabled environment.

This series focuses to attract researchers and practitioners who are working in Information Technology and Computer Science in the field of intelligent computing paradigm, Big Data, machine learning, Sensor data, Internet of Things, and data sciences. The main aim of the series is to make available a range of books on all aspects of learning, analytics and advanced intelligent systems and related technologies. This series will cover the theory, research, development, and applications of learning, computational analytics, data processing, machine learning algorithms, as embedded in the fields of engineering, computer science, and Information Technology.

Series Editor:
Souvik Pal
Sister Nivedita University, (Techno India Group), Kolkata, India

Dac-Nhuong Le
Haiphong University, Vietnam

Security of Internet of Things Nodes: Challenges, Attacks, and Countermeasures
Chinmay Chakraborty, Sree Ranjani Rajendran and Muhammad Habib Ur Rehman

Cancer Prediction for Industrial IoT 4.0: A Machine Learning Perspective
Meenu Gupta, Rachna Jain, Arun Solanki and Fadi Al-Turjman

Cloud IoT Systems for Smart Agricultural Engineering
Saravanan Krishnan, J Bruce Ralphin Rose, NR Rajalakshmi, N Narayanan Prasanth

Data Science for Effective Healthcare Systems
Hari Singh, Ravindara Bhatt, Prateek Thakral and Dinesh Chander Verma

Data Science for Effective Healthcare Systems

Edited by
Hari Singh
Ravindara Bhatt
Prateek Thakral
Dinesh Chander Verma

CRC Press
Taylor & Francis Group
Boca Raton London New York

CRC Press is an imprint of the
Taylor & Francis Group, an **informa** business

A CHAPMAN & HALL BOOK

First edition published 2023
by CRC Press
6000 Broken Sound Parkway NW, Suite 300, Boca Raton, FL 33487-2742

and by CRC Press
4 Park Square, Milton Park, Abingdon, Oxon, OX14 4RN

© 2023 selection and editorial matter, [Hari Singh, Ravindara Bhatt, Prateek Thakral and Dinesh Chander Verma]; individual chapters, the contributors
CRC Press is an imprint of Taylor & Francis Group, an Informa business

Library of Congress Cataloging-in-Publication Data
Names: Singh, Hari, 1957- editor.
Title: Data science for effective healthcare systems / edited by Hari
Singh, Ravindara Bhatt, Prateek Thakral, Dinesh Chander Verma.
Description: First edition. | Boca Raton : Chapman & Hall/CRC Press, [2023]
| Series: Internet of things: data-centric intelligent computing,
informatics, and communication | Includes bibliographical references and
index. | Identifiers: LCCN 2022003644 (print) | LCCN 2022003645 (ebook) |
ISBN 9781032105680 (hardback) | ISBN 9781032307503 (paperback) |
ISBN 9781003215981 (ebook)
Subjects: LCSH: Medicine—Data processing. | Medical informatics. |
Medicine—Information technology.
Classification: LCC R858 .D3779 2023 (print) | LCC R858 (ebook) | DDC
610.285—dc23/eng/20220401
LC record available at https://lccn.loc.gov/2022003644
LC ebook record available at https://lccn.loc.gov/2022003645

ISBN: 978-1-03-210568-0 (hbk)
ISBN: 978-1-03-230750-3 (pbk)
ISBN: 978-1-00-321598-1 (ebk)

Visit the Taylor & Francis Web site at
http://www.taylorandfrancis.com

and the CRC Press Web site at
http://www.crcpress.com

DOI: 10.1201/9781003215981

Typeset in Palatino
by codeMantra

Contents

Preface

This book primarily introduces the importance of data science in the field of healthcare. Data science has proven to be a gamechanger in the optimization of disease prevention, drug discovery, diagnosis, treatment, hospital operation, and post-care monitoring. Initially, the basic concepts, applications, and challenges related to data science will be covered to lay down a strong foundation for its importance in healthcare. A large volume of data is generated in healthcare in processes primarily from clinical trials, genetic information, electronic medical records (EMRs), billing, wearable data, care management databases, scientific articles, social media, and internet research. A global pandemic like COVID-19 has dramatically increased the need and the importance of data science and analytics.Data science in healthcare industry is mainly used for predictive analysis that uses artificial intelligence, machine learning, deep learning to predict possibility of an event occurring in the future based on known present variables and facts. The various available and emerging tools and techniques to manage this voluminous healthcare data results in improving patient outcomes and reduce healthcare costs. Various techniques such asregression and classification have been covered here for better insights into healthcare data analysis and its related advantages. This book also focuses on the importance of visual analytics to observe the medical history of a patient for further courses of action to cure the diseases. This book is also meant to enlighten the importance of data science in drug discovery, pandemic like COVID-19 needs fast simulation techniques to observe the reaction of drugs inthe body so that the drug can be approved by competent authorities and used to cure the disease.

In nutshell, the tools and techniques of data science have changed the way to manage, analyze, and leverage healthcare data for better and optimized prediction.The main motive of this book is to bring the research and findings together for clear directions for future work.

Editors

Dr Hari Singh has been an Assistant Professor (Senior Grade) in the Department of Computer Science and Engineering and Information Technology at Jaypee University of Information Technology, Solan, HP, India since 2018. He has a PhD, MTech and B.Engg.(Honors) in Computer Science and Engineering. He earned his PhD degree from Thapar University, Patiala, Punjab, India in 2017. He has more than twenty years of teaching experience that includes significant administrative and research experience. His areas of interest are Databases, Data Science, Big Data Analytics, Distributed and Parallel Computing, Grid Computing, Cloud Computing, and Machine Learning. He has many awards, honors, and recognitions to his credit. He delivered several invited/expert talks on recent research topics at renowned institutes and universities. He has published several research papers in SCI/Scopus, peer-reviewed International Journals and book chapters. He has also presented and published many research papers in National/International Conferences. Dr Singh has also worked as an editor of proceedings of various International/National Conferences. He has attended/participated in several workshops at reputed Institutes/Universities/Organizations. He has organized several Conference/Seminar/Workshops. He has supervised Post Graduate Thesis/Dissertations and handled an AICTE sponsored research project under the RPS scheme and one consultancy project. He has been a member of professional societies, such as CSI, ISTE, IEEE, and has been a member/reviewer of several Scopus-Indexed journals.

Dr Ravindara Bhatt is an Associate Professor in the Department of Computer Science and Engineering and Information Technology at Jaypee University of Information Technology, Waknaghat, India. Ravindara joined the Department of Computer Science and Engineering and Information Technology, Jaypee University of Information Technology, in 2006. Ravindara earned his PhD degree from Indian Institute of Technology, Kharagpur. Dr Ravindara has over 20 years of extensive experience in Academics and Industry. His areas of interest are Data Science, Big Data, Machine Learning, and Wireless Sensor Networks. He has published several research papers in SCI/Scopus, peer-reviewed International Journals. He has also presented and published many research papers in National/International Conferences and is a reviewer for various renowned International journals.

Mr Prateek Thakral is currently an Assistant Professor in the Department of Computer Science and Engineering, Jaypee University of Information Technology, Waknaghat Solan. He has earned a B.Tech in Information Technology and an M.Tech in Computer Engineering from Kurukshetra University, Kurukshetra in 2010 and 2013, respectively. Before joining JUIT, he was an Assistant Professor (on contract) at the National Institute of Technology Kurukshetra for four years. He has 8 years of teaching experience in total. He has published about 10 research papers as various reputed book chapters, journals and international conferences. He is currently serving as a member of the Computer Society of India (CSI).

Dr Dinesh Chander Verma holds a PhD(CSE), MTech(IT), MCA and MPhilin in Computer Science. He has more than 17 years of teaching experience that includes significant administrative, research, and industrial exposure. He has delivered many expert talks, chaired sessions, and reviewed a good number of research articles. His areas of interest include Machine Learning, MANET, IoT, and Data Science. He is a Life Member of the Indian Society for Information Theory and Applications (ISITA). He has published several research articles, book chapters in Scopus/UGC Care/ESCI indexed journals. He has authored two books for UG courses and published one patent too. He has conducted several conferences/seminars/FDPs on recent emerging technologies and has mentored many industrial live projects on emerging technologies.

1

Big Data in Healthcare: Applications and Challenges

Monika
Panipat Institute of Engineering & Technology

Pradeep Kumar and Sanjay Tyagi
Kurukshetra University

CONTENTS

DOI: 10.1201/9781003215981-1

1.1 Introduction

The healthcare industry might be considered a key source of big data. Personal information such as nationality, date of birth, location, sex, education, and income, as well as other specific data concerning the patient's history with medical datacenters, healthcare, and disease are all included in healthcare data. It is produced constantly in acute care units and surgical operating rooms, as well as inbound from every digital process in systems [1]. Figure 1.1 shows some scenarios from where big data is collected from the healthcare system.

The enormous amount of data can assist in offering improved healthcare outcomes. Big data analytics assist in analyzing huge amount of records and identifying solutions to numerous underlying problems simultaneously. When it comes to processing huge data, big data analytics can help to save money. Any disease that can exist and be cured anywhere in the world can be accurately predicted. Different statistical, data mining, and machine learning methodologies can be used in big data exploration. Using numerous analytical setups, the healthcare field has a lot of chances for offering effective disease cures [2].

According to a study after 2011, big data in healthcare surpassed 150 exabytes and data size is expected to be over 40 ZB in 2020, around 50 times what it was in 2009 [3]. At least 4% of health data was migrated in the healthcare industry to the cloud in the previous years, with that number predicted to rise to 20.5% [4].

1.2 Types of Data in Healthcare

1.2.1 Business, Organizational, and External Data

Administrative, scheduling, billing, financial, and other non-health and non-clinical data that were not previously linked.

FIGURE 1.1
Some scenarios of big data collected from healthcare.

1.2.2 Patient Sentiment and Behavior Data

Mobility sensor data includes sensor data or streaming data from home monitoring, medical monitoring, telehealth, smart devices, and sensor-based wireless. Biometric data includes fingerprints, handwriting, and iris scans.

1.2.3 Clinical Information and Notes

Eighty percent of health information is unstructured, consisting of photos, papers, transcribed notes, and clinical notes. These semi-structured to unstructured clinical records (patient discharge summaries, medical photographs, diagnostic testing reports, etc.) and papers constitute novel data sources.

1.2.4 Web- and Social Networking–Based Data

Google and other search engines, Internet consumer use, and social networking sites all contribute to web-based statistics (Twitter, LinkedIn, Facebook, blog, smartphones, and health plan websites).

1.2.5 Genomic Data

Genomic data represents a large volume of new gene-sequencing information. Genotyping, gene expression, and DNA sequencing are all examples of genomic data.

1.3 Big Data 5 V's in Healthcare

Gartner identified eight important sources of big data in health in 2016 [5]. The four V's Veracity, Volume, Velocity, and Variety have been coined by Ernst & Young and others to describe it. Similarly, McKinsey also identified five "rights" that it may provide: "right provider", "right living", "right care", "right value", and "right innovation" [6].

1.3.1 Volume

Terabytes and petabytes of data are used by healthcare systems. Personal information, 3D imaging, genomics, personal medical records, radiological images, and biometric sensor readings are all stored in these systems [7]. This complicated data structure may now be managed and analyzed by healthcare systems. Storage, manipulation, and use of such complicated data are now possible due to the advent of cloud computing. According to KPMG (Klynveld Peat Marwick Goerdeler) report, healthcare data had surpassed 150 exabytes in 2013 and is growing at a speedy rate of 1.2–2.4 exabytes each year [8].

1.3.2 Velocity

The underlying explanation for data's exponential increase is velocity [9], which states how quickly data is generated. Data is being generated at an ever-increasing rate. Due to the amount and diversity of data acquired, the speed with which unstructured and structured data is generated forces a conclusion based on its outcome.

1.3.3 Veracity

Data veracity refers to the degree of certainty that a data interpretation is consistent. Varied data sources have different levels of data reliability and dependability [10]. Unsupervised machine learning algorithms, however, are employed in healthcare to make choices that data may be useless or ambiguous [11]. The purpose of healthcare analytics is to extract useful insights from this data so that patients can be treated effectively and the best decisions can be made.

1.3.4 Variety

It refers to the data's format, whether it's unstructured or structured, medical images, video, audio, text, or sensor data. Clinical data is structured data that must be collected, stored, and analyzed using specialized equipment. Structured data accounts for only 5% to 10% of overall healthcare data. Images, audios, videos, e-mails, and healthcare data, such as prescriptions, hospital medical reports, radiographic films, and physician's observations, are examples of unstructured or semi-structured data [12].

1.3.5 Value

This V, unlike the other 4Vs, is too unique since it reflects the anticipated results of big data processing. We're continuously looking for new ways to collect and extract the true value from the vast data. Investment should be the one to store data as the quality of the governance strategy and approach determines the value of data. Another important consideration is that certain data has a different risk value at the time of collection, but that risk can change with time [13].

Five more key traits have been identified by researchers, totaling 10V's of big data. Variability, Validity, Vulnerability, Volatility, and Visualization are the five extra traits. Healthcare data is separated into structured and unstructured data, which includes Electronic Medical Records (EMR) reports, medical photographs, and so on [14]. A large amount of data helps improve the worth of healthcare by utilizing creative analyses. The huge volume of data associated to healthcare can be analyzed by distributing the process using cloud centers and big data. Not only have big data increased the size of data but it has also increased the value that can be derived from it. To put it in another way, big data has shifted the focus of Business Intelligence away from reporting and decision-making toward prediction. Understanding innovative diseases and therapies, predicting results early, taking instantaneous decisions, improving health, boosting treatment, lowering expenses, and improving healthcare quality and worth are all instances of a value in healthcare.

1.4 Big Data Analysis in Healthcare Industry

Big data analysis can change the healthcare scenario. The ability to use technological equipment by healthcare professionals and make decisions about their clinical and other data streams has been changed for better comprehend. The five processes that make up big data healthcare analytics include data acquisition, data storage, data management, data

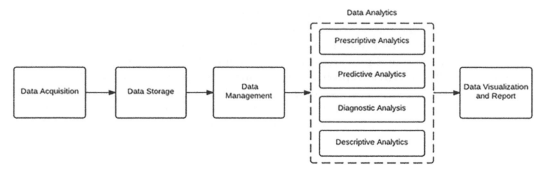

FIGURE 1.2 The process of big data analytics in healthcare [32].

analytics, and data visualization and reporting. Figure 1.2 depicts the process of big data analysis in healthcare management.

1.4.1 Data Acquisition

The type of data can be classified into unstructured, structured, or semi-structured, and it comes from both primary such as clinical decision support systems, electronic health records (EHRs), and Computerized Provider Order Entry (CPOE) and secondary resources such as laboratories, pharmacies, Health Maintenance Organization (HMOs), government sources, and insurance companies [15]. In healthcare, EHRs, social media, image processing, web-based data, and smartphones, among other things, are the most significant sources of big data.

1.4.2 Data Storage

In this epoch of technology, storage is crucial. Since the amount of data in the healthcare industry grows, we need a storage platform that is both efficient and huge. With such a big number of users, cloud computing is the most promising technology. Clouds offer the scalability and capabilities needed to obtain access to data, boost awareness, speed up the development of scalable analytics solutions, and generate income. It reduces the necessity of maintaining expensive computing gear and software.

1.4.3 Data Management

In healthcare, it encompasses structuring, cleansing, mining, and controlling the data. It also contains a mechanism for determining whether any row or omitted data exist. That information must be handled in a proper way. It aids in the risk assessment of patients and the creation of a customized discharge plan. Apache Ambari and HCatalog are the two important data management solutions. The process of obtaining files or important information from big healthcare databases is known as data retrieval. In healthcare, big data analysis usually includes information recovery and data mining [16].

1.4.4 Data Analytics

Data analytics is the procedure of converting raw data into information. The four forms of big data analytics applied in healthcare are descriptive, diagnostic, predictive, and prescriptive analytics [17].

The descriptive analysis offers specific information on each attribute such as features, number of features, and the size of the data set.

Predictive analysis aids in the "forecasting" of future events based on current data. It deciphers data insights and provides useful information to businesses in the form of recommendations. It also provides probabilistic estimates of future outcomes [18].

Prescriptive analytics makes use of predictive data outcomes to allow persons to "prescribe/determine" numerous activities to take and steer them toward a result. Before making a decision, it aims to assess the impact of future decisions and provide advice on alternative outcomes.

1.4.5 Data Visualization

Data visualization is the process of displaying analytic conclusions from healthcare data in a graphical layout to make better decisions. It can be used to interpret data patterns and associations.

1.5 Big Data Analytics Tools in Healthcare

Big data analytics is used to process the unprocessed data. The data, which is still unprocessed, is accessed, retrieved, and processed using service-oriented architecture. Another technique is data warehousing, which involves gathering data from a variety of sources and preparing it for processing, even if the data isn't available in real time. From several sources, data is processed and prepared. Although the data is unstructured or structured, the big data analytics platform can accept a variety of data formats [19]. Some of the analytics tools are listed below (Table 1.1).

1.6 Applications of Big Data in Healthcare

1.6.1 Data Analytics in COVID-19

Big data technology can save a lot of data on people who have been infected with COVID-19. It assists in gaining a complete understanding of the nature of the virus. In future, the knowledge acquired can be used to teach new preventive actions. This technology is used to save data from COVID-19 affected instances of all types (recovered, infected, and expired). This information can be used to track down cases and provide resources for better public health protection. Patient physiology, patient-reported travel, patient location, comorbidity, proximity, and existing symptoms are just a few examples of digital data modalities that can be used to provide insights at the community and population levels [24].

1.6.2 Hadoop-Based Applications

Because most of the data is unstructured, extracting relevant information about clinical operations, patient care, and research is a huge problem for the business. The Hadoop can

TABLE 1.1

Various Big data Platforms in Healthcare [20]

Platform/ Technology	Description
MapReduce	It is a programming archetype for forming Big Data applications that execute in parallel across multiple nodes. It's a method for analyzing big amounts of complex data [21].
Hadoop	Apache Hadoop is a distributed platform to deal with huge datasets through clusters of computers ranging in size from one to thousands [22].
Pig and Pig Latin	To work with a wide range of data types, Pig's programming language is used. The PigLatin programming language and its runtime version, which executes PigLatin code, are the two main modules.
Hive	Apache Hive is a query and analysis tool that runs on top of the Hadoop databases and file systems. Hive is an SQL-like Hadoop database and file system querying tool [23].
Cassandra	It is a standalone database system. It's a complex system that's meant to deal with massive volumes of data spread over several utility servers. Also, it offers continuous service and eliminates the possibility of a single point of failure.
Jaql	It is a query language for analyzing bulky data collections. It transforms "high-level queries" into "low-level queries" for parallel execution of MapReduce jobs.
Lucene	Lucene has been included in several open-source projects and is widely used for text analytics and searches. Its scope comprises the library and full-text indexing search within a Java program.
Mahout	Mahout is an open-source Apache project aimed at developing scalable machine learning models for Hadoop-based big data analytics.

assist the healthcare sector in managing this massive volume of data. In the healthcare sector, following are some of the applications of Hadoop ecosystem:

- **Genomics and Cancer Treatment:** To struggle against cancer, it is important to organize massive amounts of data efficiently. Individual genetics has an impact on cancer mutation patterns and responses, which helps to explain why some tumors are incurable. When recognizing cancer patterns, it is discovered that it is vital to provide customized therapy for certain malignancies based on patient's genetic composition. For mapping three billion DNA base pairs, researchers can use Hadoop's MapReduce technology to discover the best cancer therapy for individual patients.

- **Fraud Prevention and Detection:** In the first few years, health-based insurance companies used a variety of approaches to detect fraud and develop methods to prevent it. Companies utilize Hadoop to identify fraudsters by using data from prior health claims, voice recordings, earnings, and demographics to create apps based on a prediction model. By combining authentic medical claim bills, real-time Hadoop-based health apps, voice data recordings, weather forecasting data, and other data sources, Hadoop NoSQL database can assist in avoiding medical claim fraud at an early stage.

- **Network in Hospital:** Hadoop NoSQL database is used by various hospitals to accumulate and manage massive volumes of data from a variety of origins linked to patient care, payroll, and finances allowing them to detect risky patients along with deducting daily costs.

- **Patient's Vital Monitoring:** Using bigdata technologies, hospital employees around the world can connect their job output. Several hospitals in many parts of the world use Hadoop-based components in the Hadoop Distributed File System, such as the Impala, HBase, Hive, Spark, and Flume frameworks, to convert massive amounts of unstructured data generated by sensors that take patient vital signs, heartbeats per minute, blood pressure, blood sugar level, and respiratory rate into structured data. Without Hadoop, these healthcare professionals would be unable to analyze the unstructured data supplied by patient healthcare systems.

1.6.3 Big Data in Public Health and Behavior Research

In public behavior and health, big data concentrates on biological data collected by portable equipment, for instance vitals, electrocardiograms, wearable devices, contagion, and daily health records.

- **Electrocardiogram:** Traditional electrocardiographic tracing investigations are essential for understanding the reasons and mechanisms of arrhythmias and other related disorders; however, the data does not allow for the prediction of the initiation of cardiac damage before it occurs. As a result, new metrics must be established for use in various preclinical cardiovascular diagnoses. The introduction of Big Data which collects higher complexity information characterized by volume, variety, and velocity is making a significant contribution to the control, contrast, and management of big data sets [24].
- **Omics Data:** The term "omics" refers to large records in the molecular and organic sciences (e.g. macrobiotics, metabolomics, proteomics, genomics, etc.). The purpose of using big data is to recognize ill approaches and improve the precision of medical therapy. The advancement of genomics, proteomics, metabolomics, and other kinds of Omics knowledge in earlier eras has resulted in a massive amount of data related to molecular biology [25].

1.6.4 Source of Valuable Data

In the healthcare industry, technological advancements in the utilization of gadgets have brought with them the new possibilities for generating and collecting data. Most data repositories in healthcare, such as those in other industries and organizations, combine data from a diversity of sources, including social media, EHRs, and medical devices [26].

- **EHRs:** In a more organized sense, data in a healthcare facility is stored in EHRs to offer a multifaceted view of patients' records. The EHR is a database of electronic healthcare data that generally pertains to individuals, medical records, and administrative information. Sub-schemes such as admission, discharge, and transfer of patients' schema, recurring engagements and planning schema, the technique for inputting prescription schema, and notes on routine medical checks are all included in a traditional EHR framework [27].
- **Medical Supplies and Equipment:** Medical devices and sensors such as pulse oximeters, blood pressure monitors, glucose monitors, and other sensors generate massive amounts of data that might reveal important information about a patient's physical condition. One of the motivating factors for embracing big data

in healthcare is the explosion of the Internet of Things and its ability to provide speedy access to medical needs. Body Sensor Networks and their continued application in healthcare will offer healthcare providers the ability to scan critical parameters and, as a result, precisely predict imminent medical hazards such as epidemics and pandemics [28].

- **Social Media:** In the healthcare industry, social media is also a valuable source of information. Patient behavior data and sentiment data on patient recovery are collected. Furthermore, social media posts such as blogs, Twitter feeds, Facebook status updates, and web pages can expose and provide an indicator of a person's health, mood, and state of mind, which is important to health professionals.

1.6.5 Big Data in Medical Experiment

Molecular biology is concerned with the communication and supervision of biological activity inside cells, for example, communications between proteins, RNA, and DNA. It is an important aspect of both biological and medical research. The study of proteins and genes has a secure interaction with the features of genetics and biochemistry. Macromolecule blotting and probing, polymerase chain reaction, molecular cloning, microarrays, and other techniques are used in molecular biology. A person's body comprises organs, tissues, and cells, along with cross-sectional images of tissues and organs, which is used to display the structure of the human body for considering medical measures. Biological laboratory specimens, such as human body data sets, are collected from human bodies and stored in biorepositories. Before a new medicine, vaccine, or piece of medical equipment is used, clinical trials must be performed. A medical experiment is a form of test or study used in clinical or medical research to determine the efficacy of a new medical therapy on humans [29].

1.6.6 Medical Research Using Big Data

Research articles and organized knowledge are currently produced at a rapid rate as the medical/clinical area has developed. There are also a lot of obsolete materials under the clinical/medical section. The study creates a substantial involvement to the subject of big data in healthcare.

1.7 Challenges with Healthcare Data Management

1.7.1 Challenges Associated with Manpower

- **Human Interaction:** Despite technological advancements, there are still some areas where a human could achieve better outcomes than a machine. As a result, humans must be involved at every level of big data analytics. To offer meaningful solutions, experts from various fields (those who understand the problem and data storage) must interact with big data tools. The scarcity of skilled and knowledgeable individuals is once again an impediment to the implementation of big data analytics [30].

- **Keeping Big Data Experts:** Even though corporations may discover the greatest big data professionals with healthcare experience, hiring them is tough and expensive. Given the severe competition, retaining highly skilled data scientists and analysts is also difficult [17,31].

- **Deficiency of Talent:** When businesses choose to use big data technology, a need for qualified data analysts who can understand healthcare data arises [15]. Data scientists and analysts with experience in the healthcare field and those who can apply the right tools to the data, generate results, and analyze them to give actionable insights are in high demand. However, only a few people have the essential skills and abilities to apply analytics to healthcare [16].

1.7.2 Challenges in Data and Process

- **Data Integrity:** The authenticity and integrity of healthcare data is an issue when combining multiple forms from various origins [1,8,6]. Data from X-rays, physiological pathology reports, bedside monitors, and recordings from various tests may be used to compile patient data. Before analyzing this large amount of data, an information extraction method is required, which extracts the necessary data and delivers in an acceptable format to analyze the data. It's a technical difficulty to guarantee the accuracy and thoroughness of this process. Furthermore, sensor malfunctions and human errors may result in inadequate and incorrect data, which could result in severe health concerns and unpleasant occurrences for patients [11]. Furthermore, errors caused by poor data quality are to blame for increased expenses for healthcare companies. As a result, data cleaning and normalization, which involves removing noise and unnecessary data, is difficult in making effective utilization of data.

- **Big Data Privacy and Security:** Patient record is stored in a variety of places and can be accessed through a variety of endpoints, including medical records, pathology reports, and insurance claim information. To track patient health and enable the transmission of patient data across various parties, a variety of applications are utilized, each with varying levels of security. Out-of-date software can jeopardize the security of health data, leaving it vulnerable to cyber-attacks. Personal information, such as a person's name, occupation, and income, can cost healthcare providers a lot of money if it is accessed and misused [30]. Furthermore, disclosing private health data raises privacy concerns for patients [8,32]. Because of the unconstrained actions of data breaches, managing large data security and privacy remains a technical concern, even with the technical controls and measures in place.

- **Interoperability:** The issue of interoperability occurs when data is generated by multiple healthcare equipment and devices [1,12,5]. Because these devices use different platforms and software, the data they generate is in different formats. To make full use of this data, the devices must be able to interact and exchange data in a common format that is interoperable with other devices.

- **Data Storage and Linkage:** Traditional IT equipment in organizations were not capable to handle such vast amounts of data as the volume of healthcare data rises exponentially [8]. Furthermore, data redundancy difficulties arise as a result of data storage among multiple departments within an organization [9]. Analyzing data that is fragmented and incomplete becomes tough. Even the most advanced algorithms fail to cope with disintegrating data. The huge volume and a variety of data from various sources make it difficult to combine and aggregate these sources into repositories [10].

- **Data Collection:** Healthcare data is multidimensional and highly segmented, and it comes from a variety of sources [1]. Due to a lack of synchronization across several data sources, there may be gaps in the information provided. Furthermore, the organization of the data available from these sources varies greatly. Healthcare data, however, contains organized patient's demographic information, physician observations, diagnostic metaphors such as MRI and CT scans, and visuals that are not in a structured format. As a result, bringing together disparate data silos from many sources and transforming them into a uniform format suitable for storage in the system is difficult [14]. Furthermore, continuous data collection is difficult due to real-time or near-real-time data production [8].

1.7.3 Overall Organizational Challenges

- **Actionable Insights at the Right Time:** With correct tools and analytics solutions, big data could manage huge information or data than intuition. Actionable intuitions are much important than simple responses to the questions posed because of the activities they stimulate. As a result, the priority is to gain timely insights that inspire action. Given the importance of timely healthcare choices, another problem to consider is the development of triable information in realtime [33].

- **The Discrepancy in Technology:** Despite the increased interest in healthcare digitization, most businesses continue to rely on outdated technologies. It's a challenge to replace a historical data storage and management system with cutting-edge technology. Due to the large volume of data held in physical records in healthcare, digitalization would necessitate a significant amount of effort, human resources, and time. Another difficult task is to bridge the technological divide [34].

- **Unknown Purpose:** Lack of clarity in the aim of big data analytics to an organization has also become a hurdle in its advancement. Organizations use big data technologies as a source of competitive advantage without clearly defining their business goals. Force-fitting new technologies will result in a lack of direction. It's once again difficult to define the business goals for using big data analytics [35].

- **Identifying Useful Information and Tools:** The next step is to find and store relevant data once firms become familiar with commercial use cases for big data technology. As a result, the appropriate tools for working with such data must be discovered. It's also difficult to figure out what tools and solutions are available.

- **Sharing:** Data sharing is another stumbling block to the successful deployment of big data analytics. Organizations must exchange data with other healthcare organizations to reap the benefits of big data technology for the community. Although more openness and data availability would allow for faster judgments, firms are wary of sharing data due to competitive pressures. This obstructs the effective use of big data analytics in healthcare.

- **Economic:** The most critical initial difficulty for healthcare businesses adopting a data-driven culture is managing the expense of data warehouses and infrastructure required to hold massive amounts of data. In reality, the required computational resources also increase initial investment for performing big data analysis. Hence, for small and medium organizations, it would be costly, while major businesses are wary of making such an investment without knowing what they would get in return.

1.8 Conclusion

Big data analytics, which makes use of a plethora of heterogeneous, unstructured, and structured data sources, has a critical responsibility in the future of healthcare. A variety of analytics is already being used to aid the healthcare workers and patients. Genetic data processing, physiological signal processing, and medical image analysis are the major areas of interest. The exponential growth in the volume of healthcare data compels computer scientists to devise novel ways to process such a massive amount of data in a manageable amount of time. Big data analytics brings heterogeneous data together from various domains including medical informatics, medical imaging, sensor informatics, computational biomedicine, bioinformatics, and health informatics. Furthermore, the properties of big data give an excellent foundation in healthcare and medicine for developing applications to use promising software platforms.

Data scientists face hurdles in integrating and implementing a large volume of medical data acquired across multiple platforms. As a result, it is suggested that a healthcare revolution is required to bring analytics, health informatics, and bioinformatics together to encourage tailored and additional effective therapies.

References

1. Mukhtar, W. F., and Abuelyaman, E. S. 2020. *Opportunities and Challenges of Big Data in Healthcare. Data Analytics in Medicine: Concepts, Methodologies, Tools, and Applications*, 1989–2001. IGI Global. http://doi:10.4018/978-1-7998-1204-3.ch099
2. Russom, 2011. Big data analytics. TDWI best practices report, fourth quarter 19(4): 1–34.
3. Hong, Liang, Luo, Mengqi, Wang, Ruixue, Lu, Peixin, Lu, Wei, and Lu, Long. 2018. Big data in health care: Applications and challenges. *Data and Information Management*, 2(3): 175–197. https://doi.org/10.2478/dim–2018–0014
4. Mousannif, Hajar, Khalil, Ismail, and Kotsis, Gabriele. (2013). The cloud is not 'there', we are the cloud! *International Journal of Web and Grid Services*, 9: 1–17. http://doi:10.1504/IJWGS.2013.052854.
5. Sini, E. 2016. How big data is changing healthcare. Humanitas Hospital Italy.
6. The big-data revolution in US health care: accelerating value and innovation. 2013. Available from: https://www.mckinsey.com/industries/healthcare-systems-and-services/our-insights/the-big-data-revolution-in-us-health-care (accessed August 2021).
7. Liu, W. and Park, E.K. 2014. Big data as an e-health service: 982–988. http://doi:10.1109/ICCNC.2014.6785471.
8. KGMP report, https://assets.kpmg/content/dam/kpmg/pdf/ 2016/01/healthcare-insights-dec-2015-2.pdf (accessed July 2021).
9. Raghupathi, W., and Raghupathi, V. 2014. Big data analytics in healthcare: promise and potential. *Health Information Science and Systems*, 2: 3. https://doi.org/10.1186/2047-2501-2-3

10. Mehmood, R. and Graham, G. 2015. Big data logistics: A health- care transport capacity sharing model, *Procedia Computer Science*, 64: 1107–1114.
11. Herland, Matthew, Khoshgoftaar, Taghi, and Wald, Randall 2014. A review of data mining using big data in health informatics. *Journal of Big Data*, 1: 2. 10.1186/2196–1115–1–2.
12. MAPR, Healthcare and life science use cases. 2018. https://mapr.com/solutions/industry/healthcare-and-lifescience- use-cases/ (accessed July 2021).
13. Mallappallil, Mary et al. 2020. A review of big data and medical research. *SAGE Open Medicine*. https://doi.org/10.1177/2050312120934839.
14. Shvachko, K., Kuang, H., Radia, S., and Chansler, R. 2010. The Hadoop Distributed File System. *2010 IEEE 26th Symposium on Mass Storage Systems and Technologies (MSST)*: 1–10.
15. Al-Jarrah, O. Y., Yoo, P. D., Muhaidat, S., Karagiannidis, G. K., and Taha, K. 2015. Efficient machine learning for big data: A review. *Big Data Result*, 2: 87–93. https://doi.org/10.1016/j.Bdr.2015.04.001.
16. Andrzej Chluski, L. Z. 2015. The application of big data in the management of healthcare organizations: A review of selected practical solutions. *Bus. Informatics*, 1: 9–18. https://doi.org/10.15611/ie.2015.1.01.
17. Ahmed, I., Ahmad, M., Jeon, G., and Piccialli, F. 2021. A framework for pandemic prediction using big data analytics. *Big Data Research*, 25, 100190. https://doi.org/10.1016/j.bdr.2021.100190.
18. India Mag. 2018. https://analyticsindiamag.com/organizations-continue-to-face-challenges-with-big-data-lets-deep-dive/ (accessed August 2021).
19. PEX Process Excellence Network. 6 ways pharmaceutical companies are using big data to drive innovation & value. https://www.processexcellencenetwork.com/tools-technologies/whitepapers/6-ways-pharmaceutical-companies-are-using-big-data (accessed June 2021).
20. Haleem, A., Javaid, M., Khan, I. H., and Vaishya, R. 2020. Significant applications of big data in COVID-19 pandemic. *Indian Journal of Orthopedics*, 54(4): 526–528.
21. Song, Y., Wang, H., Li, J., and Gao, H. 2016. MapReduce for Big Data Analysis: Benefits, Limitations, and Extensions. In: Che, W. et al. (eds) *Social Computing. ICYCSEE. Communications in Computer and Information Science*, 623. Springer. https://doi.org/10.1007/978-981-10-2053-7_40
22. Abualkishik, Abedallah. 2019. Hadoop and big data challenges. *Journal of Theoretical and Applied Information Technology*, 97: 3488–3500.
23. Kan, Z., Cheng, X., Kim, S. H., Jin, Y., and Kan, Z. 2018. Apache hive-based big data analysis of health care data. *International Journal Pure and Application Mathematics*, 119(18): 237–259.
24. Cipresso, C., Rundo, F., Conoci, S., and Parenti, R. 2019. Big data in preclinical ECG alterations research. *Biomedical Journal*, 13(2): 9895 -9896, doi: DOI: 10.26717/BJSTR.2019.13.002384.
25. van Allen, E. M., Wagle, N., and Levy, M. A. 2013. Clinical analysis and interpretation of cancer genome data. *Journal of Clinical Oncology*, 31: 1825–1833.
26. Asare-Frempong, Justice and Jayabalan, Manoj 2017. Exploring the impact of big data in healthcare and techniques in preserving patients' privacy. *International Journal of Computer Science and Network Security*, 17: 143–149.
27. Saranga Jayawardena, D. B. A. 2013. A systematic literature review of security, privacy and confidentiality of patient information in electronic health information systems. *Sri Lanka Journal Bio-Medical Informatics*, 4(2): 25–31.
28. KupwadePatil, H. and Seshadri, R. 2014. Big data security and privacy issues in healthcare. *IEEE International Congress on Big Data*: 762–765.
29. Vesna, V. The Visible Human Project: Informatic bodies and posthuman medicine. 2000. 262–263. https://doi.org/10.1007/BF01205456
30. Labrinidis, Alexandros and Jagadish, H.V. 2012. Challenges and opportunities with big data. *Proceedings of the VLDB Endowment*, 5: 2032–2033. https://doi.org/10.14778/2367502.2367572.
31. Dhayne, H., Haque, R., Kilany, R., and Taher, Y. 2019. In search of big medical data integration solutions - A comprehensive survey. *IEEE Access*. 7: 91265–91290. https://doi.org/10.1109/ACCESS.2019.2927491.
32. Dash, S., Shakyawar, S.K., Sharma, M. et al. 2019. Big data in healthcare: management, analysis, and future prospects. *Journal of Big Data*, 6: 54. https://doi.org/10.1186/s40537-019-0217-0.

33. Harvey, C. Big data challenges. *Datamation*. 2017. https://www.datamation.com/big-data/big-data-challenges.html (accessed in August 2021).
34. Chander, D., Singh, H., and Gupta, A. K. 2020. A study of big data processing for sentiments analysis. *Large-Scale Data Streaming, Processing, and Blockchain Security*. IGI Global. https://doi.org/10.4018/978-1-7998-3444-1.ch001.
35. Singh, Hari and Bawa, Seema. 2020. Predicting Covid-19 statistics using machine learning regression models Li-MuLi-Poly. Multimedia Systems. https://doi.org/10.1007/s00530-021-007982.

2

Impact Analysis of COVID-19 on Different Countries: A Big Data Approach

Reema Lalit

Panipat Institute of Engineering & Technology

Nitin Sharma

Chandigarh University

CONTENTS

2.1 Introduction

Today data is being generated in terms of terabytes, petabytes, and even exabytes in many applications such as stock exchange [1], intelligent transportation system [2], and social media. Analysis of big data is a huge challenge in front of organizations. The chapter focuses on the challenges faced by organizations while analyzing big data and also the methods of handling big data [3]. In this chapter, we are going to analyze data related to COVID-19 for different countries available on GitHub [4]. In this chapter, the diverse effects of this virus on different countries and their causes are compared. To carry out this analysis, WHO dashboard data of different countries have been used [5]. The comparison graphs are drawn in python using Google Colab. "Google Colab" is a product from Google

DOI: 10.1201/9781003215981-2

Research. It allows to write and execute arbitrary python code through the browser and is especially well suited to data analysis, education, and machine learning. Section 2.2 contains the preprocessing steps of data to be considered for the analysis, Section 2.3 contains the challenges in big data analytics, Section 2.4 contains the current scenario of the countries under pandemic, Section 2.5 contains the process adopted to carry out the analysis, Section 2.6 contains major factors that can majorly affect the result of analysis, and Section 2.7 contains the conclusion.

2.2 Processing Steps of Big Data

Big data processing involves various steps which are data collection and recording, data cleaning, interrogation of data, data analytics, and modeling [6–8]. According to researchers, most of the analysis time is consumed by preparation activity. This activity is considered as the longest activity. In data preparation, we need to understand our data first as the data used for this analysis is usually raw, organized, dependable, formatted, and aggregated/compressed data but data collected from different sources is not in the same format as desired. Therefore, there is a need to convert the collected data into the appropriate form. There are a variety of methods for data preprocessing and analysis based on different data types, for example, in date–time data, POSIX format is commonly used. One commercial solution available for data preparation is Tamr. This software takes the advantage of machine learning and awareness of available data to computerize the fast fusion of data silos at scale [9]. It provides a solution for several issues in big data. Tamr works with relational database files, Comma-separated values (CSV) files, and Hadoop distributed file system (HDFS) files as input, then it generates schema mapping. Figure 2.1 shows the block diagram representation of big data processing.

2.2.1 Data Collection and Recording

Big data is acquired from several data sources. For example, social networking sites, such as Twitter and Facebook, generate an enormous amount of data. Petabytes and exabytes of data can be produced easily by scientific experiments and simulations. The world around us generates a tremendous amount of data, which has no meaning, but it can be cleaned and filtered using various techniques [10]. The biggest problem is defining the filters so that they do not dispose of meaningful information. Another challenge is to repeatedly create data about data so that it can be determined how and what data is to be recorded. Figure 2.2 shows the various tools available for data collection process.

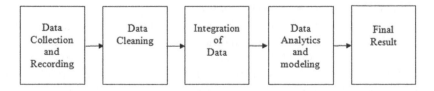

FIGURE 2.1
Data preprocessing activities.

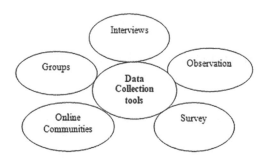

FIGURE 2.2
Tools of data collection.

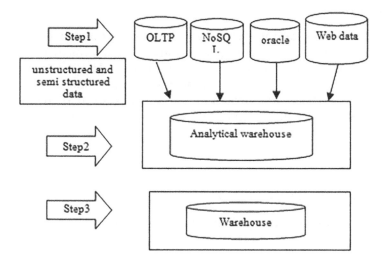

FIGURE 2.3
Data integration.

2.2.2 Data Cleaning

In data cleaning, the data is converted in such a format that is ready for analysis. During data cleaning, the missing values are filled, the corrupted or inaccurate data records are corrected or removed from the database. The main causes of inconsistencies and errors in data are generally user entry errors, data corruption during transmission, or storage. There are many strategies to fill in the missing values such as replacing it by mean or median value, or fill the missing value with a global constant.

2.2.3 Data Integration

Due to the heterogeneity of the data, it is not recommended to put data into a warehouse. Data is generated from various applications due to which it is heterogeneous. Having a cluster of datasets in a warehouse does not help in its reuse. But with enough metadata, it can be reused efficiently [11]. The biggest challenge is due to heterogeneous experimental data and differences in the record structure. Figure 2.3 shows the steps involved in data integration process. For data integration, the following steps need to be followed.

Step 1: Mine data from different data sources.

Step 2: Conversion of unstructured/semi-structured data into structure data.

Step 3: Transforming structured data into data warehouse.

2.2.4 Data Modeling

Querying and mining in big data are very diverse as compared to conventional numerical analysis methods. Big data is often unclean, dynamic, diverse, interrelated, and unreliable. However, even unreliable and dynamic big data is of greater importance than small sample since universal figures obtained from recurrent patterns and correlation analysis are more powerful than the individual samples [12].

2.2.5 Data Interpretation

Data understanding and examining depend on the assumptions made. Computers often have viruses, bugs, and worms, models generally are as accurate as their assumptions, and outcomes generally based on incorrect data. Examining big data is often half-done if user cannot appreciate the analysis. Finally, it is the duty of a decision-maker to interpret the final results [13]. This data can be further analyzed using linear regression, multi-linear regression, and polynomial regression techniques based on machine learning models [14].

2.3 Challenges of Big Data Analysis

A number of challenges are reported in big data analysis [15]. Some of the challenges are discussed below.

2.3.1 Heterogeneity and Incompleteness

Data we receive from different sources is usually incomplete and heterogeneous. The biggest task is to complete this data and make it homogeneous for analysis. For example, we have received data of employees, which include E-name, E-id, Phone no., and salary, and some fields are missing, such as some employees may not provide his or her phone number. This type of data cannot be analyzed until it is completed [15].

2.3.2 Scalability

The important point that comes to mind with big data is its huge size. Supervising large and quick-rising sizes is one of the challenging matters for several years. In the past, this challenge was overcome by the use of faster processors. But currently, there is a vibrant shift in technology. The technologies developed should work with equal efficiency irrespective of small or big data [3].

2.3.3 Timeliness

The bigger the size of data more time it will take to process and the longer it will take to analyze. Therefore, providing useful data to the organization on time is also a big challenge. Nevertheless, velocity here does not mean speed but it refers to the rate at which data is coming from various media [16].

2.3.4 Analytics of Big Data

Big data analytics is the practice of probing huge data of varying types to reveal unseen patterns, indefinite correlations, and discovering information. This information can supply viable rewards over competitive organizations and results in more business, such as added efficient advertising and enlarged profits. Innovative and advanced practicing big data, such as Hadoop, MapReduce, and HDFS, offers more efficient solutions over the conventional data warehousing [17].

Hadoop: It is a software package that allows us to run and write programs that can process enormous data. It includes (1) HBase (pre-alpha) – online access of data, (2) Hive – distributed data warehouse, which also provides an SQL-based query language, (3) HDFS – Hadoop distributed file system, (4) PIG – data flow language and execution environment, and (5) MapReduce – offline computational engine.

Hadoop gives dependable common storage space and investigation systems for large-scale data processing: storage space provided by HDFS and investigation given by MapReduce [18]. Hadoop working with big data requires mainly two things – (1) Low-cost and consistent storage, and (2) advanced tools for analyzing unstructured and structured data.

Apache Hadoop is an open-source software. It addresses both the problems more efficiently and effectively [18]. It does the following functions: (1) Hadoop implements MapReduce using HDFS, (2) MapReduce divides applications into several tiny blocks, (3) HDFS makes many replicas of data blocks for reliability, and (4) MapReduce processes the data from its location.

2.4 Current Scenario in Top Five Countries Affected by Pandemic

The five countries affected by COVID-19 are the United States of America, India, Brazil, South Africa, and Russia. In the US, around 34 million cases have been reported till now, in Brazil, the number is more than 18 million, in India, more than 30 million cases have been reported, in Russia, more than 8 million, and in South Africa, more than 5 million cases have been reported till now. Now as we can see different countries have diverse effects of COVID-19. Many factors can be responsible for that such as healthcare services, number of tests carried out in a country, political factors, immunity of the people of a particular country, country's population, timely detection, and tracing of the disease [19]. To deal with the pandemic situation, data analysis can be very helpful in planning and implementation of various strategies. Data analysis can also be used to predict damage and measures that can be considered to control the situation.

2.5 Process Adopted to Carry Out the Analysis

To carry out this study, Google Colab has been used. To be specific, Colab is a complimentary Jupyter notebook environment that runs entirely in the cloud. There is no need for

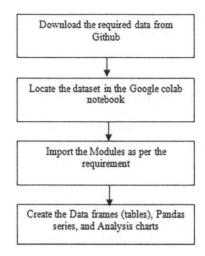

FIGURE 2.4
Data analysis process.

setup and the notebooks that are created can be shared by all the team members just like Google Docs. Colab can also support several trendy machine learning libraries which can be easily loaded in your notebook. There is no need for installation in the case of Google Colab. The COVID-19 data which was available on GitHub is also used to carry out the analysis [4]. Datasets taken for analysis are available as a repository on GitHub. Coders/ programmers across the world create GitHub repositories for their codes so that they can download and upload their work anytime from anywhere [20]. Essentially, it's like carrying data in a portable storage device. Figure 2.4 shows the process adopted for analysis.

Step 1: Download the required dataset from GitHub:
    First, it is required to download and create a copy of the dataset of COVID-19 in Colab for analysis. The python code for creating the copy and downloading the dataset is given as follows [21]:
    # Cloning the GitHub repository (*!git clone https://github.com/CSSEGISandData/ COVID-19.git*)

Step 2: Locate the Dataset in the Google Colab notebook:
    Follow these steps to get the Data path from Colab notebook. Click on the folder icon on the left-hand side of the notebook, then click on the arrow in front of the COVID-19 folder. Select the folder csse_covid_19_datafolder, then select the csse_covid_19_time_series folder. Then the CSV files will be available that contain data. Right-click on each of the CSV files and then click on the Copy path option [22].

Step 3: Importing modules as per requirement:
    The following inbuilt modules will be required pandas, pyplot, seaborn, folium, and datetime.

Step 4: Creating data frames, graphs, and maps:
    Data frame is nothing but a table; we can also restrict the table field with the following code.

```
# Creating Dataframe
conf = pan.read_csv(confirm_case)
```

```
# This code will access the top 5 rows and all the columns
conf.head()
```

Code for Graph Generation for different countries affected by Pandemic
`Plt.plot()` function is used to generate graph from the given dataset. Some other functions can also be used that can make the graph more presentable.

```
#Cases Confirmed in USA
us_case=conf_df['Country/Region']=='US'].iloc[:,4].apply(sum, axis=0)
us_cases.index=pd.to_datetime(us_cases.index)
plt.figure(figsize=(10,4))
plt.title('USA Corona cases')
plt.plot(us_cases.index,us_cases, c='g', linewidth=2,
marker='o',markersize=7)
plt.xticks(rotation=45)
plt.ylabel("in millions")
plt.grid(True,'major',linestyle='—',c='yellow')
```

Similar code can be used to generate graphs for number of coronavirus cases in Brazil, India, Russia, and South Africa; the top countries are having many coronavirus cases. Figure 2.5 shows the comparative analysis of US, Brazil, India, Russia, and South Africa. Figure 2.6 shows the ten countries most affected by the pandemic.

2.6 Major Factors that Can Majorly Affect the Result of Analysis

There are various challenges when it comes to comparing countries, such as how extensively the test for COVID-19 has been conducted by country and the population of the country.

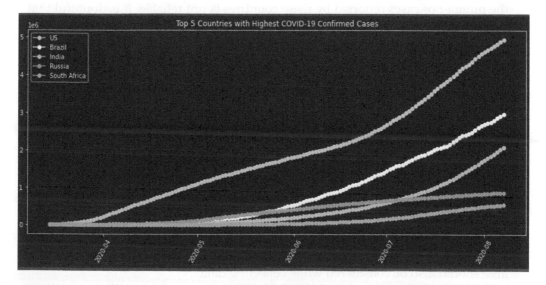

FIGURE 2.5
Comparative analysis of US, Brazil, India, Russia, and South Africa.

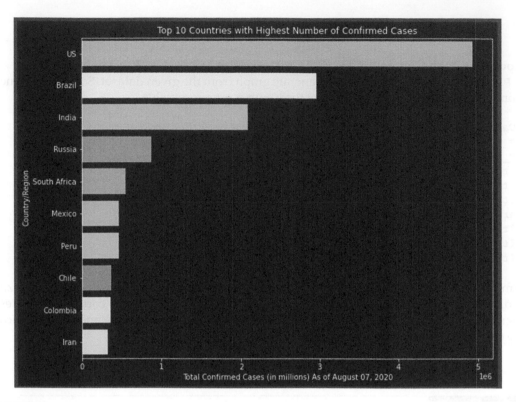

FIGURE 2.6
Graph showing ten countries most affected by the pandemic.

- *Political Factors*

  Many countries, such as Iran and China, have a firm political system. Therefore, the number of cases reported by these countries is not reliable. It is doubtful that the number of deaths recorded in these countries is far more than declared. So, the main question is can we trust this data? And the answer is no. Therefore, the accuracy of data analysis highly depends on the accuracy of data.

- *Testing Conducted*

  The countries that have done more testing during the pandemic and traced the number of contacts of infected person has shown better results in fighting against COVID-19. The number of tests done according to the population of the country can be useful statistics to predict fatality rates. Even the number of testing done shows ambiguity in data as some countries have data of many persons tested and some countries have data of number of tests carried out. Many other factors such as time of testing, where it is done should also be taken into account.

- *Country's Population*

  Data highly depends on the country's population as some countries have more population and some have less. Countries having more population are more likely to have adverse impacts of a pandemic. Demographical factors such as age and area should also be considered while collecting data.

  Comparisons have been made for studying the impact of COVID-19 on different countries. But the question is how we can compare a country with quite less population with a country having a huge population. It would make more sense if we compare countries having similar populations and demographic conditions.

- *Health Services*

    Most European countries have better health infrastructure systems compared to Asian or African countries. Health infrastructure played a vital role in efforts to control the pandemic, but they are all not the same. Some questions related to health services need to be answered: "Do people got immediate treatment?" "How easily the beds were available in the hospitals?" "Do people have to pay for their treatment or they were helped by the government?" All these questions need to be addressed while collecting data.

An additional factor is the stage of co-morbidity – it includes the number of other conditions such as or high/low blood pressure, diabetes, heart disease from which people were already suffering when they got infected.

2.7 Conclusion

Despite so much work done in big data analytics, it is still considered in its starting stage. Many research topics based on data science are open for research such as introduce Data virtualization (DV) into novel industries, responsive Business Intelligence, aggregating swarm sourcing data, aggregating cloud services and applications with DV, discrete and aligned detection of data quality semantics, and the method for creating new rules from dirty data. The current era is of big data. Hadoop's MapReduce and HDFS use easy and hearty procedures on low-cost computer systems to provide extremely high data accessibility and to examine massive information rapidly. Hadoop provides many advanced tools for organization's big data for businesses. Every opportunity provides faster advances in many technical and scientific disciplines although; several data science challenges are described in this chapter that should be considered before realizing them fully. The challenges considered in this chapter are quite obvious for almost all the applications and for all the stages of analytics such as scalability, timeliness, heterogeneity, privacy, lack of structure, error-handling, and visualization.

References

[1] M. Shastri, S. Roy, and M. Mittal, "Stock Price Prediction Using Artificial Neural Model: An Application of Big Data," *EAI Endorsed Transactions on Scalable Information Systems*, 6, p. e1, 2019.

[2] N. Sharma, P. K. Dahiya, and B. R. Marwah, "Various Automatic Licence Plate Recognition System: A Review," in Chitkara University Doctoral Consortium -2019, 2019.

[3] L. T. Yang and J. Chen, "Special Issue on Scalable Computing for Big Data," *Big Data Research*. 100, pp. 2–3, 2014.

[4] C. COVID, "Global Cases by Johns Hopkins CSSE https://github.com/CSSEGISandData/COVID-19/tree/master/csse_covid_19_data/csse_covid_19_time_series.

[5] E. Bisong, "Google colaboratory," In *Building Machine Learning and Deep Learning Models on Google Cloud Platform*, ed: Springer, 2019, pp. 59–64.

[6] R. Lalit, K. Handa, and N. Sharma, "Automated Feedback Collection and Analysis System," *International Journal of Distributed Artificial Intelligence (IJDAI)*, vol. 10, pp. 43–53, 2018.

[7] H. Zou, Y. Yu, W. Tang, and H.-W. M. Chen, "FlexAnalytics: A Flexible Data Analytics Framework for Big Data Applications with I/O Performance Improvement," *Big Data Research*, vol. 1, pp. 4–13, 2014.

[8] H. Chen, R. H. Chiang, and V. C. Storey, "Business Intelligence and Analytics: From Big Data to Big Impact," *MIS Quarterly*, pp. 1165–1188, 2012.

[9] H. Singh, R. Vasuja, and R. Sharma, "A Survey of Diversified Domain of Big Data Technologies," *Data Intensive Computing Applications for Big Data*, vol. 29, p. 1, 2018.

[10] C. V. G. Zelaya, "Towards explaining the effects of data preprocessing on machine learning," In 2019 IEEE 35th International Conference on Data Engineering (ICDE), 2019, pp. 2086–2090.

[11] X. L. Dong and D. Srivastava, "Big data integration," In 2013 IEEE 29th International Conference on Data Engineering (ICDE), 2013, pp. 1245–1248.

[12] J. T. Wassan, "Discovering Big Data Modelling for Educational World," *Procedia-Social and Behavioral Sciences*, vol. 176, pp. 642–649, 2015.

[13] N. Dey, C. Bhatt, and A. S. Ashour, *Big Data for Remote Sensing: Visualization, Analysis and Interpretation*, Cham: Springer, p. 104, 2018.

[14] H. Singh and S. Bawa, "Predicting COVID-19 Statistics Using Machine Learning Regression Model: Li-MuLi-Poly," *Multimedia Systems*, 2021/05/06 2021.

[15] M. Xiaofeng and C. Xiang, "Big Data Management: Concepts, Techniques and Challenges," *Journal of Computer Research and Development*, vol. 50, p. 146, 2013.

[16] Y. Demchenko, P. Grosso, C. De Laat, and P. Membrey, "Addressing big data issues in scientific data infrastructure," In 2013 International Conference on Collaboration Technologies and Systems (CTS), 2013, pp. 48–55.

[17] A. K. Karun and K. Chitharanjan, "A review on hadoop—HDFS infrastructure extensions," In 2013 IEEE Conference on Information & Communication Technologies, 2013, pp. 132–137.

[18] L. Jiang, B. Li, and M. Song, "THE optimization of HDFS based on small files," In 2010 3rd IEEE International Conference on Broadband Network and Multimedia Technology (IC-BNMT), 2010, pp. 912–915.

[19] B. Gross, Z. Zheng, S. Liu, X. Chen, A. Sela, J. Li, et al., "Spatio-Temporal Propagation of COVID-19 Pandemics," *EPL (Europhysics Letters)*, vol. 131, p. 58003, 2020.

[20] A. E. Azzaoui, S. K. Singh, and J. H. Park, "SNS Big Data Analysis Framework for COVID-19 Outbreak Prediction in Smart Healthy City," *Sustainable Cities and Society*, vol. 71, p. 102993, 2021.

[21] J. D. Blischak, E. R. Davenport, and G. Wilson, "A Quick Introduction to Version Control with Git and GitHub," *PLoS Computational Biology*, vol. 12, p. e1004668, 2016.

[22] D. Spinellis, Z. Kotti, and A. Mockus, "A dataset for github repository deduplication," In Proceedings of the 17th International Conference on Mining Software Repositories, 2020, pp. 523–527.

3

Overview of Image Processing Technology in Healthcare Systems

Ankit Singh
United Institute of Medical Sciences

Sivanesan Dhandayuthapani
Santosh Deemed to be University

CONTENTS

3.1 Introduction

Over the last two decades, advancements of image processing and computer vision in healthcare setting are booming gradually and play a very significant role in identifying the risk factors of various diseases and/or disorders. Identification of any particular risk factor for a specific disease and/or disorder using any type of image-based analysis, such as X-ray, CT-scan, MRI, and histological images, is one of the major limitations in the field of healthcare and becomes more challenging to the physicians while diagnosing and interpreting the results. In this modern era, the advancement of various applications including computer-based technology in the field of medical education and research system showing high satisfaction with some challenging end points. The fast growth of imaging technology in the field of medical sciences is evidenced through its utilization in various forms starting from simple two-dimensional (2D) to complex four-dimensional (4D) Doppler images to interpret the diagnostic reports. With the tremendous advances in image processing techniques, such as image recognition, analysis, and enhancement, it is now possible to count and measure the diagnostic results with an extreme level of accuracy that was proven using more applicable statistical tools as well.

Medical imaging can be simply defined as "a form of signal processing using simple photographic images or videos as input to derive a set of various characteristics and parameters as output that are highly related to input sources." The process trails for the management and identification of any disease and disorders. It is also worth noting that the process of image processing includes the usage of radiological imaging where electromagnetic energies (X-rays and gamma), sonography, magnetic, scope, and thermal and isotope imaging are chiefly used. Even though with a handful of technologies available to record information related to body function and location, all the techniques have its own limitations compared to those produce images and modulate images [1]. Medical imaging produces images of the body's internal structures without the use of invasive devices by employing quick precursors that include the arithmetical and logical conversion of energies to signals [2]. These signals will eventually be transformed into digital images to represent various types of tissues throughout the body.

Image Segmentation, Image Storage, and Image Transmission: The major goal of image segmentation is to separate an image into distinct homogeneous parts based on common properties such as spatial position, colour, form, texture, and motion (in case of video segmentation). It's still difficult to replicate the human visual system's capacity and segment or partition of an image into meaningful sections, and it has been studied extensively since computer vision's early days. While many works have been published in the literature to review segmentation algorithms, semantic segmentation techniques, and medical image segmentation, few have been dedicated to interactive image segmentation (IIS) methods, even though research in this area is very active and a recent periodic overview is still required. The task of extracting an image region or item of interest from the background (BG) using prior knowledge provided by human input is referred to as IIS, "supervised segmentation," and "semiautomatic segmentation." This interaction allows the user to provide good constraints (on size, colour, location, and objective) to guide the segmentation process, either in the form of some points or scribbles to mark the object of interest and/or the BG, either using a bounding box or polygon to delimit the region of interest (ROI) [3]. When compared to automatic segmentation approaches, this can improve outcomes while also saving runtime.

A computer system for finding, exploring, and retrieving images from a huge database of digital images is referred to as image retrieval. Because of the variety of contents and the growing size of image collections, annotation has become both unclear and time-consuming. This switched the focus to content-based image retrieval (CBIR), which indexes images based on their visual content. The retrieval of images based on visual attributes including colour, texture, and shape is known as CBIR. These traditional image indexing methods have become obsolete, ranging from storing an image in a database and identifying it with a keyword or number to associating it with a classified description, which is not CBIR. In CBIR, each image that is stored in the database has its features extracted and compared to the features of the query image. It involves two steps as follows:

1. **Feature Extraction:** the extraction of recognizable visual features is the initial step in the procedure, and
2. **Matching:** the second phase entails matching these qualities to produce a visually similar output.

Large image databases for a number of purposes are becoming feasible as processors get more powerful and memories become less expensive. Databases containing art works, satellite, and medical imaging have been attracting an increasing number of users from a variety of professions. Examples of CBIR applications are Crime Prevention, Security Check, Medical Diagnosis, and Intellectual Property.

3.2 Computer-Based Technology

Long ago, educational developers demonstrated that computers might be programmed to act as drill instructors, tutors, testers, and schedulers of instruction in schools. However, most schools could not afford computer-based teaching methods until recently. Computer prices have declined considerably in the previous decade, thanks to the development of small, rapid, and inexpensive microcomputers. Majority of researchers think there is only one correct answer to this question, and that is to compare the results of the students who learnt with and without the use of the computer [4]. When writing and reading were first offered as educational instrument, no one attempted to quantify their impact. No statistical approaches were utilized to predict or influence outcomes.

Image Processing Algorithms with Efficiency in Terms of Time Complexity and Space Complexity: In our day-to-day life, we are experiencing many issues and trying to find ways to solve them by identifying the more suitable ways. In some cases, it is easy to solve the problem very efficiently and in a few cases, the solutions may be less efficient. Besides, it is quite normal to use the most easiest and efficient way to approach the solution. For example, even though there will be "n" number of paths to reach a particular destination from our start point, anyone will prefer to use a quite easy and less complicated path to be there on time, i.e. the efficient way. It is quite logical to apply the same approach in the case of **computational problems** or **problem-solving** when there is an advancement in technologies, such as **computer technology**. To solve one computational problem, it is possible to design various paths, i.e. **algorithm(s)** to approach the solution, but choosing the more efficient and shortest algorithm is the wise way to solve the issue.

3.3 Image Recognition, Analysis, and Enhancements

Convolution neural network (CNN), a form of deep learning (DL), is a well-suited image analysing technique, which is more particular to analyse the results of X-rays or MRI. CNNs are intended with an assumption that it will process images based on the expertise of a computer science expert and allow the networks to operate more efficiently while handling larger images. As an output, some CNNs are similar or even surpassing the precision of a human diagnostics expert while identifying important features in the field during diagnosis using image studies. A recent study published in the Annals of Oncology showed that a well-trained CNN on analysing the images from dermatology has identified melanoma, a form of skin cancer, with 10% more specific than the clinicians [5]. Even though the clinicians are equipped with more detailed BG information about the patients, such as demographic variables and the specific site of suspect feature, a well-trained CNN could perform like a dermatologist as close as nearly 7%. Therefore, it is clear that algorithm may be a more suitable tool to aid the physicians in detecting melanoma irrespective of their experience and training. Therefore, the DL tools are faster and more accurate.

Development of Standard in Medical Imaging Field: DL is a subtype of representation learning in which sophisticated data representations are represented using smaller hierarchized structures defined by a collection of unique qualities. With the advent of powerful parallel computing hardware based on graphical processing units and the availability of large data sets, DL has emerged as a state-of-the-art technique in computer vision. In the domain of medical services, DL is especially effective for evaluating both organized and unstructured data. The application of DL algorithms to multiple imaging modalities and organs has substantially benefitted medical image processing over the last decade. DL algorithms can be used to automate certain tasks usually handled by radiologists, such as lesion identification, segmentation, classification, and monitoring. DL has been used in abdominal radiology for a variety of tasks, organs, and illnesses [4].

3.4 Role of Machine Learning and DL in the Field of Medical Diagnosis

Healthcare is considered as an important industry which offers value-based care to millions of people and becoming top revenue earners over the globe. Nowadays, the healthcare setting in the United States earns US$1.668 trillion. Compared to other developed or developing countries, several countries spend more on healthcare per capita. Quality, Value, and Outcome are three words that are always associated with healthcare and promise a lot. Healthcare experts and stakeholders all around the world are seeking for new ways to deliver on this promise. Technology is allowing healthcare professionals to build alternate staffing models, Intellectual Property (IP) capitalization, provide smart healthcare, and reduce administrative and supply expenses, in addition to playing a crucial role in patient care, billing, and medical records. In the healthcare industry, machine learning (ML) is one such subject that is gradually gaining traction. Researchers are utilizing DL to identify skin cancer, while Google has built a ML algorithm to identify malignant tumours in mammograms [6]. In healthcare, ML may help assess hundreds of different data points and suggest outcomes, as well as provide fast risk scores and exact resource allocation among other things. Some of the major applications of ML in healthcare and how they will impact the way we see the healthcare industry in 2018 and beyond will be covered in this chapter under the subheading applications.

Capsule Networks: The New DL Network: While constructing any objects with the help of rendering in computer graphics, specifications such as geometric information can tell the system about how to draw the object, the scale and angle for it along with other required spatial information and thereby representing it all on the screen as an object. However, when the same is extracted just by having a look at an object, then the process that capsule network based on is inverse rendering. The logic behind the CNNs can be explained on noticing the architectural failure that can be easily understood by the picture depicted here. This is because that the CNNs won't pay much attention to the pose of the object. Therefore, it is very clear that any object can often be created by giving some sort of parameters that computer graphics applications will render it [7]. However, with the use of capsule networks, the network by itself acquires how to inversely render an image by having a look at an image and thereby predict with instantiation parameters to make use of it efficiently. As seen in Figure 3.1, the final result is determined with the use of all possible pose parameters. As it is clear, a typical neuron of a neural network performs scalar operations such as weighting of inputs, sum of the weighted inputs, and non-linearity.

Within capsules, these operations are somewhat modified and executed as follows:

1. Input vectors are multiplied with weight matrices in a matrix. The spatial correlations between the low-level and high-level characteristics in the image are particularly critical for such a matrix multiplication encodes.

FIGURE 3.1
Irregular shape of an object.

2. Weighting of the input vectors and passing of the output through the current capsule will be decided by a process called **dynamic routing**.

3. Sum of the weighted input vectors. (Nothing special about this).

4. Non-linearity using the "squash" functions. A maximum and minimum length of 1 and 0, respectively, that will be determined while retaining its direction is defined as non-linearity using the squash function.

Metrics for Comparing Different Algorithms: Evaluation of the ML algorithm is one of the essential parts of any project because the results obtained from the model will be up to the satisfaction level. However, most of the time the classification accuracy will be used to measure the performance of any model but it is not sufficient enough for a true judgement. Below are the different types of evaluation matrices that are available such as classification accuracy, logarithmic loss, confusion matrix, area under curve (AUC), F1 Score, Mean Absolute Error, and Mean Squared Error (MSE).

Classification Accuracy: It is the ratio of the number of correct predictions to the total number of input samples. It executes well only if there are equal number of samples among the same class.

Logarithmic Loss: Logarithmic loss, often known as log loss, is a type of loss that operates by disciplining incorrect classifications. It performs admirably in multi-class categorization. When using Log Loss, the classifier must assign probability to each of the classes for all the data.

Confusion Matrix: It produces a matrix as an output, which describes the model's overall performance. Let's pretend we're dealing with a binary classification problem. We have some samples that fall into one of the two categories: yes or no. We also have our own classifier that guesses the group of any input sample.

AUC: One of the most often used metrics for evaluation is the AUC. It's used to solve problems with binary categorization. The likelihood that a classifier would score a randomly chosen positive example higher than a randomly chosen negative example is equal to the AUC of the classifier.

F1 Score: The Harmonic Mean between the precision and recall with a range of [0, 1] is defined as F1 Score. It tells you how precise your classifier and also how robust it is. The higher the "F1 Score," the better the performance of our model. F1 Score aims to strike a balance between recall and precision.

- **Precision:** The number of correct positive results divided by the number of positive results predicted by the classifier equals the number of correct positive outcomes.

- **Recall:** It's calculated by dividing the number of valid positive results by the total number of relevant samples (all samples that should have been identified as positive).

Mean Absolute Error: The difference between the Original and Predicted Values is averaged to get the Mean Absolute Error. It tells us how close the forecasts were to the final result.

MSE: The sole difference between MSE and Mean Absolute Error is that MSE takes the average square of difference between the original and predicted values, whereas Mean Absolute Error takes the average of difference between the original and predicted values.

3.5 Development in Remote Healthcare with Mobile Phone and Telemedicine Systems

There is a growing demand for e-health systems (e.g. remote patient monitoring (RPM), electronic health record systems, mobile health, telemedicine, e-visits, e-consultations, and so on). Continuous monitoring, diagnosis, prediction, and therapy are all possible with such systems. As a result, they serve to reduce healthcare costs by allowing patients to go about their daily routines while having their vital signs monitored continuously. Furthermore, these systems allow doctors to communicate with patients not only when they are physically present at the hospital but at any time. In hospitals, however, PM systems are crucial; they may be used to rate patients based on their statuses, allowing hospitals to prioritize critical patient care. The increasing usage of smart mobile devices has had a substantial impact on the number of people who seek medical help. As a result, RPMs have a considerable impact on patients across a wide range of domains. The Internet of Things has a significant impact on a variety of domains, with the medical sector being the most appealing [7,8].

Development of Analysis Models Based on Discrete Time Markov Chain (DTMC): The design of communication protocols becomes more complex as communication networks evolve. Insights into approaches for optimizing future communication protocols can be gained by evaluating the performance of present networks. Simulation, empirical data analysis, and analytical models are among the most used methodologies (e.g. channel models). Understanding network behaviour and designing communication protocols both require accurate modelling of network events, particularly error behaviour, at the link layer and above. Video and audio codecs, for example, can do real-time predictive rate management by estimating traffic conditions in real time using a model of network traffic characteristics [9]. Creating a Gilbert model (i.e. a two-state discrete Markov chain) based on acquired network traffic traces is the standard network modelling technique to error modelling. This model can then be used to dynamically produce false network traces for the network under investigation, which can then be used to simulate and better understand the performance of existing and emerging network protocols and applications.

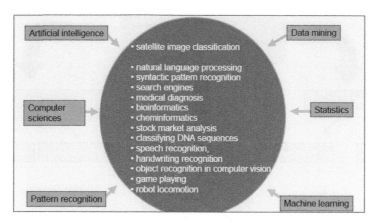

FIGURE 3.2
Detailed classification and its applications. (ESA Advanced Training Course.)

Development of Models for Such Medical Systems and Comparison with Recent Literature: People are gradually shifting from characters to visuals as computer processing power increases. Statistics show that today's information, particularly internet information, transmits and stores more than 80% of all information. As a result, doing relevant application research on picture digital media is very vital in order to make the usage of image information safer and more convenient. Denoising, encryption, compression, storage, and many other facets of digital media image processing technologies are all covered. Image clarity is harmed by noise, which is a significant influence [4,9]. A mean filter method, an adaptive Wiener filter method, a median filter, and a wavelet transform method are all common image noise removal approaches. For example, the image denoising approach utilized in the literature by the neighbourhood averaging method is a mean filtering method that is suited for reducing particle noise in a scanned image.

Classification: As shown in Figure 3.2, labelling of a single or group of pixel(s) based on its grey value termed as classification is one of the most often used methods to extract the information based on the requirements. Usually, multiple features are used for a set of pixels under classification, i.e. many images of a particular object are needed. In Remote Sensing area, for an electromagnetic spectrum with good registration for composing the picture of a particular geographic area, this procedure will be highly useful. Furthermore, specially designed algorithms are used for extracting information and primarily rely on the analysis of spectral reflectance properties of such descriptions to perform various types of "spectral analysis."

Quite interestingly, multispectral classification can be accomplished using either of the two methods, namely Supervised or Unsupervised. Uniqueness and locality of some of the land cover types, such as urban, wetland, and forest, are known as priori through a combination of field works and top sheets are commonly known as specified classification. The analyst's attempt to find specific areas in remotely sensed data indicates homogeneous examples of various land cover classes. TRAINING SITES are so called because the spectral properties of these well-known locations are utilized to "train" the classification algorithm for the eventual land cover mapping of the image. As a result, a computer is necessary to divide pixel data into different spectral classes based on statistical criteria. Figure 3.3 clearly depicts the basic description of various possibilities of categorizing the classifiers; further, the details of the supervised and unsupervised

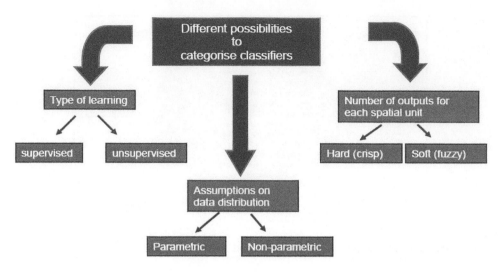

FIGURE 3.3
Detailed descriptions of different possibilities to categorize classifiers.

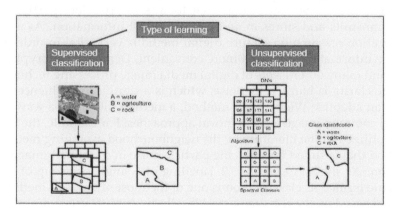

FIGURE 3.4
Description of type of learning. (CCRS.)

classifications are represented in Figure 3.4. Labelling of cells based on their shape, size, colour, and texture is one of the most important elements of comparison in the medical field mainly for MRI images.

Role and Current Trends: Image processing is emerging as a biomedical tool in the healthcare sector these days, and it is making a significant contribution to the improvement of human health. "Picture analysis, image segmentation, image enhancement, noise reduction, geometric transformations, and image registration" may all be done with ease with these tools. Any expert may analyse photos and videos, examine a section of pixels, modify colour and contrast, generate contours or histograms, and control ROIs using visualization of functions and apps. Processing, displaying, and navigating larger images can be achieved with the support of toolbox. The ready-to-use software-based solutions have been shown to be a more promising lifesaver in the diagnosis and management of patients' diseases. In India, using image processing technology is still in its early stages, with applications limited to institutional or research settings [10]. There are few applications in real-time patient management of illness grading.

Imaging Analytics and Diagnostics: CNN, a type of DL, is a well-suited image analysing technique, which is more particular to analyse the results of MRI or X-rays. Images of the structures and activities inside your body can be created using a range of machines and procedures. Your doctor's choice of imaging relies on your symptoms and the part of your body being checked.

Image Processing – Basis Concept: Image processing is simply a compatible formatting of the composed images with the aid of available software. Integrated team of experts with doctors and biomedical engineers is required for the pilot work. Specified images collected and arranged in folders by the doctors can be processed by the engineers and biomedical experts using suitable software such as Minitab and Catia according to the order set. Such technology will be highly helpful in disease grading and management as a prognostic tool and further, the borderline cases can be easily organized with high accuracy. Therefore, image processing is an important tool that can be utilized to achieve grading and classification.

Image Processing in India: The application of computer-based technology is being equally worthwhile and interesting in medical education system [6]. Introduction of various material-based learning aids including computer applications in the form of applicable software, internet, and telecommunications has greater potency in changing the surface of medical education. Moreover, India is obviously in its initial phases in the biomedical field due to the educational patterns developed and adopted. The doctors are even very less interested in interdisciplinary approach. Nowadays, this scenario of failure is slowly changing with the arrival of internet, entry of interdisciplinary journals, and access of private sectors. However, the growing young researchers in India are now more interested and aggressive with in-depth knowledge. Additionally, the need and importance of involvement of biomedical engineering and the challenges facing are highly underlined by junior researchers. The increasing number of diseases can be very easily interpreted and understood using the advancements of image processing technologies starting from two-dimensional (2D) images to complex four-dimensional (4D) Doppler images. "With the aid of 2D images such as X-ray images related to lung disorders, such as tuberculosis, lung emphysema, and pneumonia, can be easily collected and processed and thereby the chest disorders can be graded and formatted according to the Indian pattern. Various bone disorders such as cervical spondylitis, bony fractures, malignancies, and subclinical bone material changes can also be assessed and processed." Cervical spondylitis, usually an age-related chronic condition, which normally affects the joints and neck, develops as a result of the wear and tear of the cartilage and bones of the cervical spine. Even though physicians diagnose the patient of cervical spondylitis based on symptoms, disease grading would be one the major challenges with the use of digital X-rays. The same will be applicable to other bone disorders as well.

3.6 Applications in Health Research

Breast Cancer Detection Using Mammograms: Breast cancer is one of the most common types of carcinomas in developed countries in the Western world, according to the American Cancer Society, which advises mammography after 40 years of age as a routine screening tool for all women. Breast cancer indicators are misinterpreted in 52% of cases, with 43% of those errors being caused by disregarding signs of anomalies based on scan findings [6]. One of the most common errors during the interpretation of results using mammography is where sensitivity changes the quality of images and expertise of the diagnosing radiologist. Therefore, efforts are being continuously made to standardize with automated technologies.

Retinopathy Detection Using Retina Images: Image processing techniques, similar to breast mammography, have been found to be beneficial in cases with retinopathy. Normally, the images obtained will be subjected to a set of procedures for data analysis and interpretation. Image is an increasingly significant source of sensory observations about human activity and the urban environment. Image Scape is a software tool that is available for processing, clustering, and browsing large sets of images. Diabetic retinopathy is one of the severe and widely spread eye diseases that is widely proven and accepted as one of the commonest causes of legal blindness in the working-age population of developed countries [12,13]. There are three different ways in which it can contribute: image enhancement, mass screening (including detection of pathologies and retinal features), and monitoring. Efficient algorithms for the detection of the optic disc and retinal exudates have been presented with robustness and accuracy in comparison to human graders on a small image database.

Image Enhancement and Segmentation: Image enhancement and segmentation plays a very significant role and it is vast and dynamic field not only in the healthcare setting but also in the field of computer vision and satellite imagery. The main purpose of image segmentation is to divide image into various regions for a meaningful task. It is important to use maximum prior information during segmentation to develop robust interpretation systems. There are many segmentation approaches which further classified according to the characteristics and techniques used including the grey values (brightness), texture, and gradient magnitudes. Segmentation techniques can be further divided into contextual and non-contextual techniques.

Furthermore, contextual techniques exploit the association between image characteristics and identify group of pixels that might have similar grey levels which becomes close to one another or have similar gradient values [3]. It includes two techniques such as region-based techniques and boundary-based techniques in which region-based technique deals as a region-growing approach where connected regions are found based on the relationship of the pixels, whereas boundary-based techniques are used to describe the boundaries between regions and other methods such as active contours and watershed segmentation. On other side, non-contextual techniques ignore the association that exists between characteristics of an image, features in an image; pixels are simply grouped together on the basis of some aspect such as grey level.

Need for Image Processing in Radio Diagnosis: There are currently complicated programmes that allow users to visualize and even control medical images. These applications are extremely interesting in the field of radiology, both in terms of training and teaching. Furthermore, some of these applications are referred to as Free Open-Source (FOS) Software because they are free and their source code is easily accessible, making them suitable for PCs. OsiriX Lite and 3D Slicer are two notable examples of FOS software [14]. However, the use of this category of freely downloadable programmes is constrained.

Merits and Demerits of Image Processing: Digital image processing in the most understandable terms is the image editing used to improve its visual appearance but not limited to it. There are various merits and demerits of image processing; among them, the major merits are that it can be processed by digital computers. It can be flattened and allows weather forecasting, industries to remove defective products from the production line, and robots to have vision. It is used to analyse medical images, cells, and their composition. The authors would say the only disadvantages to something which develops new information for your processing (as thresholding does) are (1) the computational time and resources needed to compute the new data set and (2) the new data takes up space in your memory image. Therefore, it is worthless to do it unless the information is highly needed. For example, maybe your prototype applied a threshold to the entire image, but by reordering operations, you might be able to perform this operation only in particular ROIs. This is purely hypothetical and may be not very good examples, as thresholds are often used for detecting ROIs.

3.7 Conclusion

Images can display more clear, visible, and precise method of expression of data in the pictorial form. It consists of various small elements called pixels. Each pixel has a unique value and position. The most significant type is geometric image, which denotes an image created arithmetically using geometrical primitives such as lines. Each image is recorded in a unique file format that is made up of two parts: a heading and data. In this chapter, some of the recent and simpler analytical tools used to elaborate images have been discussed. It has been observed from the literature that image processing techniques can detect certain features/lesions in images and generate good results, but don't provide the quality required in healthcare systems. Furthermore, various complicated image analysis techniques are detected for the quantification of previously difficult to assess characteristics and to improve existing techniques.

References

1. Gonzalez, R, Eddins, S (2008) "4". *Digital Image Processing Using MATLAB* (2nd ed.). McGraw Hill. p. 163.
2. Burke, JA, Estrin, D, Hansen, M, Parker, A Nithya, RA, Reddy, S, Srivastava, M. (2006) Participatory Sensing. Workshop on World-Sensor-Web (WSW): Mobile Device Centric Sensor Networks and Applications; pp. 1–6.
3. Chen, LC, Barron, JT, Papandreou, G, Murphy, K, Yuille, AL. Semantic image segmentation with taskspecific edge detection using CNNS and a discriminatively trained domain transform. In: *Proceedings of the IEEE Conference on Computer Vision and Pattern Recognition*, 2013; pp. 4545–4554.
4. Saladra, D, Kopernik, M (2016) "Qualitative and quantitative interpretation of SEM image using digital image processing." *Journal of Microscopy*, vol. 264, no. 1, pp. 102–124.
5. Armi, L and Fekri-Ershad, S (2019) "Texture image analysis and texture classification methods—a review." *International Online Journal of Image Processing and Pattern Recognition*, vol. 2, no. 1, pp. 1–29.
6. Ganesan, K, Acharya, UR, Chua, CK, Min, LCi, Abraham, KT and Ng, KH (2012) "Computer-aided breast cancer de tection using mammograms: a review." *IEEE Reviews in Biomedical Engineering*, vol. 6, pp. 77–98.

7. McGlynn, EA, McDonald, KM, Cassel, CK (2015) "Measurement is essential for improving diagnosis and reducing diagnostic error: a report from the institute of medicine." *JAMA*, vol. 314, pp. 2501–2502.

8. Farmer, A, Gibson, O, Hayton, P, Bryden, K, Dudley, C, Neil, A, Tarassenko, L (2005) "A real-time, mobile phone-based telemedicine system to support young adults with type 1 diabetes." *Journal of Innovation in Health Informatics*, vol. 13, no. 3, pp. 171–177.

9. Srivastava, M, Hansen, M, Burke, J, Parker, A, Reddy, S, Saurabh, G, Allman, M, Paxson, V, and Estrin, D (2006) "Wireless urban sensing systems". Assessed from: http://www.icir.org/mallman/papers/urban-sensing-ucla-tr65.pdf

10. Spiroskostopoulos, P Ravazoula, PA (2017) "Development of a reference image collection library for histopathology image processing, analysis and decision support systems research." *Journal of Digital Imaging*, vol. 30, no. 3, pp. 1–9.

11. Prescott, JW (2013) "Quantitative imaging biomarkers: the application of advanced image processing and analysis to clinical and preclinical decision making." *Journal of Digital Imaging*, vol. 26, no. 1, pp. 97–108.

12. Walter, T, Klein, J-C, Massin, P, Erginay, A (2002) "A contribution of image processing to the diagnosis of diabetic retinopathy-detection of exudates in color fundus images of the human retina." *IEEE Transactions on Medical Imaging*, vol. 21, no. 10, pp. 1236–1243.

13. De Fauw, J, Ledsam, JR, Romera-Paredes, B, Nikolov, S, Tomasev, N, Blackwell, S, et al. (2018) "Clinically applicable deep learning for diagnosis and referral in retinal disease." *Nature Medicine*, vol. 24, pp. 1342–1350.

14. Malay, T, Pakhira, K (2011) *Digital Image Processing and Pattern Recognition* (1st ed). PHI Learning Pvt. Ltd.

4

Artificial Intelligence to Fight against COVID-19 Coronavirus in Bharat

Pushpendra Kumar Verma

IME Group of Colleges

Preety

Swami Vivekanad Subharti University

CONTENTS

4.1 Introduction

Artificial intelligence (AI) surveillance can used to determine whether people are following social distancing during the COVID-19 epidemic in the country. Right now, this technology is being officially ascertained in Telangana to monitor whether or not people are wearing masks and are giving priority to social distancing [1,2].

Using AI in CCTV is a technical solution based on images; hardware changes may be required in very old CCTV setups [1].The presence of masks on the faces of people standing in the coverage area of the CCTV camera can be identified. At the same time, it can also be used to identify whether social distancing is being followed according to the government guidelines or the people are standing as close as before. COVID-19 outbreak is still passionately deliberated by the world; the spread of this virus is growing very fast; and it is difficult to find a cure for it or detect it early (Figure 4.1). However, scientists are aware that AI can help find a solution in the future [2,3].

AI has been used to accelerate genome sequencing to make diagnosis faster and perform analysis with scanner robots. The contributions of AI have eliminated the need for clinical trial phases and have completely outpaced human skills. Emergency measures that use technological solutions, including AI, should be assessed at the end of the crisis and, as regards those who violate individual freedom, should not be trivialized under the pretext of better protection of the population [4]. The pandemic is causing problems to people, and

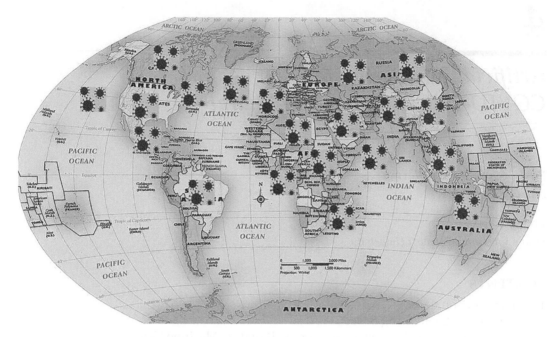

FIGURE 4.1
COVID-19 infection around the whole world.

experts are looking to get rid of them using AI technologies [5,6]. All have to follow the pandemic guidelines [7,8], and governments have to develop strategies and build health infrastructure and emergency services [7,9].

Some regions in China are developing AI+ new coronary pneumonia remote system under their R&D projects [10]. Such a new intelligent image evaluation system for coronavirus pneumonia developed by Shanghai Public Health Clinical Center medical personnel can upload CT images of patients to the system for rapid diagnosis and analysis.

4.2 Viral Gene Sequencing Based on AI

COVID-19 belongs to the genus β-coronavirus and infects humans in combination with influenza virus, par influenza virus, adenovirus, respiratory tract cytoviruses, rhinoviruses, and human metapneumovirus, and SARS and MERS viruses have certain similarities [8,9]. Now the gene sequencing of coronavirus is the key to distinguish the new coronavirus from other pathogens. It's critical to figure out what's causing the pneumonia pandemic, develop testing tools, and look for viable therapies. Gene sequencing of the new coronavirus is a dynamic and time-consuming process. AI can effectively solve the problem of increased time consumption and can considerably reduce the heavy workload of manual sequencing. The platform can quickly sequence and determine the samples of virus-infected patients as compared to the reagent diagnosis technology. It can greatly prevent the missed detection of virus mutations due to manual sequencing and can greatly improve the detection speed [11,12].

4.3 Diagnosis of New Coronary Pneumonia Based on Machine Vision

The diagnosis of new coronavirus infection depends on the detection of viral nucleic acid. Although this method has strong specificity, it has low understanding. The lung imaging of asymptomatic patients with new coronary pneumonia can find infection earlier, and there will be obvious abnormalities in the imaging findings.

The segmental or sub-segmental ground-glass shadow is dominant, the lesions in the advanced stage increase, the scope expands, the lungs develop multiple lobe involvement, and the ground-glass shadow and the real shadow of severe patients show diffuse lesions of both lungs, showing "white lung" and other shapes [13]. The training of machine vision models requires a large amount of clinical data. But most of the previous systems used in some hospitals suffer from the problem of insufficient sample sets, which limit the clinical significance [9]. A large number of studies have pointed out that using CT imaging for the diagnosis of pneumonia and bronchitis gives high accuracy. The application of AI in medical CT imaging based on distance transformation can quickly advance link soft tissue layered display processing to extract the outer contour and cutting depth of objects in the CT image(s) [14]. AI-based detection and three-dimensional segmentation of lung nodules for primary lung cancer perform with reliable accuracy and three-dimensional segmentation of lung infections, and diagnosis rate reaches 90.4%. However, it is only suitable for the detection of lung nodules; the detection of advanced lung tumors and segmentation is not accurate enough [12]. AI can provide high-efficiency and high-accuracy diagnosis of new coronary pneumonia.

4.4 New Coronary Drug Screening Based on AI+ Big Data

The vaccine and drug development process is long and complicated and requires strain isolation, sequencing analysis, target identification and validation, compound screening and optimization, evaluation studies and animal experiments, preparation synthesis, clinical trials, and other steps. It is a long process and usually takes more than 5 years [13]. In the face of urgent situation of new coronary pneumonia, it is difficult to quickly develop new drugs. "New medicine" is a key method for the development of new disease drugs. AI has efficient algorithms and powerful computing power. According to the characteristics of the new coronavirus, it is possible to screen out possible drugs from a large number of existing drugs and then shorten the development cycle of new drugs and increase the success rate of drug development. AI and natural language processing are used in many medical applications to create pneumonia consultation robots to assist doctors in solving simple diseases (Figure 4.2).

4.5 Using Computer Vision to Detect Coronavirus Infection

Health personnel use a thermometer gun to visually check a person / traveler for fever, and they perform tests of cough and breathing related to COVID-19. Computer vision

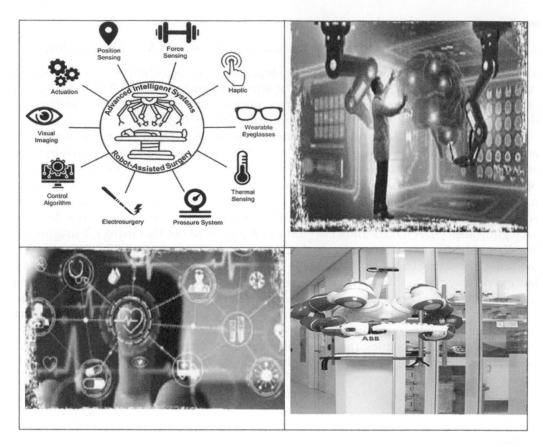

FIGURE 4.2
Robots to assist doctors in solving simple diseases.

algorithms can perform the same operations on a large scale. The AI system developed by Baidu uses cameras equipped with computer vision and infrared sensors to predict the temperature of people in public areas. The system can screen up to 200 people per minute and detect their temperature with accuracy in the range of 0.5°C. The AI will mark persons with temperature above 37.3°C. The technology is now used at the Beijing Qinghe Railway Station [15].

Alibaba has developed an AI system that can detect coronavirus in a chest CT scan. According to the researchers who developed the system, the accuracy of the AI is 96%. The AI received training on 5,000 cases of corona virus cases and can perform tests within 20 seconds, while experts need 15 minutes to complete the diagnosis. It can also distinguish between coronavirus and common viral pneumonia. This algorithm can help medical centers that are already under great pressure to screen patients for COVID-19 infection. According to reports, the system has been adopted in 100 hospitals in China [15]. Digital information is also evolving not only to inform doctors about the status quo but also to help them decide what to do next. The software will predict whether a patient is likely to be admitted to the ICU and, if so, when that admission will be necessary, as well as the probable date of discharge [16]. This information will help clinicians make better use of ICU bed capacity, on-site staffing, and the number of ventilators available.

4.6 AI in Other Areas

Digital technologies, including information technology and AI, are therefore proving to be important tools to help build a coordinated response to this pandemic. The multiple uses of AI illustrate the limits of the promises from which we cannot expect to compensate for structural difficulties, such as those experienced by many health institutions around the world. The search for efficiency and cost reduction in hospitals, often supported by information technologies, must not reduce the quality of services or compromise universal access to care, even in exceptional circumstances.

Finally, it should be possible to evaluate the emergency measures taken at the end of the crisis to identify the benefits and pitfalls that the use of digital tools and AI entails. In particular, temporary mass control and monitoring measures of the population through technologies should not be trivialized and become permanent.

Data protection rules, such as the Council of Europe Convention 108+, must continue to be fully applicable in all circumstances: Whether it is the use of biometric data, geolocation, facial recognition, or the exploitation of health data, the use of emergency applications must take place in consultation with the data protection authorities and respecting the dignity and privacy of users. The different biases of the various types of surveillance operations must be considered, as they can cause significant discrimination [12,14].

Now that COVID-19 has spread across the globe as a pandemic, the status of its infection must continue to be monitored. BlueDot, which develops software to detect infectious disease risk, predicted before WHO that COVID-19 would spread from Wuhan and made a warning. Detecting signs of a new type of pneumonia in Wuhan, BlueDot warned from air passenger data in December 2019 that 11 cities, including Tokyo and Seoul, were at high risk of infection [15].

Metabiota also uses AI for natural language processing to analyze news and reports on infectious diseases issued by public institutions and predict the number of infected people in China, Italy, Iran, and the USA. In addition, Stratifyd uses social media posts against public information to assess the risk of infection [15].

4.7 Conclusions

There are a number of application areas of AI-based expert systems that have been studied for verifying social distancing norms, disease diagnosis and analysis, genome sequencing, clinical trials, drug discovery, and a lot others. AI and other technologies can be very efficient where human speed and accuracy are limited.

References

1. Kong W, Li Y, Peng M, Kong D, Yang X, Wang L, Liu M (2020) SARS-CoV-2 detection in patients with influenza-like illness. *National Microbiology*, 5(5): 675–678. doi: 10.1038/s41564-020-0713-1.

2. Coronavirus disease (COVID-19): situation report–121. World Health Organization. 2020. [2020–04–19]. https://www.who.int/docs/default-source/coronaviruse/situation-reports/20200520-covid-19-sitrep-121.pdf.

3. Chen Y, Li L (2020) SARS-CoV-2: Virus dynamics and host response. *Lancet Infect Disease*, 20(5): 515–516. doi: 10.1016/S1473-3099(20)30235-8. http://europepmc.org/abstract/MED/32213336.

4. Del Rio C, Malani PN (2020) COVID-19-new insights on a rapidly changing epidemic. *JAMA*, 323(14): 1339–1340. doi: 10.1001/jama.2020.3072.

5. Fontanarosa PB, Bauchner H (2020) COVID-19-looking beyond tomorrow for health care and society. *JAMA*, 323(19): 1907–1908. doi: 10.1001/jama.2020.6582.

6. Yang P, Wang X (2020) COVID-19: A new challenge for human beings. *Cellular and Molecular Immunology*, 17(5): 555–557. doi: 10.1038/s41423-020-0407-x. http://europepmc.org/abstract/MED/32235915.

7. Ting DSW, Carin L, Dzau V, Wong TY (2020) Digital technology and COVID-19. *National Medical*, 26(4): 459–461. doi: 10.1038/s41591-020-0824-5. http://europepmc.org/abstract/MED/32284618.

8. Contreras I, Vehi J (2018) Artificial intelligence for diabetes management and decision support: Literature review. *Journal Medical Internet Research*, 20(5): e10775. doi: 10.2196/10775. https://www.jmir.org/2018/5/e10775/.

9. Shaw J, Rudzicz F, Jamieson T, Goldfarb A (2019) Artificial intelligence and the implementation challenge. *Journal Medical Internet Research*, 21(7): e13659. doi: 10.2196/13659. https://www.jmir.org/2019/7/e13659/.

10. van Hartskamp M, Consoli S, Verhaegh W, Petkovic M, van de Stolpe A (2019) Artificial intelligence in clinical health care applications: Viewpoint. *Interact Journal Medical Research*, 8(2): e12100. doi: 10.2196/12100. https://www.i-jmr.org/2019/2/e12100/.

11. Bullock J, Luccioni A, Hoffman Pham K, Sin Nga Lam C, Luengo-Oroz M Mapping the landscape of artificial intelligence applications against COVID-19. arXiv. Preprint posted online March 25, 2020. doi: 10.1613/jair.1.12162.

12. Duan Y, Edwards JS, Dwivedi YK (2019) Artificial intelligence for decision making in the era of big data–evolution, challenges and research agenda. *International Journal Information Management*, 48: 63–71.

13. "Coronavirus disease 2019 (COVID-19) situation report—80", April 2020 [online]. Available: https://www.who.int/docs/default-source/coronaviruse/situation-reports/20200409-sitrep-80-covid-19.pdf?sfvrsn=1b685d64.

14. Hong J-W, Williams D (2019) Racism, responsibility and autonomy in HCI: Testing perceptions of an AI agent. *Computer Human Behaviour*, 100: 79–84.

15. Russell S, Norvig P (2010) *Artificial Intelligence: A Modern Approach*, third edition. Upper Saddle River, NJ: Prentice Hall.

16. Alimadadi A, Aryal S, Manandhar I, Munroe PB, Joe B, Cheng X (2020) Artificial intelligence and machine learning to fight COVID-19. *Physiology Genomics*, 52(4): 200–202. doi: 10.1152/physiolgenomics.00029.2020. http://europepmc.org/abstract/MED/32216577.

5

Classification-Based Prediction Techniques Using ML: A Perspective for Health Care

Meenakshi Malik, Aditi Kaushik, and Rekha Khatana

Starex University

CONTENTS

5.1 Introduction

Machine Learning (ML) is a broad multidisciplinary term that incorporates ideas from statistics, cognitive science, computer science, optimization theory, engineering and a variety of several math and science domains [1]. ML has several applications, but data mining remains the most important among these [2]. Supervised ML and unsupervised ML are the two primary kinds of ML. Unsupervised ML is used to derive conclusion from data sets that contain input data without labelled response [3]. The goal of supervised ML approaches is to discover the link between input attributes "independent variables" and a target attribute "dependent variable" [4]. There are two primary groups of supervised techniques: (1) "Regression" and (2) "Classification". In regression, the output variable accepts continuous values, whereas the output variable takes class labels in classification [5]. Classification is a data mining (ML) technique for predicting data instance group membership [6]. Although there are other ML approaches available, classification is the most extensively utilized technique [7]. Classification is a well-liked ML task, particularly

DOI: 10.1201/9781003215981-5

in future planning and invention of knowledge. Researchers in the fields of ML and data mining consider classification to be one of the most studied problems [8]. Both regression and classification processes might be hampered by missing values in data collection [9]. Missing data issues may be overcome by the following ways: data miners may oversee omitting data, switch full omitting values with some individual global constant, for a given class switching an omitting value with its feature, physically observing sample with omitting values and inserting a probable or feasible value [10]. Applications of ML have presently backed enormously in the areas of health care throughout the world for improving its features, quality and for keep on contributing the same [11]. During critical situations, the ideal strategy is to utilize ML-based decision-making in the health care sector. Hence, there is a necessity for the field of "emergency ML" in today's society [12].

The purpose of this chapter is to describe the participation in computational decision-making of ML algorithms in the health sector. The chapter is ordered in a sequence having related work presented in Section 5.2, and Section 5.3 comprises two sub-sections where ML and the use of ML have been discussed in health care. Section 5.4 presents the scope and contribution of ML in disease prediction and detection. Section 5.5 covers the performance metrics of the classification methods. Section 5.6 explains the applications of classification in health care. Challenges and Opportunities for ML in health care have been covered in Section 5.7.

5.2 Related Work

In [13], Jason D. M. Rennie mentioned text classification using a Naïve Bayes (NB) text classifier, although the usage of a NB text classifier did not guarantee the output precision of 100%. The classifier's predictions aren't always accurate. T. Mouratis suggested the use of a classifier in his study [14], which boosted the precision of the output. However, the difficulty with it was that it didn't clearly assess the noun, verb and adjective during classification, so it might give erroneous value at times. B. Rosario employed Hidden Markov models to recognize entities in [15]. This covers the conversion of biomedical data into structural representation. It entails the transformation of natural language text into a structured framework. Their work employs ML to extract data. Text classification is used to generate medical abstract extraction. Words are classified with semantic classes in semantic lexicons, allowing associations to be made between them, which aids in extracting the essential sentences linked to the question. The precision and recall of the results gained are displayed in a graph. In this work, the authors employed co-occurrence of sentence and the NB algorithm to retrieve semantic relations such as Gene/Protein from MEDLINE abstracts. Individual sentences were treated as instances by M. Craven in [16], and the NB classifier was used to process them. Each incident is treated as a positive training set in this case. Relational learning allows for alternative relation extraction. Using NB, the authors were able to extract words from the abstracts of MEDLINE. Oana Frunza's [17] work entails the automatic extraction of relationships between medical ideas. For sentence classification, a medical dictionary is used. Semantic parser is used to automatically parse the sentences. Post application of semantic extraction, a set of extraction, alteration and validation criteria are used to separate the true semantic relation to be extracted. However, the usage of only one ML method, NB, may result in poor output precision L. Hunter uses natural language processing for biomedical words processing in [18]. By parsing user statements using natural language processing, this study carries an illness name and gives the resolution that has been entered in a database for that disease, but disease diagnosis is not supported. Jeff Pasternack [19] includes extracting words based on their occurrence in the article; extracting a particular word from the web depending on the occurrence of certain number of words by a certain number of times. The work utilized a bag of words to eliminate verb and adjective from the article, but it does not utilize natural language processing during extraction. Abdur Rehman [20] includes automatic extractions of relations between concepts. For sentence classification, a medical dictionary is used. Semantic parser is used to automatically parse the sentences. It extracts words using some classification algorithms: Decision Tree, NB, Complement Naïve Bayes (CNB), Adaptive, Support Vector Machine (SVM) and so on, but it does not provide data on disease diagnosis. Other classifiers exceed AdaBoost classifier in Adrian Canedo-Rodriguez's paper [21]. OanaFrunza used a pipelined approach in [22] to find and extract the association between the given MEDLINE abstract. The main goal is to discover the best prediction model and the secondary objective is to establish a reasonable data representation. Numerous predictive algorithms and textual representation strategies are considered to accomplish these tasks. Decision-based models, probabilistic models "NB, CNB", Adaptive learning, linear classifiers such as SVMs and a classifier which mostly forecasts the majority class in training data are among the six classification algorithms employed. All six categorization algorithms are addressed in terms of their benefits and drawbacks.

According to the time stamp of each occurrence, the sequence-based representation method creates an electronic health record sequence for each patient. Then, to identify temporal patterns as phenotypes, frequent pattern mining techniques can be used [23,24]. According to classic learning, the amount of training data required rises as the complexity of the learning algorithm rises [25,26]. As a result, execution of neural networks outside of typical domains with access to enormous Internet-scale data sets offers a hurdle. Particularly it is relevant in clinical applications, as several predicting jobs face challenges due to high-class imbalance because of the underlying nature of most disorders. To avoid such issues and enhance efficiency, one solution is to leverage side information such as class hierarchy. However, relatively limited research work is there in the deep learning community exploiting the utilization of such priors for neural network training. In [27], blend of a deep architecture with a tree-based prior for encoding relationships between dissimilar labels and label categories has been shown. However, the research is constrained to modelling a restricted class of side information.

5.3 Unlocking the Power of Classification and Prediction Techniques using ML in Health Care

5.3.1 Machine Learning

In the earlier days, human intervention is being used to analyse the data; however, this is ineffective and many hidden patterns are not detected within the data [28]. ML's iterative nature permits the machine to adjust its processes and outputs to new situations and data [29–31].

In unsupervised ML, the machine should explore the data and attempt to develop a few types of patterns or structures; models must be developed from scratch, and no proper

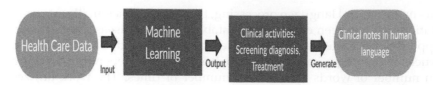

FIGURE 5.1
ML in health care.

outputs should be given. This is frequently used to determine and differentiate outliers [28]. There are presently a number of areas where ML is widely used. In financial area, supervised ML is being utilized for the prediction of whether the credit card dealings are expected to be falsified and such algorithms spontaneously direct the credit card holder a message for checking fraudulent charge. It is also often used in the retail industry. Users can assess what customers would like next using predictive ML-driven analytics and create an online experience that meets the customer needs [28].

5.3.2 ML in Health Care

The prevalence of ML to analyse data is gaining momentum in a rising business in which fitbits, smartwatches and devices continually collect a host of health data [32]. A lot of data has currently become available in the field of health care. This contains electronic medical records containing structured or unstructured data [33]. Figure 5.1 depicts a general ML model (classification approaches) in health care. The discussion between the doctor and the patient is very difficult to quantify and categorize; the conversation is highly personalized and can take many separate directions [30]. Since medication is connected to narration type, modern ML methodologies must seek to organize and relate mass quantities of unstructured raw data. The capability to use and understand this sort of data in an extensive range is extremely useful for the application of ML technologies in the health sector [34].

If used effectively, ML can help doctors diagnose near-perfectly, selecting the best medication for the patient, determining high-risk patients for poor drug outcomes and improving the general health of patients while lowering costs [30]. ML may be utilized in helping to diagnose patient and lead them to appropriate cure while guiding patients to keep away from costly, time-intensive emergency care centres [35].

5.4 ML in Disease Prediction and Detection

"Prevention is better than cure" is a wise saying. In order to make a smart health care system, early prediction of the disease is necessary instead of the diagnosis as some cases can appear before the early diagnosis of a disease. ML has facilitated the correct identification of various ailments and diagnoses (Figure 5.2).

   i. **Input from Patients**: First, the data about their past medical history is collected from patients. After receiving the data, it is sent to the database for its storage.
  ii. **Applying ML Algorithm**: Since the raw data can't be used directly, the ML algorithm is applied to generate the information/data sets from the data. There are

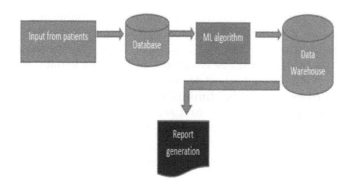

FIGURE 5.2
General working framework of ML in disease prediction.

many ML algorithms which may be functional on the data to generate information such as NB, Decision tree, Random Forest, K-nearest neighbour (KNN) and ANN.

iii. **Storage of the Generated Data Sets**: In this phase, the generated data sets are stored in the data warehouse from where the processing, reading, writing and managing of these large data sets can be performed efficiently. Hive is better to work with the integration of R/Python.

iv. **Report Generation**: After processing the large data sets, the report is generated that carries information related to disease prediction.

ML algorithms, such as NB, Decision tree and Random Forest, read the clinical data through patient's input. The clinical data can be the disease data that includes physiological measurements and information about known diseases, the symptoms, or it can be the environmental data that contains information about the person's exposure to smoking, sunbathing, different weathers, etc. or the genetic data containing the DNA sequence of the patient.

ML plays an important role in the prediction of very dangerous diseases. Many researchers have worked in this area. Let's explore some of the related works of ML in disease prediction.

5.4.1 ML in Diabetes Prediction

The high amount of blood sugar causes diabetes. It is caused by the absence or low amount of insulin produced by the pancreas as insulin helps glucose from food to get into the cell to produce energy in the body. The first symptoms of diabetes are frequent urination, increased thirst, extreme hunger, fatigue, blurred vision and slow healing of cuts.

Mujumdar et al. [36] proposed the diabetes prediction model to better classify the diabetes by considering factors such as glucose, body mass index, age and insulin. They divided the proposed system into five phases: data set collection of 800 records and ten attributes to understand the data and patterns, data pre-processing to handle inconsistent and missing data for accurate and precise results, clustering phase using K-means on glucose and age parameters to classify the patients into diabetic and non-diabetic groups. The next phase was of model building in which they have implemented a set of algorithms with pipelining. From the results, they concluded that logistic regression gave the highest accuracy.

Sisodia et al. [37] proposed the design of a model that is capable of predicting the probabilities of occurrences of diabetes in patients with maximum accuracy. For the model, they have used Decision tress, SVM and NB. To perform the experiment, University of California, Irvine (UCI) ML repository is utilized to extract the data. From the outcomes, they concluded that NB gave the highest accuracy of 76%.

The risk factor of diabetes may be diminished and controlled if the prediction made is strong in nature and provides precise and accurate results. Ref. [38] proposed a robust framework to predict the chances of occurrences of diabetes by including outlier rejection, filling the missing values, feature selection and classifiers. To improve the accuracy of the prediction, the area under receiving operating characteristic (ROC) curve is used.

5.4.2 ML in Cancer Prediction

Lung cancer occurs when cells divide uncontrollably in the lungs, causing the tumours to grow. To control this, an early prediction is needed based on the symptoms in the patient's body. Kadir and Gleeson [39] have provided a review of different approaches for lung cancer prediction and challenges in the development of powerful techniques.

Classifications using ML have improved magically in the area of disease predictions and in supporting the doctors in timely diagnoses. Cervical cancer is a type of gynaecological cancer that can affect a human body in most dangerous ways. It becomes important to analyse the important factors associated with it to timely predict the disease. Nithya and Ilango [40] presented a deep analysed work on the factors by applying ML techniques such as Random Forest, rpart, KNN and SVM in R. To better evaluate the performance and accuracy of these algorithms, maximum possibilities were explored. Based on the experimentation, it is concluded that C5.0 and Random Forest have performed good with better accuracy.

Nowadays, breast cancer has emerged as the major cause of death among women. The need is to study and extract the patterns from the data sets that can help to build systems for predicting this disease on time. Kumari and Singh [41] have designed a prediction system which is able to forecast the illness at an initial phase based on the symptoms and by analysing the data sets. For the analysis and experimentation, Wisconsin Breast Cancer data set is used. The outcome confirms the 99.28% of accuracy.

5.4.3 ML in Heart Disease Prediction

The number of heart disease patients is growing drastically even at juvenile ages. The need is to put a system that can detect the symptoms of this disease at an early stage to provide better controlling. Gavhane et al. [42] projected a structure that reduces the need of undergoing ECG test for a common man and that is handy and can provide results in a reliable time. The application predicts the vulnerability on the basis of some parameters such as age, sex and pulse rate. For the experimentation, they have used a neural network as it is a reliable and accurate algorithm.

As per the reports of Indian Heart Association, the rate of deaths due to heart problems is increasing uncontrollably. It has become necessary to develop a system and analyse the algorithms that can accurately predict the chances of this developing disease in a person.

Kannan and Vasanthi [43] have examined and compared the accuracy of different ML algorithms with the ROC curve.

Many researchers have proposed the decision support systems working with ANN. But many of these techniques are focussing only on the pre-processing of the features.

TABLE 5.1

Analysis of related works

References	Disease	Analysis
[36]	Diabetes	Applied K-means for clustering into diabetic and non-diabetic. Logistic regression gave the highest accuracy amongst other algorithms.
[37]	Diabetes	Used Decision trees, SVM and Naïve bayes on UCI ML repository. Naïve bayes gave the highest accuracy.
[38]	Diabetes	Focused on outlier rejection, feature selection, classifications. Are under ROC curve Is used for better accuracy.
[39]	Lung Cancer	Review on different approaches applied in this area and the challenges needs to be resolved.
[40]	Cervical cancer	Implemented Random Forest, rPart, KNN and SVM C5.0 in R. C5.0 and Random Forest provided the better accuracy.
[41]	Breast Cancer	Applied integrated algorithms and generated 99.28% of accuracy
[42]	Heart	Performed neural network on data recorded on the basis of factors like age gender, pulse rate.
[43]	Heart	Drawn a comparative analysis on various algorithms with Receiving operating curve.
[44]	Heart	Proposed a hybrid model based on X^2-DNN that works on features refinement and gives 93.33 % of accuracy.

Liaqat et al. [44] have proposed a hybrid model named X^2-DNN that works on the refinement of features and elimination of problems. For the elimination of unnecessary features, the authors have used X^2 statistical model and DNN for search strategy. Experimentation results show the accuracy of 93.33% of the proposed model. Table 5.1 shows the brief analysis of these works.

5.5 Applications of Classification in Health Care

The classification algorithm is a supervised learning technique which is utilized to identify the category of new observations on the basis of training data [45]. In these algorithms, a programme is made to learn by providing it a data set which is then classified into new data and observations, classes or groups. Classification plays a major role in various application areas of health care (Figure 5.3) as described below:

(a) **Disease Prediction and Detection**
"Prevention is better than cure" is a wise saying. In order to make a smart health care system, early prediction of the disease is necessary instead of the diagnosis as some cases can appear before the early diagnosis of a disease. ML has made the process of identification and detection of different diseases easier with maximum accuracy and precision as discussed earlier.

(b) **Medical Imaging and Diagnostics**
Medical imaging consists of various processes and techniques that shape up the visualization of inner organization of the body and of some organs and tissues. It covers X-ray, ultrasound, MRI, etc. The main motive of medical imaging is

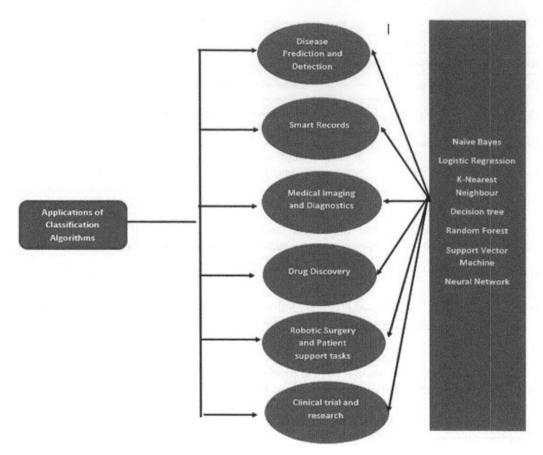

FIGURE 5.3
Applications of classifications.

to provide accurate results to the doctors so that it can be detected on time what was wrong with the internal organs of the body. But again, the imaging generates a lot of data that can't be handled by the medical team efficiently and may be liable to suffer from errors that might be caused by various factors such as lack of expertism and stress. ML is the solution to this problem. ML provides (1) *High accuracy image processing*, (2) *Localization of organs involving the conversion of 3D space into 2D space*, (3) *Content-based image retrieval for understanding rare disorders*, (4) *Normalization, enhancement and completion of data with pattern discovery* and (5) *Image data and report combination*.

(c) **Smart Records**

Managing the huge data of patient's records is tedious and complex. Since this huge data is stored in the data warehouse in an unstructured way, it becomes inefficient to read and analyse them. For the rescue, ML comes to the role to enable efficient and effective reading and analysis of this huge unstructured data.

In the conventional approach, the users categorize the data during the creation phase. But this approach doesn't scale with the volume of data as this would lead to low productivity and erroneous classifications. With this, the need for a smart technology arose and thus ML is employed. ML can be defined as a process

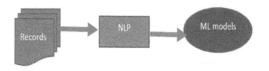

FIGURE 5.4
Working framework of smart record creation.

that with the use of statistical techniques or models, it can predict the categories of records.

As shown in Figure 5.4, the records are inputted to the natural language processing phase to convert them into machine-readable forms. After this, the information is fed into the ML models to classify and categorize them accordingly. Smart Records using ML provide many benefits such as (1) *Automated classification and processing*, (2) *Automation of manual process*, (3) *Efficient data extraction*, (4) *Document clustering*, (5) *Unstructured to structured data* and (6) *Safe and secure access.*

(d) **Drug Discovery**

Since the pharmaceutical companies collect a vast amount of data for the drug discovery, ML suits the best here to efficiently handle this huge data. ML plays varied roles in the drug discovery process: (1) in drug design by predicting the 3D structure and interactions between drug–protein, (2) in prediction of reaction synthesis and (3) in drug screening by predicting the toxicity, bioactivity and classification of target cells.

(e) **Robotic Surgery and Patient Support Tasks**

In recent times, we have seen how perfectly the robotic machines handle the surgeries by assisting the surgeons in the execution of surgical procedures. This all has become possible with the use of ML as it uses real-time data and information from the previous successful operations and surgeries and previous medical records to improve the efficiency and accuracy of the robotic tools and thus reduces human error, helps in carrying out more complex procedures, for example, spine surgery and unclogging blood vessels. Robots can provide help to paralyzed patients by making them enable to regain their walking ability, providing medication and companionship to them and many more.

(f) **Clinical Trial and Research**

Clinical trials are time-consuming and can take years to complete in many cases. By applying ML techniques, this time can be reduced to much extent as ML performs real-time monitoring of data of the trial participants and on the basis of this, it provides the best sample size for testing by ensuring reduced data-based errors.

5.6 Challenges and Opportunities for ML in Health Care

In this segment, the challenges that should be considered in ML systems for health care applications and the future opportunities that ML can provide to the health care system are covered (Table 5.2).

TABLE 5.2

Challenges and Opportunities

Challenges	Opportunities
• Governing the data	• Pattern imaging analysis
• Transparency in working algorithms	• Personalized treatment and behavioural modification
• Optimization of e-records	• Robotic surgery
• Reliability	• Predicting epidemic outbreak
• Cybersecurity	• Collection of data through crowdsourcing
• Data and ownership rights	

5.6.1 Challenges in Health Care System

The following factors should be considered while designing the ML systems for health care:

1. **Governing the Data**: Medical data of a patient is personal and access protected, and not everybody is in favour of sharing their medical history publicly. The need is to create a system that will store this confidential information securely and protect it from unauthorized access.

2. **Transparency in Working Algorithms**: The working algorithms necessarily should be transparent so that people can understand, how actually these algorithms work while designing drug in medical imaging, clinical trial, etc.

3. **Optimization of e-Records**: The accuracy of an experiment depends on the quantity and quality of data in use. Since the medical data consists of a huge amount of unstructured, fractured and unwanted data, the need is to optimize this ocean of data so that only qualitative data can be used for performing experimental work. Optimization of these e-records will also provide benefits of easy storage of these data.

4. **Reliability**: The accuracy of a system depends directly on the data provided to it. On the one hand, if a data is reliable and valid, the machine will learn well and perform well with higher accuracy. But on the other hand, unreliable and garbage data can cause a serious problem in the processing and learning of the machine.

5. **Cybersecurity**: As this century is witnessing many emerging powerful technologies, there is a high chance of integrating ML with Internet of Things to operate and connect the health care services via the internet. With this, the threat of vulnerability of these systems to cyber-attacks will also arise. The need is to apply the cybersecurity mechanisms with these ML systems to protect them from any kind of malware or cyber-attacks.

6. **Data and Ownership Rights**: Data acts a fuel to any learning system. The big data creates challenges that needs to be addressed such as intellectual property rights, safe access to data, copyright and contracts.

5.6.2 Unlocking the Opportunities of ML in Health Care

There are many opportunities in health care that can change the whole scenario of the health care system. In this part, the emerging opportunities of ML in health care are framed.

1. **Pattern Imaging Analysis**: ML can help in even the minor changes in the scans and thus helping the radiologists in detecting and diagnosing health issues at the early stages.

2. **Personalized Treatment and Behavioural Modification**: The huge amount of data of patients' health history serves as a fuel in the analysis of patients' health. ML can help in the compilation of these records and health care providers to detect and access health issues better.

    However, behavioural modification using ML can enforce a positive behaviour attitude in the patients towards their treatment. By analysing and monitoring the physical and mental states of a patient, physicians can better understand their behaviour and can finalize the right kind of treatment and lifestyle changes for them.

3. **Robotic Surgery**: In recent times, robotic surgery has proven its applications and importance in various areas of health care. Still many developments and advancements are needed in this area. More precision and accuracy of surgical tools are in demand that can be achieved using ML algorithms.

4. **Predicting Epidemic Outbreak**: The Covid-19 epidemic has shown the world the urgent need for the system that can predict the outbreaks of dangerous diseases. Many health care organizations are working on applying ML by doing data collection from satellites or collecting data from social media updates and surveys to perform timely monitoring and predict the possible epidemic outbreaks.

5. **Collection of Data through Crowdsourcing**: This technique helps the researchers in collecting data through cheaper modes such as questionnaires and surveys. The success of crowdsourcing depends on the size of the network of contributors. If it is a large network then more data will be collected and thus more accurate results will be generated otherwise lesser data will generate low accurate results. It should be kept in mind that technology constraints might affect the data collection in rural areas. Therefore, for rural areas, different approaches should be used. The following points should be considered while working with crowdsourcing:

    • Careful following of the network growth as the accuracy of the result depends directly on the crowd data.

    • The trade-off between sample size and issues should be handled carefully; sometimes due to rigorous sampling, the crowdsourcing is affected unknowingly.

5.7 Conclusion

The ability to capture, share and supply data has become a top priority as digitalization impacts every industry, including health care. The challenges involved can be addressed by ML, big data and the "artificial intelligence". ML can also help organizations to meet growing medical requirements, improve operations and reduce costs. ML innovation can help health professionals more efficiently and with more precision and personalized care to detect and treat diseases on the bedside. A review of ML in health care reveals how innovation in technology can lead to more effective, holistic treatment strategies that can improve patient's treatment outcomes. The primary goal of this chapter was to assess classification-based prediction approaches towards the functionality of health system.

A comprehensive discussion of the various classification algorithm strategies in ML has further supported our aim. It also aimed to identify numerous techniques and applications used in classification-based prediction in the field of health care. This chapter explained how ML can be utilized to predict and detect ailments. Furthermore, we have attempted covering ML applications in health care. A detailed description of all classification algorithms widely used in the field of health care has been provided. We also discussed further ML possibilities and challenges in health care. This chapter also described classification performance measures of ML algorithms.

References

1. Ghahramani, Z. (2004) Unsupervised Learning. In: Bousquet, O., von Luxburg, U., Rätsch, G. (eds) *Advanced Lectures on ML*. ML 2003. Lecture Notes in Computer Science, vol. 3176. Springer, Berlin, Heidelberg. https://doi.org/10.1007/978-3-540-28650-9_5.

2. Kotsiantis, S., Zaharakis, I., and Pintelas, P. (2006) ML: A Review of Classification and Combining Techniques. *Artificial Intelligence Review*, 26, 159–190. https://doi.org/10.1007/s10462-007-9052-3.

3. Zhang, D., and Nunamaker, JF. (2003) Powering E-Learning in the New Millennium: An Overview of E-Learning and Enabling Technology. *Information Systems Frontiers*, 5, 207–218. https://doi.org/10.1023/A:1022609809036.

4. Maimon, O., and Rokach, L. (2005) Introduction to Supervised Methods. In: Maimon, O., Rokach, L. (eds) *Data Mining and Knowledge Discovery Handbook*. Springer, Boston, MA. https://doi.org/10.1007/0-387-25465-X_8.

5. Supervised Learning. https://see.stanford.edu/materials/aimlcs229/cs229-notes1.pdf.

6. Kesavaraj, G., and Sukumaran, S. (2013) "A Study on Classification Techniques in Data Mining", *2013 Fourth International Conference on Computing, Communications and Networking Technologies (ICCCNT)*, Tiruchengode, India, pp. 1–7.

7. Singh, M., Sharma, S., and Kaur, A. (2013) Performance Analysis of Decision Trees. *International Journal of Computer Applications*, 71, 10–14.

8. Baradwaj, BK., and Pal, S. (2012) Mining Educational Data to Analyze Students' Performance. arXiv preprint arXiv:1201.3417.

9. Dunham, MH. (2006) *Data Mining: Introductory and Advanced Topics*. Pearson Education India, New Delhi.

10. Kantardzic, M. (2019) *Data Mining: Concepts, Models, Methods, and Algorithms*, 3rd Edition. Wiley-IEEE Press, New York. ISBN: 978-1-119-51607-1.

11. Sánchez Martínez, S., Camara, O., Piella, G., Cikes, M., González Ballester, MÁ., Miron, M., Vellido, A., Gómez, E., Fraser, A., Bijnens, B. (2019) ML for Clinical Decision-Making: Challenges and Opportunities. https://doi.org/10.20944/preprints201911.0278.v1.

12. Debnath, S., Barnaby, D.P., Coppa, K. et al. (2020) ML to Assist Clinical Decision-Making during the COVID-19 Pandemic. *BioMed Central*, 6, 2332–8886.

13. Rennie, JDM., Shih, L., Teevan, J., and Karger, DR. (2003) "Tackling the Poor Assumption of Naïve Bayes Text Classifier", *Proceedings of the Twentieth International Conference on ML (ICML-2003)*, Washington DC.

14. Mouratis, T., and Kotsiantis, S. (2009) "Increasing the Accuracy of Discriminative of Multinominal Bayesian Classifier in Text Classification", *ICCIT'09 Proceedings of the 2009 Fourth International Conference On Computer Science And Convergence Information Technology*, Seoul, South Korea.

15. Rosario, B., and Hearst, MA. (2004) "Semantic Relation in Bioscience Text", *Proceedings of the 42nd Annual Meeting on Association for Computational Linguistics*, Barcelona, Spain, Vol. 430.

16. Craven, M. (2009) "Learning to Extract Relations from Medline", *Proceedings of the Association for the Advancement of Artificial Intelligence*. https://doi.org./10.35940/ijeat.F1289.0886S219.
17. Frunza, O., Inkpen, D., and Tran, T. (2011) A Machine Learning Approach for Identifying Disease-Treatment Relations in Short Texts. *IEEE Transactions on Knowledge and Data Engineering*, 23, 801–814. https://doi.org/10.1109/TKDE.2010.152.
18. Hunter, L., and Cohen, KB. (2006) Biomedical Language Processing: What's Beyond Pubmed? *Molecular Cell*, 21–25, 589–594.
19. Pasternack, J., and Roth, D. (2009) "Extracting Article Text from Webb with Maximum Subsequence Segmentation", WWW 2009 MADRID.
20. Rehman, A., Babri, HA., and Saeed, M. (2012) "Feature Extraction Algorithm For Classification of Text Document", *ICCIT 2012*, University of Chittagong, Bangladesh.
21. Canedo-Rodriguez, A., Kim, JH. et al. (2012) Efficient Text Extraction Algorithm Using Color Clustering for Language Translation in Mobile Phone. *Journal of Signal and Information Processing*, 3(2), Article ID: 19574, 10 pages. http://doi.org/10.4236/jsip.2012.32031.
22. Frunza, O., Inkpen, D., and Tran, T. (2011) A ML Approach for Identifying Disease Treatment Relations in Short Texts. *IEEE Transactions on Knowledge and Data Engineering*, 23(6), 801–814.
23. Gotz, D., Wang, F., and Perer, A. (2014) A Methodology for Interactive Mining and Visual Analysis of Clinical Eventpatterns Using Electronic Health Record Data. *Journal of Biomedical Informatics*, 48, 148–159.
24. Perer, A., and Wang, F. (2014) "Frequence: Interactive Mining and Visualization of Temporal Frequent Event Sequences", *Proceedings of the 19th International Conference on Intelligent User Interfaces*. ACM, pp. 153–162. https://doi.org/10.1145/2557500.2557508.
25. Vapnik, V. (2000) *The nature of statistical learning theory*. Springer Science & Business Media, New York.
26. Bartlett, PL., and Mendelson, S. (2002) Rademacher and Gaussian complexities: Risk bounds and structural results. *Journal of Machine Learning Research*, 3, 463–482.
27. Srivastava, N., and Salakhutdinov, RR. (2013) "Discriminative Transfer Learning with Tree-Based Priors", *NIPS*, Lake Tahoe, Nevada, December 5–10, 2013, Volume 2, pp. 2094–2102.
28. Machine Learning. https://www.sas.com/en_in/insights/analytics/machine-learning.html (Online).
29. Machine Learning. https://en.wikipedia.org/wiki/Machine_learning.
30. Maddux, D. (2014) *The Human Condition in Structured and Unstructured Data*. Acumen Physician Solutions. https://acumenmd.com/blog/human-condition-structured-unstructured-data/.
31. Brownlee, J. (2020) "What is ML: A Tour of Authoritative Definitions and a Handy One-Liner You Can Use". https://www.machinelearningmastery.com.
32. Dolley, S. (2018). Big Data's Role in Precision Public Health. *Frontiers in Public Health*, 6. https://doi.org/10.3389/fpubh.2018.00068.
33. King, AJ., Cooper, GF., Clermont, G., Hochheiser, H., Hauskrecht, M., Sittig, DF., and Visweswaran, S. (2019) Using Machine Learning to Selectively Highlight Patient Information. *Journal of Biomedical Informatics*, 100, 103327. ISSN 1532-0464.
34. "Challenges in ML from Electronic Health Records", NIPS 2015 *Workshop on Machine Learning in Healthcare*, MLHC. https://neurips.cc/Conferences/2015/ScheduleMultitrack?event=4922.
35. Dolley, S. (2015) Big Data Solution to Harnessing Unstructured Data in Healthcare. IBM Report.
36. Mujumdar, A., and Vaidehi, V. (2019) Diabetes Prediction using ML Algorithms. *Procedia Computer Science*, 165, 292–299. https://doi.org/10.1016/j.procs.2020.01.047.
37. Sisodia, D., and Sisodia, DS. (2018) Prediction of Diabetes using Classification Algorithms. *Procedia Computer Science*, 132, 1578–1585. ISSN 1877-0509, https://doi.org/10.1016/j.procs.2018.05.122.
38. Diabetes Prediction Using Ensembling of Different ML Classifiers MD. Kamrul Hasan 1, MD. Ashraful Alam1, Dola Das2, Eklas Hossain 3, (Senior Member, IEEE), and Mahmudul Hasan 2.
39. Kadir, T., and Gleeson, F. (2018) Lung Cancer Prediction Using ML and Advanced Imaging Techniques. *Translational Lung Cancer Research*, 7(3), 304–312. https://doi.org/10.21037/tlcr.2018.05.15.

40. Nithya, B., and Ilango, V. (2019) Evaluation of ML Based Optimized Feature Selection Approaches and Classification Methods for Cervical Cancer Prediction. *SN Applied Sciences*, 1, 641. https://doi.org/10.1007/s42452-019-0645-7.

41. Kumari, M., and Singh, V. (2018) Breast Cancer Prediction system. *Procedia Computer Science*, 132, 371–376, ISSN 1877-0509. https://doi.org/10.1016/j.procs.2018.05.197.

42. Gavhane, A., Kokkula, G., Pandya, I., and Devadkar, K. (2018) "Prediction of Heart Disease Using ML", *2018 Second International Conference on Electronics, Communication and Aerospace Technology (ICECA)*, pp. 1275–1278. https://doi.org/10.1109/ICECA.2018.8474922.

43. Kannan, R., and Vasanthi, V. (2019) "ML Algorithms with ROC Curve for Predicting and Diagnosing the Heart Disease", *Soft Computing and Medical Bioinformatics*. Springer Briefs in Applied Sciences and Technology. Springer, Singapore. https://doi.org/10.1007/978-981-13-0059-2_8.

44. Ali, L., Rahman, A., Khan, A., Zhou, M., Javeed, A., and Khan, JA. (2019) An Automated Diagnostic System for Heart Disease Prediction Based on χ^2 Statistical Model and Optimally Configured Deep Neural Network. *IEEE Access*, 7, 34938–34945. https://doi.org/10.1109/ACCESS.2019.2904800.

45. Classification Algorithm in Machine Learning. https://www.javatpoint.com/classification-algorithm-in-machine-learning.

6

Deep Learning for Drug Discovery: Challenges and Opportunities

Aarti

Lovely Professional University

CONTENTS

6.1 Introduction

Drug discovery and advancement are the most imperative translational science activities [1] that add to human well-being and prosperity. However, the advancement of a new drug [2] is an incredibly lengthy, exorbitant, demanding and inefficient method which requires by and large of 10–15 years. It normally costs 2.6 billion USD. Any disappointment is a huge monetary harm, and indeed, disappointments are not uncommon. Notwithstanding propels in innovation and a generally excellent comprehension of biological systems, over the most recent 20 years, the pharmaceutical business has seen an undeniably debilitating innovative work efficiency because of developing expenses, while unquestionably the quantity of recently

DOI: 10.1201/9781003215981-6

endorsed drugs has consistently reduced due to over expansion of administrative issues and mounting trouble in finding the following blockbuster drug (either in another illness region or a far better medication) [3]. So, how to diminish the expenses and accelerate new medication discovery has become a difficult and required question in business. Artificial intelligence (AI) is an expansive branch in computer science that tries to make human intelligence using machines, of which machine learning (ML) is fundamental to accomplish this objective [4]. As of late, a subset of ML, deep learning (DL), is arisen as a method equipped for accomplishing high accuracies from large information, while dealing with both organized and unstructured information. AI-based strategies [2] are additionally acquiring increasing prevalence in the drug business since they suggested the capacity to speed up and conduct the medicine improvement pipeline in preclinical investigations along with successive clinical preliminaries [5–11]. ML as a subfield inside AI intends to create and use methods that gain from raw information. ML models [12] can be categorized as either supervised or unsupervised, named for the datasets for which the strategies work. In supervised learning, it is a numerical association among factors found in a dataset with known information and yield factors [13]. The most notable illustration is a linear regression between two known factors; in any case, models can be altogether more complex. On the one hand, virtual screening expectations [14], disease diagnosis [15] or drug adequacy [16] and assimilation, conveyance, digestion, discharge and toxicity forecast [17] are the output examples of supervised ML. On the other hand, unsupervised learning discovers designs hidden inside input information and make bunches dependent on intrinsic models or connections among data points. Undoubtedly, joining the two kinds of model based on the equivalent dataset is progressively utilized in this field.

The two different sorts of ML are unsupervised and reinforcement learning. When input-only information is given and the method attempts to discover something helpful in the information then it is an unsupervised learning. Disease target discovery from feature-finding approaches [18] is the output of unsupervised learning. In reinforcement learning, the agent collaborates with the environment for settling a successive decision task and alters its activity approaches to maximize its performance [19]. The yields from this include de novo drug design and exploratory design where both are reachable through quantum chemistry [20]. A recent application of reinforcement learning is Deep Q-network-Docking, an algorithm that is applicable to the context of protein-ligand docking forecast [21]. There are various different ML models. However, in view of their expanding prominence in the field, artificial neural networks (ANNs) deserve extraordinary mention and they have a place with their own subset of ML techniques known as DL [22,23] which are propelled by biological neural networks (NNs) in that they included many associated nodes with every association communicating signal between them, similar to a synapse where the signal is a number, and every neuron plays out some nonlinear functions of the amount of its sources of information [12]. As the network does a few efforts to gain proficiency in a job, the numerical weighting of each nodal association is resolved dependent on that nodes commitment to an effective result [24]. ANNs and DL overall have been effective in an assortment of tasks, from computer vision, mobile publicizing to patient result forecast [23,25].

6.2 Principles of DL

DL is a part of ML in view of the utilization of various ANN methods, through a series of numerous layers with nonlinear handling units [26] to understand high-level deliberations

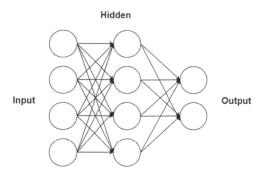

FIGURE 6.1
Structure of ANN.

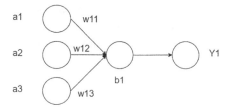

FIGURE 6.2
The interrelationship among input and output values.

for information portrayals [20]. The structure of ANN is depicted in Figure 6.1 and is propelled by the design of the human brain. The layers in ANN are the input, hidden and output layers where the nodes are known as neurons, and adjoining layers are either completely associated or partially associated.

Input factors are taken by input nodes, changed through hidden nodes and yield esteems are determined at yield nodes. Figure 6.2 depicts the interrelationship of a hidden unit. The yield esteem Y_i of the node i is determined as displayed in equation 6.1.

$$Y_i = g\left(\sum_j W_{ij} * a_j\right) \tag{6.1}$$

where a_j alludes to the input factors, W_{ij} is the weight of input node j on node i and g is the nonlinear type of activation function.

The preparation of an ANN is done by iterative alteration of the weight esteems in the network to optimize blunders among anticipated and genuine value ordinarily through the backpropagation (BP) techniques [27]. The advanced ANN algorithm was created during the 1980s. However, the conventional ANN technique experienced issues, for example, diminishing gradients and overfitting issue that was generally changed with support vector machine such as ML algorithms. There are likewise numerous algorithmic upgradations in DL, for instance, utilizing the Dropout [28] strategy to address the overfitting issue. TensorFlow, PyTorch and Keras are among the most well-known DL programming packages and the majority are open-sourced.

It is a versatile ML approach equipped for scaling the information size [29] of large number of information samples. A plethora of studies give proof that DL has accomplished advanced results [30] in different fields. Itis dramatically acquiring interest in innovative work (R&D) group at the scholarly community and business as they are likewise being vigorously contributed by software and hardware companies such as Google and Intel [31]. DL is the capacity to become familiar [29] with the deep structures of NN by utilizing BP. When DL is applied to ANN it is known as deep neural network (DNN) [32]. DL has acquired enormous achievement [20] in a wide scope of applications [2], for example, PC games, computer vision, speech recognition, self-driving cars and natural language processing among others. Most would agree that DL is changing our regular day-to-day existence.

6.3 DL Methods for Drug Discovery

The most popular methods of DL are categorized into supervised and unsupervised learning [4]. Methods that will be examined are DNN, convolutional neural network (CNN) [33], recurrent neural network (RNN) [2], auto encoder (AE) and deep belief network (DBN) [29]. Underneath, the illustration is also provided about how these DL advancements are utilized in research of drug discovery.

6.3.1 DNN

DNN consists of various hidden layers where every layer [20] includes many nonlinear interaction units (Figure 6.3). It can take enormous quantity of input highlights and the neurons in various layers can automatically extricate features at various progressive levels. As a direct expansion of ANN, DNN has been acquainted to handle high-dimensional information along with unstructured information for machine vision [33].

In various studies, DNN outperformed several traditional AI strategies in foreseeing compound toxicity, Absorption, Distribution, Metabolism, Elimination, Toxicity (ADMET) properties and solubility. To deal with high-dimensional information, a few feature extraction techniques and dimension reduction systems have been incorporated into assorted DL structures such as CNN, RNN and AE.

6.3.2 CNN

It is one of the notable structures of DL which [29] was first applied to image acknowledgment. It has made a momentous accomplishment in the field of image acknowledgment [2].

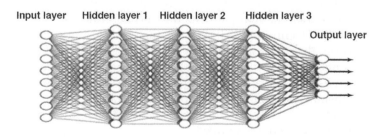

FIGURE 6.3
DNN.

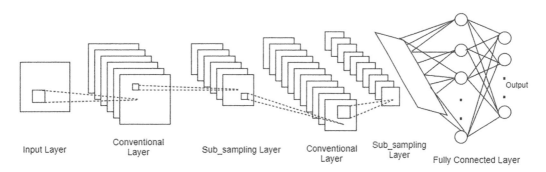

FIGURE 6.4
CNN.

They are propelled by the vertebrate's visual cortex that consists of tiny neuron cells. Hubel and Wiesel showed in their investigations that some particular neuronal cells in the brain reacted just within the sight of edges or lines of a specific direction. For instance, a few neurons reacted when presented with vertical edges and diagonal or horizontal edges, which gave off an impression of being spatially arranged in columnar designs, can deliver visual insight. This thought of a particular model inside a framework having explicit tasks is the premise of CNN. The model of CNNs is the neocognitron, which was imagined in the mid-1980s [1]. Specifically, the CNN is a mainstream [33] DL system for imaging analysis that comprises various convolutional, max-pooling layer and fully associated multi-layer perceptron layers (Figure 6.4).

The reason behind the first two layers is to extricate local repeating designs from the picture information to adjust the input measurement of the fully associated layers. It usually consists of several convolutional and subsampling layers [33] where the convolution layer comprises a bunch of filters having a small open field and learnable boundaries. The subsampling layer is utilized to decrease the size of feature maps which are linked into completely associated layers in the end. The last layer is by and large a completely associated layer [2] which is a multi-layer perceptron that uses an activation function.

A CNN to a great extent diminishes the quantity of free boundaries learned due to the sharing of same boundaries for each filter, in this manner bringing down the consumption of memory and increasing the speed of learning. CNN currently comprise a structure for a broad scope of applications [1] such as video analysis and speech recognition.

6.3.3 RNN

It is a variation of ANN in which yield from the past state [33] is utilized as an input for the present state (Figure 6.5). Hence, this detailing has an old-style relationship to the hidden Markov model, a kind of belief network. The prerequisite to show consecutive information likewise incited the advancement of RNN. It has been applicable for de novo molecule design by "memorizing" from Simplified Molecular Input Line Entry Specification (SMILES) string in sequence form.

It incorporates feedback segments that allow signals from one layer to be taken care of back to a past layer. Also, they are the only NN with an inward memory, the utilization of which is important to eliminate challenges of figuring out how to store long-term data. On account of the memory, they are capable of perusing an arrangement and its specific situation. RNNs can accept consecutive information as input highlights, which is entirely

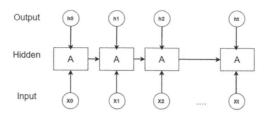

FIGURE 6.5
RNN.

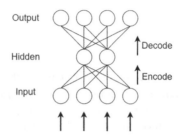

FIGURE 6.6
AE.

reasonable for time-subordinate assignments [34]. However, the fundamental model suffers from gradient vanishing and exploding issue. Accordingly, more sophisticated structures have been suggested to overcome the limitations of basic RNNs by utilizing the innovation called the Long Short-Term Memory (LSTM) [35]. The current applications are the expert systems, hydrological prediction and navigation [36].

6.3.4 AEs

AE [29] is a NN used for an unsupervised DL model [20] which apply a BP algorithm for training. It is applied to nonlinear dimensionality reduction, denoising applications [37], data compression, feature extraction and picture or information production (generative models). The chain structure is identical to a multi-facet ANN in which the yield is set to be equivalent to the input [2]. The basic design incorporates three parts: an input layer, a hidden layer and a yield layer (Figure 6.6).

It is also a data-driven technique that comprises encoder and decoder where encoder is an NN that can change the data got from the input layer into a predetermined number of hidden units, and afterward couples a decoder NN with the yield layer having similar number of nodes as the input layer [20]. Rather than anticipating labels of input examples, the reason for the decoder NN is to reproduce its own contributions from a lesser number of hidden units. Commonly, the reason for AE is for nonlinear dimensionality decrease. Currently, the AE idea has become more generally utilized to learn generative models from information [38].

6.3.5 DBN

DBN was at first suggested and trained [29] using BP by Hinton et al. [32,39] as a deep unsupervised learning method utilizing greedy pre-prepared piled up layers of Restricted

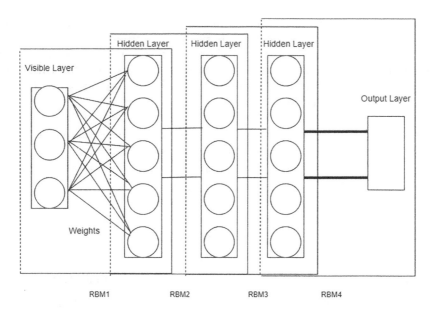

FIGURE 6.7
DBN.

Boltzmann machine (RBM).DBNs comprised multi-facets of neurons which are further divided into hidden and visible layers. Visible layers get information, while hidden layers extract features, so they are known as feature locators. An RBM comprises a visible and hidden layer unit (Figure 6.7). This system can be prepared in a supervised and unsupervised style and can address countless highlights of the data sources.

DBN [39] can be utilized not only to distinguish and classify information but also to deliver information [2]. It is made of many layers of RBM where a single hidden layer cannot extricate every attribute from the input data, as it cannot decide the connection between the factors. Subsequently, various layers of RBMs are utilized in a steady progression to extricate nonlinear highlights. Modeling of this comprises greedy, unsupervised, layer-by-layer pre-preparation along with a supervised and global fine-tuning process. The hybrid preparation method as far as builds the generative exhibition and discriminative force of the organization. Thus, it turns out to be progressively complex and profoundly attractive for handling classification issues. The public application areas are human emotion discovery, sustainable power source forecast and financial estimating [36].

6.4 Opportunities and Challenges

The opportunities and challenges in drug discovery are described in the following.

6.4.1 Drug Safety

Ensuring the safety of drug is one of the basic issues in the drug discovery process. Analyzing data of the known impacts of medications and anticipating their results are complicated assignments. Analysts and architects from research and medicine organizations, such as Roche and Pfizer, have been attempting to utilize DL to get significant data from clinical information acquired in clinical preliminaries that are the costliest phase of drug production. In order to decrease their expenses, it is essential to utilize the experience acquired during past clinical preliminaries in the beginning phases of drug advancement that can be accomplished in two stages:

- Biomedical information from research tests could be investigated and deciphered utilizing AI to foresee the impacts of a medicine.
- Information from scientific preliminaries examined with AI should uphold the understanding of biological information.

With these two growing methodologies, it is feasible to plan better preclinical trials to yield with the best treatments with the least reaction [40].

6.4.2 Integration of Biomedical Information with Computational Methodologies

While developing ML methodologies to integrate biomedical information, several difficulties emerge. Biological and clinical datasets have intrinsic complexity beyond their enormous sizes. Biomedical datasets are likewise heterogeneous, high-dimensional, biased, dynamic, incomplete and noisy. Biomedical information is often high-dimensional yet inadequate too. These differentiations with huge datasets in different areas, such as computer vision, social networks and natural language, normally contain countless high-quality examples.

AI could assist with streamlining treatment by coordinating biomedical and scientific information with computational approaches. It can be utilized to make software for testing the medicines and combinatorial treatments. Such type of models and methods that help in the combination of scientific information are yet under development.

6.4.3 Genetically Analysis of Data and Customized Medication

Numerous drug industries and new companies are centered around hereditary information translation and customized drug. Reviewing the patient's hereditary description assists with offering proper medications and treatment. Building computational ways to deal with the investigation of hereditary information and propose novel treatments could be progressed with ML.

It incorporates finding novel biomarkers of medication reaction and AI-dependent computational devices utilized in the scientific method. These devices are utilized to gauge the protection from individual medications to combinatorial treatments dependent on genotype investigation.

6.4.4 Building and Getting Knowledge from Databases

Researchers utilize general storehouses of clinical information to handle enormous issues in clinics to assist clinical specialists in their daily job, as clinical information can be extricated from general storehouses which could likewise be utilized for medicine disclosure objective to consider scientific data for the beginning phase of medicine advancement.

Efforts have been made to address clinical information by utilizing DNNs. Information planned with AI may likewise be simpler to coordinate with biomedical information dissected with AI, because of better similarity in the information structures produced with comparative methodologies. New accomplishments in building databases for existing AI reasons are additionally encouraging. Nonetheless, there are numerous issues in medication and drug discovery which are hard to respond only based on public information.

6.4.5 ML Methods for Genetics and Genomics

ML algorithms such as supervised ML, semi-supervised and unsupervised are used to investigate hereditary information like microarray. They can find out ailment and healthy phenotypes that could be additionally utilized to reveal the methods of activity of medicines. In any ML strategy, the analyst should choose which information to give as a contribution to the method to respond to intricate biomedical inquiries.

6.5 Applications of DL in Drug Discovery

ML algorithms can be incorporated in all phases of the process of medicine discovery. The areas where DL can benefit and promote drug discovery are mainly divided into different categories.

6.5.1 Drug Properties Prediction

It is a supervised ML issue where a drug is an input and drug property (such as drug toxicity) is the yield. Here 0–1 mark depicts if a medicine has certain features. It can likewise be outlined as a regression task [30]. So, there are various approaches to address a medicine.

- Molecular fingerprint
  It is one of the ways to address a medicine in the input pipeline of the ML structure. The most prevalent sort of fingerprint is a progression of binary digits that address the presence or absence of specific bases in the particle. Hence, medicine is portrayed as a vector of 0s and 1s.

- Text-based portrayal
  SMILES code is another approach to address a particle by encoding a design as a text. It is the method of transforming graph-structured data into textual-based data and utilizing the content in the ML pipeline.

- Graph structure
  The popularity of DL on graph-structured information, for example, graph convolution network has made it conceivable to utilize graph information straightforwardly as a contribution to the DL pipeline. PyTorch-Geometric and PyTorch-BigGraph are devoted to this work.

6.5.2 De Novo Drug Design

Another interesting application of DL with regard to chemoinformatics is the production of new chemical structures through NNs. For example, to design a compound that can bind to a particular protein, modify some pathways and do not interact with other pathways, and also have some physical property such as the specific range of solubility. This type of problem cannot be tackled with the toolkits but can be best realized in the realm of generative models. Generative models from the autoregressive algorithm, normalizing flows, variational AEs and generative adversarial networks have gotten prevalent and broad in the ML group to handle such category.

6.5.3 Drug–Target Interaction Prediction

One significant issue in computational medication discovery is foreseeing whether a specific medication can tie to specific proteins or not. This concept is known as drug–target interaction (DTI) prediction and has gotten critical consideration within ongoing years. Most of the DL frameworks for DTI prediction take both compound and protein information as the input, but the difference is what representations they are using to feed the NNs. Depending on the input representation, various architectures can be used to handle the DTI prediction. In order to utilize a text-based representation for both compounds and proteins, the RNN-based architectures are used.

6.6 Conclusion

In particular, DL has seen a significant resurgence in popularity and can possibly revolutionize numerous areas of human undertaking. There is no doubt drug discovery can acquire advantage from the accomplishments of DL. But it is a prolonged, expensive and arduous task where DL can be utilized to make this process quicker and less expensive through their methods suggested with regard to drug discovery. In drug discovery, computational solutions can help notably to lower the expenses of familiarizing the drugs in the market. Utilization of ML algorithms in designing new medicines has gotten more feasible than ever due to complicated biomedical data. In this chapter, a thorough analysis of DL in drug discovery and their opportunities and challenges are provided.

References

1. Stephen Chan, HC, Hanbin Shan, Thamani Dahoun, Horst Vogel, and Shuguang Yuan. "Advancing drug discovery via artificial intelligence." *Trends in Pharmacological Sciences* 40, no. 10 (2019), 801. doi:10.1016/j.tips.2019.07.013.
2. Lavecchia, Antonio. "Deep learning in drug discovery: opportunities, challenges and future prospects." *Drug Discovery Today* 24, no. 10 (2019), 2017–2032. doi:10.1016/j.drudis.2019.07.006.
3. Nao Nitta, Takeaki Sugimura, Akihiro Isozaki, Hideharu Mikami, Kei Hiraki, Shinya Sakuma, Takanori Iino, Fumihito Arai, Taichiro Endo, Yasuhiro Fujiwaki, Hideya Fukuzawa, Misa Hase, Takeshi Hayakawa, Kotaro Hiramatsu, Yu Hoshino, Mary Inaba, Takuro Ito, Hiroshi Karakawa, Yusuke Kasai, Kenichi Koizumi, SangWook Lee, Cheng Lei, Ming Li, Takanori Maeno, Satoshi Matsusaka, Daichi Murakami, Atsuhiro Nakagawa, Yusuke Oguchi, Minoru Oikawa, Tadataka Ota, Kiyotaka Shiba, Hirofumi Shintaku, Yoshitaka Shirasaki, Kanako Suga, Yuta Suzuki, Nobutake Suzuki, Yo Tanaka, Hiroshi Tezuka, Chihana Toyokawa, Yaxiaer Yalikun, Makoto Yamada, Mai Yamagishi, Takashi Yamano, Atsushi Yasumoto, Yutaka

Yatomi, Masayuki Yazawa, Dino Di Carlo, Yoichiroh Hosokawa, Sotaro Uemura, Yasuyuki Ozeki, Keisuke Goda. "Intelligent image-activated cell sorting." *Cell*. 175 no.1 (2018), 266–276. doi: 10.1016/j.cell.2018.08.028.

4. Elbadawi, Moe, Simon Gaisford, and Abdul W. Basit. "Advanced machine-learning techniques in drug discovery." *Drug Discovery Today* 26, no. 3 (2021), 769–777. doi:10.1016/j.drudis.2020.12.003.

5. Lavecchia, Antonio. "Machine-learning approaches in drug discovery: methods and applications." *Drug Discovery Today* 20, no. 3 (2015), 318–331. doi: 10.1016/j.drudis.2014.10.012.

6. Huang, Zhengxing, Jose M. Juarez, and Xiang Li. "Data Mining for Biomedicine and Healthcare." *Journal of Healthcare Engineering* 2017 (2017), 1–2. doi:10.1155/2017/7107629.

7. Zhang, Yinsheng, Guoming Zhang, and Qian Shang. "Computer-Aided Clinical Trial Recruitment Based on Domain-Specific Language Translation: A Case Study of Retinopathy of Prematurity." *Journal of Healthcare Engineering* 2017 (2017), 1–9. doi: 10.1155/2017/7862672.

8. Merk, Daniel, Lukas Friedrich, Francesca Grisoni, and Gisbert Schneider. "De Novo Design of Bioactive Small Molecules by Artificial Intelligence." *Molecular Informatics* 37, no. 1–2 (2018), 1700153. doi:10.1002/minf.201700153.

9. Menden, Michael P, Francesco Iorio, Mathew Garnett, Ultan McDermott, Cyril H Benes, Pedro J Ballester, and Julio Saez-Rodriguez. "Machine learning prediction of cancer cell sensitivity to drugs based on genomic and chemical properties." *PLoS One* 8, no. 4 (2013), e61318. doi:10.1371/journal.pone.0061318.

10. Schneider, Gisbert. "Automating drug discovery." *Nature Reviews Drug Discovery* 17, no. 2 (2017), 97–113. doi:10.1038/nrd.2017.232.

11. Leber, Andrew, Raquel Hontecillas, Vida Abedi, Nuria Tubau-Juni, Victoria Zoccoli-Rodriguez, Caroline Stewart, and Josep Bassaganya-Riera. "Modeling new immunoregulatory therapeutics as antimicrobial alternatives for treating Clostridium difficile infection." *Artificial Intelligence in Medicine* 78 (2017), 1–13. doi:10.1016/j.artmed.2017.05.003.

12. John, W Cassidy. "Applications of machine learning in drug discovery I: target discovery and small molecule drug design." *Artificial Intelligence in Oncology Drug Discovery and Development*, 2020. doi:10.5772/intechopen.93159.

13. Vamathevan, Jessica, Dominic Clark, Paul Czodrowski, Ian Dunham, Edgardo Ferran, George Lee, Bin Li, et al. "Applications of machine learning in drug discovery and development." *Nature Reviews Drug Discovery* 18, no. 6 (2019), 463–477. doi:10.1038/s41573-019-0024-5.

14. Jiménez, Fernando, Horacio Pérez-Sánchez, José Palma, Gracia Sánchez, and Carlos Martínez. "A methodology for evaluating multi-objective evolutionary feature selection for classification in the context of virtual screening." *Soft Computing* 23, no. 18 (2018), 8775–8800. doi:10.1007/s00500-018-3479-0.

15. Gunčar, Gregor, Matjaž Kukar, Mateja Notar, Miran Brvar, Peter Černelč, Manca Notar, and Marko Notar. "An application of machine learning to haematological diagnosis." *Scientific Reports* 8, no. 1 (2018). doi: 10.1038/s41598-017-18564-8.

16. Li, Haiqing, Wei Zhang, Ying Chen, Yumeng Guo, Guo-Zheng Li, and Xiaoxin Zhu. "A novel multi-target regression framework for time-series prediction of drug efficacy." *Scientific Reports* 7, no. 1 (2017). doi:10.1038/srep40652.

17. Maltarollo, Vinícius G., Jadson C Gertrudes, Patrícia R Oliveira, and Kathia M Honorio. "Applying machine learning techniques for ADME-Tox prediction: a review." *Expert Opinion on Drug Metabolism & Toxicology* 11, no. 2 (2014), 259–271. doi:10.1517/17425255.2015.980814.

18. Young, Jonathan D., Chunhui Cai, and Xinghua Lu. "Unsupervised deep learning reveals prognostically relevant subtypes of glioblastoma." *BMC Bioinformatics* 18, no. S11 (2017). doi:10.1186/s12859-017-1798-2.

19. Arulkumaran, Kai, Marc P Deisenroth, Miles Brundage, and Anil A Bharath. "Deep Reinforcement Learning: A Brief Survey." *IEEE Signal Processing Magazine* 34, no. 6 (2017), 26–38. doi:10.1109/msp.2017.2743240.

20. Chen, Hongming, Ola Engkvist, Yinhai Wang, Marcus Olivecrona, and Thomas Blaschke. "The rise of deep learning in drug discovery." *Drug Discovery Today* 23, no. 6 (2018), 1241–1250. doi: 10.1016/j.drudis.2018.01.039.

21. Serrano, Antonio, Baldomero Imbernón, Horacio Pérez-Sánchez, José M Cecilia, Andrés Bueno-Crespo, and José L. Abellán. "Accelerating Drugs Discovery with Deep Reinforcement Learning." Proceedings of the 47th International Conference on Parallel Processing Companion, 2018. doi:10.1145/3229710.3229731.

22. Batool, Maria, Bilal Ahmad, and Sangdun Choi. "A Structure-Based Drug Discovery Paradigm." *International Journal of Molecular Sciences* 20, no. 11 (2019), 2783. doi:10.3390/ijms20112783.

23. Dubourg-Felonneau, Geoffroy. "Flatsomatic: a method for compression of somatic mutation profiles in cancer." ArXiv.org. Accessed July 5, 2021. https://arxiv.org/abs/1911.13259.

24. Pérez-Sánchez, Horacio, Gaspar Cano, and José García-Rodríguez. "Improving drug discovery using hybrid soft computing methods." *Applied Soft Computing* 20 (2014), 119–126. doi:10.1016/j.asoc.2013.10.033.

25. Bengio, Y. "Learning Deep Architectures for AI." *Foundations and Trends® in Machine Learning* 2, no. 1 (2009), 1–127. doi:10.1561/2200000006.

26. Schmidhuber, Jürgen. "Deep learning in neural networks: an overview." *Neural Networks* 61 (2015), 85–117. doi:10.1016/j.neunet.2014.09.003.

27. Dreyfus, S. "The computational solution of optimal control problems with time lag." *IEEE Transactions on Automatic Control* 18, no. 4 (1973), 383–385. doi:10.1109/tac.1973.1100330.

28. Srivastava, Nitish, Geoffrey Hinton, Alex Krizhevsky, Ilya Sutskever, and Ruslan Salakhutdinov. "Dropout: a simple way to prevent neural networks from overfitting: The Journal of Machine Learning Research: Vol 15, No 1." ACM Digital Library. Last modified January 1, 2014. https://dl.acm.org/doi/10.5555/2627435.2670313.

29. Dargazany, Aras R., Paolo Stegagno, and Kunal Mankodiya. "WearableDL: Wearable Internet-of-Things and Deep Learning for Big Data Analytics—Concept, Literature, and Future." Publishing Open Access Research Journals & Papers, Hindawi. Last modified November 14, 2018. https://www.hindawi.com/journals/misy/2018/8125126/.

30. Fooladi, Hosein. "Review: Deep Learning in Drug Discovery." Medium. Last modified February 27, 2020. https://towardsdatascience.com/review-deep-learning-in-drug-discovery-f4c89e3321e1.

31. "Dl analytics for healthcare: UCSF, Intel join forces to develop deep learning analytics for health care." n.d. https://www.ucsf.edu/news/2017/01/405536/ucsf-intel-join-forces-developdeep-learning-analytics-health-care

32. Hinton, Geoffrey. "Deep belief networks." *Scholarpedia* 4, no. 5 (2009), 5947. doi:10.4249/scholarpedia.5947.

33. Lo, Yu-Chen, Gui Ren, Hiroshi Honda, and Davis, KL (2020) "Artificial intelligence-based drug design and discovery." *Cheminformatics and Its Applications*. doi: 10.5772/intechopen.89012.

34. Gawehn, Erik, Jan A. Hiss, J. B. Brown, and Gisbert Schneider. "Advancing drug discovery via GPU-based deep learning." *Expert Opinion on Drug Discovery* 13, no. 7 (2018), 579–582. doi:10.1080/17460441.2018.1465407.

35. Gawehn, Erik, Jan A. Hiss, and Gisbert Schneider. "Deep learning in drug discovery." *Molecular Informatics* 35, no. 1 (2015), 3–14. doi:10.1002/minf.201501008.

36. Aarti, Er. "Generative adversarial networks and their variants." *Generative Adversarial Networks for Image-to-Image Translation*, 2021, 59–80. doi:10.1016/b978-0-12–823519-5.00003-8.

37. Li, Yujia, Daniel Tarlow, Marc Brockschmidt, and Richard Zemel. "Gated graph sequence neural networks." ArXiv.org. n.d. https://arxiv.org/abs/1511.05493.

38. Kingma, Diederik P., and Max Welling. "Auto-encoding variational Bayes." ArXiv.org. n.d. https://arxiv.org/abs/1312.6114.

39. Hinton, Geoffrey E., Simon Osindero, and Yee-Whye Teh. "A fast learning algorithm for deep belief nets." *Neural Computation* 18, no. 7 (2006), 1527–1554. doi:10.1162/neco.2006.18.7.1527.

40. "Machine Learning in Drug Discovery." Deepsense.ai. Last modified January 5, 2021. https://deepsense.ai/machine-learning-in-drug-discovery/

7

Issues and Challenges Associated with Machine Learning Tools for Health Care System

Parul Chhabra and Pradeep Kumar Bhatia

G. J. University of Science & Technology

CONTENTS

7.1 Introduction...69
7.2 Machine-Learning–Based Prediction Schemes for Healthcare Industry....................71
7.3 Automated Decision Support System..72
7.4 Drug Discovery and Human Trials using Machine Learning..................74
7.5 Surgical Operations with Machine Learning Assistance...........................75
7.6 Conclusion..75
References..76

7.1 Introduction

Traditional healthcare services produce a large-scale clinical data and its manual processing may delay the diagnosis process. The usage of advanced technology in medical industry provides solutions for automated diagnosis but it is quite difficult to manage or interpret a huge volume of medical data manually. Therefore, it raises the requirement of a smart medical system to process/manage the medical data and investigators presented a framework, termed Healthcare System (HCS) which can retain all types of data (Text/Image) digitally and it can also offer data processing techniques. For the interpretation of images, researchers introduced image processing procedures. Medical history of a patient can be tracked by establishing an association between text and visual data (Figure 7.1).

The image form of clinical data consists of medical images. These images can be produced using different technologies as given below ("As of September 24, 2021, home page listed for radiology and healthcare sites").

Figure 7.2 shows the CT scan of lungs that is produced using multiple X-ray images having different angles/cross-sections. Figure 7.3 shows the Magnetic Resonance Imaging (MRI) scan of the brain that is produced using radio waves and magnetic fields. Figure 7.4 shows the ultrasound image of Lever that is produced using high-frequency sound waves and Figure 7.5 shows the X-ray image of chest that is produced using ionization radiation. As per requirements, practitioner refers the scan type to each patient. Text form of clinical data consists of metadata: laboratory test report, patient's personal information, current health status, medical history, feedback, disease, diagnosis and treatment details. The above-discussed data is used to build a complete medical record of patients and AI can be used to extract the customized facts with the help of various machine learning algorithms.

DOI: 10.1201/9781003215981-7

69

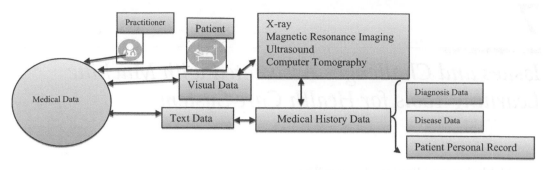

FIGURE 7.1
Healthcare system.

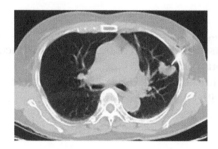

FIGURE 7.2
CT scan of lungs.

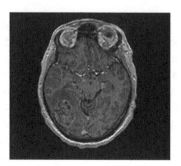

FIGURE 7.3
MRI scan of brain.

These facts may be used for the prediction of disease and diagnosis through medical image processing and clinical text data mining, development of automated decision support system, surgical operations using robotics and drug discovery and human trials. Various approaches that can be adapted for machine learning to achieve the above-discussed points are supervised learning; in this, input datasets are used for training, whereas it is not required by unsupervised learning and for semi-supervised learning, labelled datasets are used. Reinforcement learning uses feedback values to refine the output (Alsuliman et al., 2020; Ben-Israel et al., 2020;Lalmuanawma et al., 2020; Smiti, 2020; Waring et al., 2020). Combination of machine learning approaches with HCS can boost the overall diagnosis

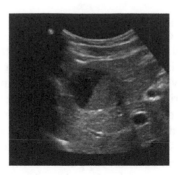

FIGURE 7.4
Ultrasound image of lever.

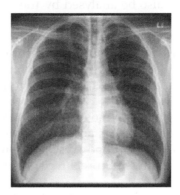

FIGURE 7.5
X-ray of chest.

process and can also enhance the decision-making process. Machine learning methods cannot process the medical data directly. Raw medical data is collected and categorized as required then training models are prepared, and desired machine learning method is selected for its processing. Finally, outcomes are used for decision and diagnosis purpose. Sections given below explore the contribution of various researchers for different stakeholders (practitioners/patients).

7.2 Machine-Learning–Based Prediction Schemes for Healthcare Industry

Using clinical data, training datasets can be developed and estimation about current disease stage and health status can be determined using machine learning algorithms that can enhance the proficiency disease detection and diagnosis process. The following section describes the machine-learning–based prediction for healthcare services:

Samadet et al. (2019) explored the machine-learning–based methods that can predict the survival accuracy using a limited set of input variables for echocardiography outcomes. A study found that traditional methods use Ejection Fraction and Comorbidities-based prediction models which are less accurate as compared to the machine learning algorithms.

Xue et al. (2018) developed a prediction model for patient readmission and compared its performance to the Support Vector Machine/Random-Tree–based methods and analytical results indicate that Functional Independence Measure method outperforms as compared to traditional methods. For training and validation was performed using existing clinical data and accuracy and sensitivity both were adjusted by finding the optimal cutoff point of receiver operating characteristic curve. Results state that it can reduce the overall treatment cost and can also improve the quality of healthcare services.

Clim et al. (2018) investigated the relation between chest sounds and level of hypertension and found that prediction scheme based on Kullback–Leibler Divergence is more accurate and can enhance the clinical decision support as compared to traditional methods.

Olsen et al. (2020) investigated the role of machine learning algorithms in diagnosis of heart diseases. A study indicates that these methods can assist the practitioners for diagnosis and can also be used to develop prediction models as per patient's classification. Large-scale disease dataset can also be analysed by the integration of these algorithms with BigData framework.

Qin et al. (2020) developed a prediction framework for the health analysis of elderly patients. It builds the predicates by perfuming the feature classification. Finally, a dataset is used for training and validation purpose. Experimental results show that it outperforms in terms of prediction accuracy as compared to traditional schemes (Artificial Neural Network/Super Vector Machine).

Du et al. (2020) developed a prediction model for the detection of cancer symptoms in patients at early stages. It uses both linear and non-linear models to process the input parameters and analysis shows that the proposed scheme outperforms in terms of various parameters, i.e. sensitivity, specificity, F1-Score, Precision and Recall/ROC cutoff as compared to traditional methods.

Qureshi et al. (2020) utilized a mobile platform to collect the patient data that can be used for the forecasting heart disease. As compared to existing methods (Neural Network/Support Vector Machine/Native Bayes), it outperforms in terms of optimal accuracy, sensitivity, and specificity. It can be further extended to analyse the impact of various brain-related injuries over the human beings.

Akbulut et al. (2018) developed a prediction scheme that utilizes clinical datasets to predict the anomaly status using different binary classification models. Experimental results show that decision-tree-based model is more accurate as compared to others (Boosted Decision Tree, Averaged Perceptron, Decision Forest, Bayes Point Machine, Decision Jungle, Logistic Regression, Locally-Deep Support Vector Machine and Neural Network). It can be further migrated to the mobile platform to analyse the large-scale datasets.

Kunze et al. (2020) developed a random forest approach to predict the patient's dissatisfaction after knee surgery. It considers various facts, i.e. age and allergy from medicines as input for prediction chart. Experimental results indicate that risks related to health and dissatisfaction level can be accurately predicted and patient's health status can be optimized using feedback. However, lack of data validation is still an open issue and it can be resolved in the future.

7.3 Automated Decision Support System

In case of primary healthcare system, practitioners manually examine the clinical data that may be error-prone and its processing is quite complex and time-consuming. All these factors degrade the efficiency of decision-making and also affect the diagnosis process. Traditional process of medical data examination for decision-making can be altered using machine learning algorithms. The section below discusses the contribution of the researchers in these areas.

Eremeev et al. (2018) analysed that for decision-making, there is a need to process the medical data at a large scale that may be available in the form of images or text and it is also quite complex to store and correlate the facts in this data. The study shows that NoSql databases are more suitable to store this type of datasets and supports optimal response time for query execution and can be easily integrated with machine learning tools as compared to traditional databases.

Shailaja et al. (2018) did a study of various machine learning methods that can be used for diagnosis and decision support of various diseases (heart disease, diabetes, and cancer). Analysis shows that different schemes have different accuracy level for each type of disease, i.e. Naive Bayes has the highest accuracy level for the diseases related to heart, whereas classification- and regression-based methods provide more accurate results for diabetic patients and cancer; support vector machine provides the highest prediction accuracy. Analytical data of this study can be utilized further to improve the accuracy level of other machine learning tools.

Mansilla et al. (2020) presented a decision support framework that can analyse the risk of infection after surgery and practitioners can use the alternative treatment type to avoid these side effects. It uses the combination of support vector machine and decision tree to balance the accuracy level in results. Experimental outcomes show that estimation of infection risk can optimize the diagnosis strategies.

Yahyaoui et al. (2019) developed a decision support framework for diabetic patients that use deep learning approach for disease prediction and diagnosis support. Experimental results show its performance in terms of prediction accuracy as compared to traditional approaches (Random Forest/Support vector machine). Its accuracy can be further enhanced by integrating deep feature extraction.

Comito et al. (2019) developed an automated decision support system that can assist practitioners as per the available datasets that are built using different medical data resources (Laboratory test/patient health records). Experimental results show that using deep learning, at early stage, symptoms can be detected and diagnosis plan can be suggested for identified diseases.

Triantafyllidis et al. (2020) explored the integration of machine learning schemes with electronics health records and decision support system to predict and manage the childhood obesity. Analysis shows that prediction accuracy can be achieved using decision tree/neural networks and effective treatment plans can be designed to prevent the obesity at early stages. Analytical data of this study can be used for mobile diagnosis platform.

Hollosy et al. (2018) used supervised learning methods (Decision Tree/Boosted Tree/Random Forest) to develop a decision support framework to diagnose patients suffering from low back pain. Analysis shows that during testing and data validation, few parameters vary (accuracy/sensitivity/precision/specificity). However, overall time of diagnosis process can be reduced using this framework and it can be integrated with large-scale datasets at the global level.

Smadja et al. (2020) investigated the support of machine learning methods for decision support system. A study found that the performance of these schemes depends on the input datasets having limited facts about symptoms and for each disease type, accuracy of decision-making may differ.

Diwakar et al. (2021) studied various approaches for the detection of heart disease using various methods, i.e. machine learning/ classification/image fusion. Outcomes show that decision-making can be enhanced using these methods and the data produced by this study can be reused for the development of new methods.

7.4 Drug Discovery and Human Trials using Machine Learning

Drug development is a quite complex and time-consuming process and it has a direct relation with the type of disease, symptom, dose, intake frequency, etc. All these factors play an important role for human drug trial as new drug may have some side effects over human body, so there is a need to recognize the risk factors associated with its development process and reactions over patient's health/ disease, etc. Machine learning offers an automated platform for drug development process and its trial. The section given below explores the solutions developed by other researchers in relevant domain.

Zhao et al. (2020) investigated the challenges associated with pharmaceutical research and drug development. A study found few facts (data source/quality/format/validity/authenticity/data rate/volume/values) having direct influence over drug development cost. Large-scale data related to drug can be analysed through the integration of machine learning/deep learning algorithms over big data platform thus may lead to the reduction of overall R&D cost of drugs.

Réda et al. (2020) did a survey to find out the association of the diseases with different drugs and its impact over the drug development process. Analysis shows that complete knowledge-base of diseases can be acquired using machine learning algorithms and it may reduce the research cost and human trials may be conducted at earlier stages and feedback from number of successful trials can be utilized to refine the drug modelling process/dose/accuracy level etc.

Ietswaart et al. (2020) developed a random forest approach–based model to find out the association of drug reactions over patients. The number of drugs used for training purpose and its performance was verified using different parameters (accuracy/correlation coefficient/recall curve/precision, etc.) and outcomes show that large-scale analysis of drug reaction associations can optimize failure rate of drug trials, and machine learning provides a platform for random experiments and no human/animal is required.

Issa et al. (2020)explored the drug development issues related to cancer/tumour and found that using existing large-scale cell datasets can be processed through machine learning algorithms and drug repurposing strategies can be defined to diagnosis this disease as well as drug development cost can be optimized. Analysis shows that using feedback, training datasets can be updated to maintain the accuracy of experiments.

Ali et al. (2019) investigated the number of machine learning approaches that can extract the cell-related data from cancer patients and can prepare training datasets for detection and diagnosis purpose. Analysis states that feature extraction of cells and drug response to patient's health, both can be used to predict the response of cancer drugs and these outcomes can optimize the drug development cost also.

Bannigan et al. (2021) conducted a survey to know the impact of machine-learning–assisted drug discovery. A study found that automation of drug discovery may boost the medicine industry and more efficient drugs can be developed in minimum time interval. Analysis shows that drug development time, cost and efforts can be optimized using machine learning methods.

Adlung et al. (2021) conducted a depth survey to find out the advantages of automated methods over traditional methods of decision-making. The study indicates that accuracy of manual processing of clinical data can be improved using machine learning assistance.

Joshi et al. (2021) did a survey to know the impact of machine learning in surgical operations and found that it can assist the practitioners to analyse the current patient health and it can also provide suggestions for diagnosis.

7.5 Surgical Operations with Machine Learning Assistance

Surgery is a complicated operation through which patients may be recovered or not. Even after surgical operation, it may have side effects over the patient health. So, there is a need to investigate the risk and side effects of surgery over patient's health. Machine learning algorithms can be utilized to overcome these issues as described below.

Štěpánek et al. (2018) investigated the role of machine learning in plastic surgery and multiple facial expression dataset was used to perform multivariate linear regression using R language. Experimental results indicate that higher accuracy for facial geometry can be achieved using neural network and Bayesian naive classifiers/decision trees can be used to map the facial image to emotions.

Loftus et al. (2020) explored the risk associated with the surgical wards where quick assessment of high-risk patients is essential and error-prone diagnosis and treatment recommendations may lead to the failure of healthcare services. For such types of risks, real-time health analysis and electronic health records can be generated using wearing sensors and medical data can be further processed using machine learning schemes to recognize the symptoms at earlier stages and to achieve higher accuracy in diagnosis.

Schwartz et al. (2019) studied the virtual-reality-based surgical operations and investigated its integration with machine learning schemes. Analysis found that the combination of both technologies can be utilized to develop a large-scale knowledgebase to help the stakeholders.

Štěpánek et al. (2018) did an analysis of facial features extraction and their classification using machine learning algorithm that can refine the outcomes of facial plastic surgery. Analytical data shows that geometry features along with sufficient datasets as evidence both can be enforced to maintain the quality of facial attractiveness.

Merath et al. (2019) analysed the compilations associated with different types of surgical operations (Liver/pancreatic/colorectal) and develop a solution to predict the complications using decision tree models. Experimental results show its performance in terms of higher prediction accuracy and efficient risk analysis related to diagnosis. Its scope can be enhanced using electronic health record system.

7.6 Conclusion

In this chapter, issues and challenges associated with the AI and machine learning tools were reviewed. Various researchers recognized the potential of these approaches and contributed their efforts to build modern healthcare system. It includes various prediction models that can be used to predict readmission, hypertension, heart diseases/cancer symptoms, health status of elderly patient's mental disorders, anomaly status and patient's dissatisfaction after surgical operations, children healthcare & malnutrition level, etc.

Machine learning schemes can be integrated with traditional decision support system and practitioners can utilize the existing datasets as a benchmark for training, validation and diagnosis purpose. Study indicates that diagnosis process can be refined by maintaining electronics health records, wearable sensors can be used to monitor real-time patient's data and treatment strategies can be enhanced accordingly.

Machine learning algorithms can be used to identify the disease behaviour over the patients and reaction of drugs over the patient health. Automated drug trials can reduce the overall drug development cost as well as drug's trials can be performed without using live entities (human/animal). Study found various parameters related to drug discovery and development i.e. quality, data rate, cost, impact of different drugs over diseases, trial success rate, etc.

Machine learning can be used to assist the surgeons during operations and these can also be used to analyse the side effects of these operations over patient health as well as complications associated with different surgeries can be predicted in advance to minimize the risk level. Patient's feedback can be used to refine the diagnosis process. Study found that the association of health risks with surgery, classification of facial expression and role of virtual reality in these operations.

Traditional healthcare services and the way medical data is examined both can be upgraded using Machine learning methods and large-scale clinical data processing cost and diagnosis cost can be optimized. Overall study fo und few open challenges associated with diagnosis accuracy, treatment cost, validation of input data, processing of large medical data prediction models for disease detection, drug modelling and integration of medical data with automated system, etc. In future, a machine learning framework will be developed to improve healthcare services.

References

Adlung, L., Cohen, Y., Mor, U., and Elinav, E. Machine learning in clinical decision making. *MED* 2 (2021): 1–24.

Akbulut, A., Ertugrul, E., and Topcu, V. Fetal health status prediction based on maternal clinical history using machine learning techniques. *Computer Methods and Programs in Biomedicine* 163 (2018): 87–100.

Ali, M., and Aittokallio, T. Machine learning and feature selection for drug response prediction in precision oncology applications. *Biophysical Reviews* 11, no. 1 (2019): 31–39.

Alsuliman, T., Humaidan, D., and Sliman, L. Machine learning and artificial intelligence in the service of medicine: Necessity or potentiality? *Current Research in Translational Medicine* 68, no. 4 (2020): 245–251. https://doi.org/10.1016/j.retram.2020.01.002

Anakal, S. and Sandhya, P. "Clinical decision support system for chronic obstructive pulmonary disease using machine learning techniques." In *2017 International Conference on Electrical, Electronics, Communication, Computer, and Optimization Techniques (ICEECCOT)*, pp. 1–5. 2017.

Bannigan, P., Aldeghi, M., Bao, Z., Häse, F., Aspuru-Guzik, A., and Allen, C. Machine learning directed drug formulation development. *Advanced Drug Delivery Reviews* 13 (2021): 1–24.

Ben-Israel, D.W., Jacobs, B., Casha, S., Lang, S., Ryu, W.H.A., de Lotbiniere-Bassett, M., and Cadotte, D.W. "The impact of machine learning on patient care: A systematic review." *Artificial Intelligence in Medicine* 103 (2020): 101785.

Casolla, G., Cuomo, S., Di Cola, V. S., and Piccialli, F. Exploring unsupervised learning techniques for the Internet of Things. *IEEE Transactions on Industrial Informatics* 16, no. 4 (2019): 2621–2628.

Clim, A., Zota, R.D., and TinicĂ, G. "The Kullback-Leibler divergence used in machine learning algorithms for health care applications and hypertension prediction: A literature review." *Procedia Computer Science* 141 (2018): 448–453.

Comito, C., Forestiero, A., and Papuzzo, G. (2019) "A clinical decision support framework for automatic disease diagnoses." In *2019 IEEE/ACM International Conference on Advances in Social Networks Analysis and Mining (ASONAM)*, pp. 933–936. IEEE, 2019.

Diwakar, M., Tripathi, Kapil Joshi, Minakshi Memoria, and Prabhishek Singh. "Latest trends on heart disease prediction using machine learning and image fusion." *Materials Today: Proceedings* 37 (2021): 3213–3218.

Du, Xinsong, Jae Min, Chintan P. Shah, Rohit Bishnoi, William R. Hogan, and Dominick J. Lemas. "Predicting in-hospital mortality of patients with febrile neutropenia using machine learning models." *International Journal of Medical Informatics* 139 (2020): 104140.

Eremeev, A. P., Ivliev, S. A., Vagin, and V. N. "Using nosql databases and machine learning for implementation of intelligent decision system in complex vision patalogies." In: *3rd Russian-Pacific Conference on Computer Technology and Applications (RPC)*, Vladivostok, pp. 1–4. IEEE, 2018.

Ietswaart, R., Seda Arat, A.X., Chen, S., Farahmand, B., Kim, W., DuMouchel, D., Armstrong, A., Fekete, J.J. Sutherland, and Urban, S. "Machine learning guided association of adverse drug reactions with in vitro target-based pharmacology." *EBioMedicine* 57 (2020): 102837.

Issa, N.T., Stathias, V., Schürer, S., and Dakshanamurthy, S. Machine and deep learning approaches for cancer drug repurposing. *Seminars in Cancer Biology* 68 (2021): 132–142.

Joshi, R.S., Lau, D., and Ames, Christopher P. "Machine learning in spine surgery: Predictive analytics, imaging applications and next steps." *Seminars in Spine Surgery* 33, no. 2, (2021): pp. 1–10.

Kunze, Kyle N., Evan M. Polce, Alexander J. Sadauskas, and Brett R. Levine. "Development of machine learning algorithms to predict patient dissatisfaction after primary total knee arthroplasty". *The Journal of Arthroplasty* 35, no. 11 (2020): 3117–3122.

Lalmuanawma, S., Hussain, J., and Chhakchhuak, L. Applications of machine learning and artificial intelligence for Covid-19 (SARS-CoV-2) pandemic: A review. *Chaos, Solitons, and Fractals* 139 (2020): 110059. https://doi.org/10.1016/j.chaos.2020.110059

Loftus, T. J., Tighe, P. J., Filiberto, A. C., Balch, J., Upchurch, G. R., Jr, Rashidi, P., and Bihorac, A. Opportunities for machine learning to improve surgical ward safety. *American Journal of Surgery* 220, no. 4 (2020): 905–913. https://doi.org/10.1016/j.amjsurg.2020.02.037.

Mansilla, Harold R., Solano, Geoffrey A., and Lapitan, Marie Carmela M. "A clinical decision-support tool for surgical site infection prediction." In: *International Conference on Artificial Intelligence in Information and Communication (ICAIIC)*, pp. 367–372. IEEE, 2020.

Merath, K., Hyer, J. M., Mehta, R., Farooq, A., Bagante, F., Sahara, K., Tsilimigras, D. I., Beal, E., Paredes, A. Z., Wu, L., Ejaz, A., and Pawlik, T. M. Use of machine learning for prediction of patient risk of postoperative complications after liver, pancreatic, and colorectal surgery. *Journal of Gastrointestinal Surgery* 24, no. 8 (2020): 1843–1851. https://doi.org/10.1007/s11605-019-04338-2.

Olsen, Cameron R., Mentz, Robert J., Anstrom, Kevin J., Page, David, and Patel, Priyesh A. Clinical applications of machine learning in the diagnosis, classification, and prediction of heart failure. *American Heart Journal* (2020).

Oude Nijeweme-d'Hollosy, W., van Velsen, L., Poel, M., Groothuis-Oudshoorn, C., Soer, R., and Hermens, H. Evaluation of three machine learning models for self-referral decision support on low back pain in primary care. *International Journal of Medical Informatics* 110 (2018): 31–41. https://doi.org/10.1016/j.ijmedinf.2017.11.010.

Peiffer-Smadja, Nathan, Rawson, Timothy Miles, Ahmad, Raheelah, Buchard, Albert, Georgiou, P., Lescure, F-X., Birgand, Gabriel, and Holmes, Alison Helen. Machine learning for clinical decision support in infectious diseases: A narrative review of current applications. *Clinical Microbiology and Infection* 26, no. 5 (2020): 584–595.

Qin, Fang-Yu, Lv, Zhe-Qi, Wang, D.N., Hu, B., Wu, C. Health status prediction for the elderly based on machine learning. *Archives of Gerontology and Geriatrics* 90 (2020): 104121.

Qureshi, Kashif Naseer, Sadia Din, Gwanggil Jeon, and Francesco Piccialli. An accurate and dynamic predictive model for a smart M-Health system using machine learning. *Information Sciences* 538(2020): 486–502.

Réda, Clémence, Kaufmann, Emilie, and Delahaye-Duriez, Andrée. Machine learning applications in drug development. *Computational and Structural Biotechnology Journal* 18 (2020): 241–252.

Samad, Manar D., Alvaro Ulloa, Gregory J. Wehner, Linyuan Jing, Dustin Hartzel, Christopher W. Good, Brent A. Williams, Christopher M. Haggerty, and Brandon K. Fornwalt. Predicting survival from large echocardiography and electronic health record datasets: Optimization with machine learning. *JACC: Cardiovascular Imaging* 12, no. 4 (2019): 681–689.

Shailaja, K. M., Seetharamulu, B., and Akhil Jabbar, M. "Machine learning in healthcare: A review." In: *2018 Second International Conference on Electronics, Communication and Aerospace Technology (ICECA)*, pp. 910–914. 2018.

Smiti, A. When machine learning meets medical world: Current status and future challenges. *Computer Science Review* 37 (2020): 100280, ISSN 1574-0137. https://doi.org/10.1016/j.cosrev.2020.100280.

Štěpánek, Lubomír, Kasal, Pavel, and Mestak, Jan. "Evaluation of facial attractiveness for purposes of plastic surgery using machine-learning methods and image analysis." In: *2018 IEEE 20th International Conference on e-Health Networking, Applications and Services (Healthcom)*, pp. 1–6. IEEE, 2018.

Štěpánek, Lubomír, Měšťák, Jan, and Kasal, Pavel. "Machine-learning at the service of plastic surgery: A case study evaluating facial attractiveness and emotions using R language." In: *Federated Conference on Computer Science and Information Systems (FedCSIS)*, pp. 107–112. IEEE, 2019.

Tan, Z., and Karakose, M. Optimized deep reinforcement learning approach for dynamic system." In: *2020 IEEE International Symposium on Systems Engineering (ISSE)*, pp. 1–4. IEEE, 2020.

Tian, Yuan, and Compere, Marc. "A case study on visual-inertial odometry using supervised, semi-supervised and unsupervised learning methods." In: *2019 IEEE International Conference on Artificial Intelligence and Virtual Reality (AIVR)*, pp. 203–2034. IEEE, 2019.

Triantafyllidis, A., Polychronidou, E., Alexiadis, A., Rocha, C. L., Oliveira, D. N., da Silva, A. S., Freire, A. L., Macedo, C., Sousa, I. F., Werbet, E., Lillo, E. A., Luengo, H. G., Ellacuría, M. T., Votis, K., and Tzovaras, D. Computerized decision support and machine learning applications for the prevention and treatment of childhood obesity: A systematic review of the literature. *Artificial Intelligence in Medicine* 104 (2020): 101844. https://doi.org/10.1016/j.artmed.2020.101844

Waring, Jonathan, Lindvall, Charlotta, and Umeton, Renato. "Automated machine learning: Review of the state-of-the-art and opportunities for healthcare." *Artificial Intelligence in Medicine* 104 (2020): 101822.

Winkler-Schwartz, A., Bissonnette, V., Mirchi, N., Ponnudurai, N., Yilmaz, R., Ledwos, N., Siyar, S., Azarnoush, H., Karlik, B., and Del Maestro, R. F. Artificial intelligence in medical education: Best practices using machine learning to assess surgical expertise in virtual reality simulation. *Journal of Surgical Education* 76, no. 6 (2019): 1681–1690. https://doi.org/10.1016/j.jsurg.2019.05.015.

Wosiak, A., Zamecznik A., and Niewiadomska-Jarosik, K. "Supervised and unsupervised machine learning for improved identification of intrauterine growth restriction types." In: *Federated Conference on Computer Science and Information Systems (FedCSIS)*, pp. 323–329. 2016.

Xue, Y., Liang, H., Norbury, J., Gillis, R., and Killingworth, B. Predicting the risk of acute care readmissions among rehabilitation inpatients: A machine learning approach. *Journal of Biomedical Informatics* 86 (2018): 143–148.

Yahyaoui, Amani, Jamil, Akhtar, Rasheed, Jawad, and Yesiltepe, Mirsat. "A decision support system for diabetes prediction using machine learning and deep learning techniques." In: *1st International Informatics and Software Engineering Conference (UBMYK)*, pp. 1–4. IEEE, 2019.

Zhao, L., Ciallella, H. L., Aleksunes, L. M., and Zhu, H. Advancing computer-aided drug discovery (CADD) by big data and data-driven machine learning modeling. *Drug Discovery Today* 25, no. 9 (2020): 1624–1638. https://doi.org/10.1016/j.drudis.2020.07.005.

8

Real-Time Data Analysis of COVID-19 Vaccination Progress Over the World

Bijan Paul
University of Liberal Arts

Aditi Roy
Insightin Technology Bangladesh Ltd.

Khan Raqib Mahmud and Mohammad Rifat Rashid
University of Liberal Arts

CONTENTS

8.1 Introduction

Coronavirus disease 2019 (COVID-19) was first reported in the city of China named Wuhan [1], and the virus is considered dangerous worldwide according to the information of the World Health Organization (WHO) published on December 31, 2019. The virus is spreading drastically when a human gets in touch with an infected person, and the other reasons are still vague. The primary symptoms and signs of coronavirus cases are fever, dry cough, fatigue, and shortness of breath [2,3]. In the preliminary stage of coronavirus epidemic, hydroxychloroquine and antipyretic and anti-viral drugs were suggested for treatment. It is recommended to maintain a safe distance of around 1 m, wear a mask while

DOI: 10.1201/9781003215981-8

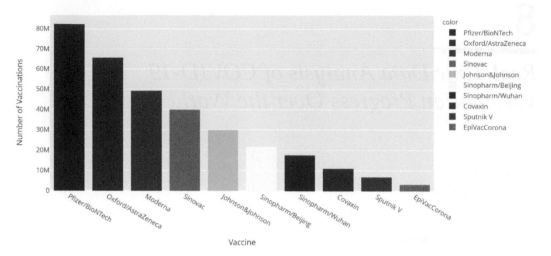

FIGURE 8.1
Number of vaccinations with a certain vaccine [4,5].

going outside, and regularly wash hands with soap for 20 seconds to control the chances of being infected by the virus. Afterward, the exact cure for corona was analyzed by different paramedical companies and they have already developed vaccines for the disease. Currently, in many countries, people are taking doses of vaccines for the prevention of the disease. In the meantime, globally, thousands of people are being tested positive daily and are isolated for 12–15 days. Even though the vaccination process is in progress, the number of COVID-19 cases is increasing drastically and handling the current situation has become a significant health concern in many parts of the world. The governments of different countries face difficulties in controlling the coronavirus as all of the medical units are full of corona patients. It is necessary to analyze the data to detect and identify the disease by analyzing the text and image data. However, a massive amount of data analyses is the preliminary step to determine the current situation of coronavirus before starting the prediction of the disease. In this chapter, we have analyzed the world data of coronavirus collected from Kaggle [4,5] data source and represented the vaccination progress in different regions of the world. According to the data analysis, the vaccine developed by Pfizer/BioNTech is widely used (around 82 million) in many parts of the world. Sinovac is used by approximately 40 million, and EpiVacCorona vaccine is used by a minimum of about 3 million around the world.

The number of COVID cases is increasing at a high rate, especially in Bangladesh (ranked eighth in the population) [6]. To control and restrict the extreme spread of coronavirus, a nationwide lockdown was imposed on March 27, 2020 [7]. However, due to the economic condition of the nation and as most people depend on income from daily-wage work, the government couldn't afford to go on with an extended period of lockdown.

Day by day, the COVID-19 situation is becoming more complex. More specifically, the neighborhood South Asian Association for Regional Cooperation (SAARC) nations are facing severe consequences of corona. Six months ago, the COVID-19 cases created a drastic effect in India; consequently, Bangladesh also faced the same issues, and the death rate attained a higher value than ever before. The primary problem is that people are not concerned about the effects of the virus though the government enforced lockdown. The main issue is the economic condition because most people lead their daily lives based on their daily labor activities.

This chapter is organized as follows: Section 8.2 provides the literature review. The data analysis framework is presented in Section 8.3, and the experimental results based on coronavirus data are shown in Section 8.4. The conclusions of the work are presented in Section 8.5.

8.2 Literature Review

The rapid increase in daily COVID-19 cases is a major concern worldwide, and it is one of the most stressful, unpredictable scenarios in the world. The primary concern of governments of different countries is how to maintain and increase the economic growth in the COVID-19 crisis?

The research on COVID-19 is one of the top priorities in the computer science community. The researchers are trying to analyze data and predict future outcomes to help governments plan and execute appropriate actions and make decisions at the right time to control the situation. The data are crucial and essential in the machine learning research of COVID-19 to identify confirmed cases, death rates, number of recoveries, and number of daily vaccinations. The most critical research challenges are lack of data availability, and without accurate and appropriate data, a model cannot be adequately trained.

There are several types of research on COVID-19 issues. One of the researches done by F. Rustam [8] identified confirmed cases, death rates, and recovered cases. Another research work done by Gupta [9] identified the growth rate of infection and the negative impacts of lockdown on the number of infected patients. The research of Sujath [10] forecasted the Indian COVID-19 cases using the dataset of Kaggle and John Hopkins GitHub Repository [11].

Remarkable studies have been done by researchers of different countries based on several approaches not only for China [12–17] but also for Italy [17–20], France [17,21], the USA [22–24], and South Korea [25,26].

Findings from other researches:

- The data forecasting is limited as it is used for specific country data.
- The overall outlook of COVID-19 vaccination data has not yet been provided for all countries over the world. It is still under process.

In our research work, we have focused on demonstrating the overall corona cases and the vaccines used by different countries using data analysis.

8.3 Methodology

8.3.1 Data Collection

The coronavirus has created a pandemic situation worldwide. The WHO considered this as an emergency of the health sector and suggested imposing lockdown to control extreme cases. Many countries imposed lockdown based on the statistical data of affected cases. Researchers especially do the data analysis, and they are collecting data from several reliable open-source resources. We have collected data from the popular data source portal Kaggle [4,5] for our research. We have collected data on the vaccination status and population of different countries. The analysis is based on the data from 236 countries and territories over the world and focuses on various data attributes such as country, population, median age, urban population percentage, world region, total vaccinations, daily vaccinations, and vaccines used by different countries. The data for the duration of around 2 months from January 10, 2021, to March 10, 2021 were taken from Kaggle for analyses.

8.3.2 Data Preprocessing

The source of data is needed before starting the data processing, especially in machine learning.

There are several steps of preprocessing, for example data cleaning by removing pointless text. The two processes lemmatization and punctuation are used to purify data in a better way. Several resources such as links and URLs, stop words, and unwanted symbols are removed for better exactness of data. Our primary aim was to analyze the progress in the vaccination across the world based on the available data.

8.3.3 Feature Engineering

To process data, feature extraction is considered as an essential part. We identified appropriate features by which data can be processed effectively in data analysis. Using these features, we have analyzed our data for finding our research outcomes.

8.4 Data Analysis

8.4.1 World Data Analysis

The condition of COVID-19 is unpredictable and frequently shifting in the current time. The research work is related to several aspects such as identifying and predicting the different vaccine types used by different countries, total vaccinations, daily vaccinations, daily vaccinations of a particular vaccine type used by different countries, how many vaccinations with a specific vaccine, how many vaccines with a particular vaccine, top 30 countries of total vaccinations, countries with high total vaccination rate, top total vaccinated countries and vaccinations used, and which country has vaccinated more people. The dataset has 5,825 rows of vaccination records of different countries.

8.4.2 Vaccines Used by Different Countries

Table 8.1 and Figure 8.2 represent the different types of vaccines used by different countries. According to the data analysis, **Pfizer/BioNTech** was the most widely used in many countries (75 countries use this vaccine). In addition, it was also the most widely used in terms of the number of daily vaccinations. In contrast, daily vaccination with **EpiVacCorona** was minimal and it was used only in Russia.

TABLE 8.1

Different Vaccines Used by Different Countries

Vaccines	Daily Vaccinations	Total Countries
Pfizer/BioNTech	82,496,840.0	75
Oxford/AstraZeneca	65,780,194.0	69
Moderna	49,270,293.0	32
Sinovac	39,943,347.0	12
Johnson & Johnson	29,933,049.0	2
Sinopharm/Beijing	21,712,749.0	17
Sinopharm/Wuhan	17,670,440.0	2
Covaxin	11,128,018.0	1
Sputnik	69,27,555.0	17
EpiVacCorona	32,73,940.0	1

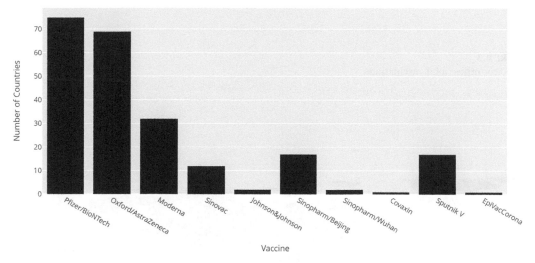

FIGURE 8.2
Countries with a particular vaccine.

8.4.3 Vaccination of World's Top 30 Countries

According to data analysis (Figure 8.3), around 96 million people were vaccinated in the USA. At the same time, approximately 52 million and 25 million were vaccinated by China and India, respectively. However, in Bangladesh (Figure 8.4), only around 4 million were vaccinated.

8.4.4 Top Ten Vaccinated Countries' Vaccination Information

The vaccination process is in progress in many parts of the world. According to the data analysis, the top ten countries' vaccination data are shown in Table 8.2. The maximum vaccinated country was the USA with a total number of vaccinations of around 96 million, and daily vaccinations were approximately 2.2 million.

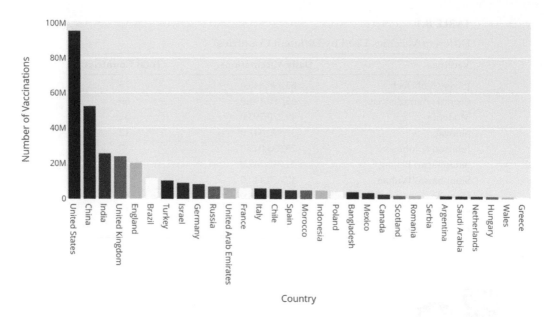

FIGURE 8.3
Top 30 countries' total vaccinations.

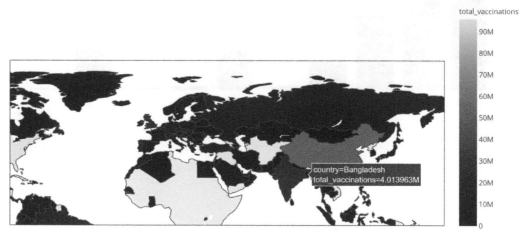

FIGURE 8.4
Total vaccinations of Bangladesh.

The second country was China and approximately 52 million people were vaccinated, and vaccination was nearly 1.9 million per day. The most vaccinated Asian Country was India, and the total vaccinations and vaccinations per day were around 25 million and 1.3 million, respectively. The other countries in the top ten positions were the UK, Brazil, Turkey, Israel, Germany, United Arab Emirates, and Russia.

In contrast, the vaccination process was very slow in Bangladesh (Table 8.3). The total vaccination in Bangladesh was around 4 million only. According to the data analysis, only 3 out of 100 people were vaccinated. The vaccination was only approximately

TABLE 8.2

Countries with a High Total Vaccination Rate [5]

Rank	Country	Vaccines	Total Vaccinations	Total Vaccinations per Hundred	Daily Vaccinations	Daily Vaccinations per Million
1	The USA	Johnson & Johnson, Moderna, Pfizer/ BioNTech	95,721,290	28.62	2,169,981	6,488
2	China	Sinopharm/Beijing, Sinopharm/Wuhan, Sinovac	52,520,000	3.65	1,916,190	1,331
3	India	Oxford/AstraZeneca	25,685,011	1.86	1,295,566	939
4	The UK	Pfizer/BioNTech	24,064,182	35.45	445,204	6,558
5	Brazil	Oxford/AstraZeneca, Sinovac	11,756,131	5.53	359,495	1,691
6	Turkey	Sinovac	10,360,283	12.28	435,596	5,165
7	Israel	Pfizer/BioNTech	9,072,077	104.81	184,792	21,350
8	Germany	Moderna, Oxford/AstraZeneca	8,431,264	10.06	221,093	2,639
9	Russia	EpiVacCorona, Sputnik	7,048,129	4.83	222,684	1,526
10	UAE	Oxford/AstraZeneca, Pfizer/BioNTech	6,325,211	63.95	160,020	16,179

TABLE 8.3

Vaccination within Bangladesh [5]

Country	Vaccines	Total Vaccinations	Total Vaccinations per Hundred	Daily Vaccinations per Million
Bangladesh	Oxford/AstraZeneca	4,013,963	2.44	1,195

1,200 per million, which was very low compared with other developed countries such as the USA or China.

8.4.5 Top Vaccinated Countries and Vaccines Used

As shown in Figure 8.5, the USA was the most vaccinated country and the Johnson & Johnson, Moderna, Pfizer/BioNTech vaccines were used. China was the second most vaccinated country and the vaccines used were Sinopharm/Beijing, Sinopharm/Wuhan, and Sinovac. India and Bangladesh used Oxford/AstraZeneca vaccine. However, Covaxin was also used in India.

8.4.6 Daily Vaccination in Bangladesh

We already know that the total vaccination in Bangladesh over the period of 2 months from January 10, 2021, to March 10, 2021, was around 4 million. Figure 8.6 demonstrates the daily vaccination in Bangladesh over time. According to the graph, the daily vaccination was initially minimal, but over the period, it reached a peak (around 195k) on February 18, 2021.

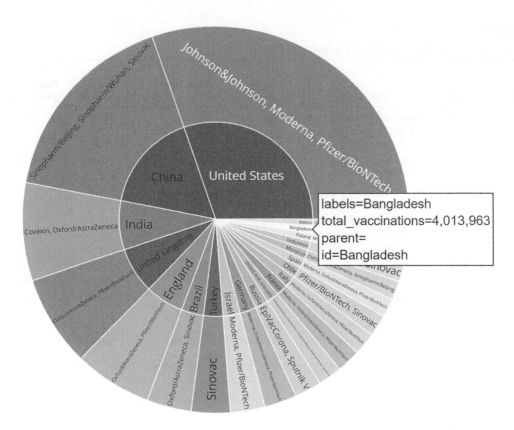

FIGURE 8.5
Top vaccinated countries with vaccination type and vaccines used in Bangladesh.

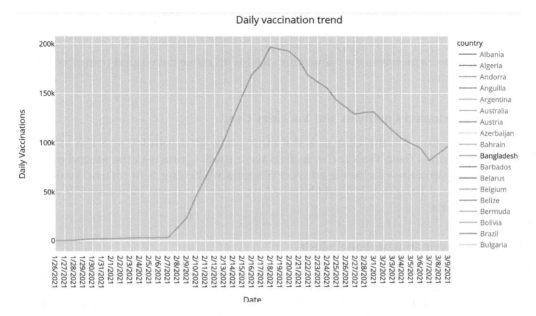

FIGURE 8.6
Daily vaccination trend in Bangladesh.

8.5 Conclusions

In the year 2020, COVID-19 caused a high amount of mortality and it affected news on a daily basis due to the unavailability of vaccines or drugs. Various researchers worked on vaccine creation, and currently, different types of vaccines are used in different countries of the world. We have analyzed the vaccination on progress based on the analysis of real-time data. Machine learning approaches were used for data analysis. We used the overall procedures such as data collection, preprocessing, and feature analysis and then analyzed the data. The research outcome represents the overall vaccination progress worldwide. Further research using machine learning can use the results based on our research. It would also be helpful for the inspection of current and any future coronaviruses.

References

[1] N. Zhu, D. Zhang, W. Wang, X. Li, B. Yang, J. Song, X. Zhao, B. Huang, W. Shi, R. Lu, et al., "A novel coronavirus from patients with pneumonia in China, 2019," *New England Journal of Medicine*, vol. 382, no. 8, p. 727–733, 2020.

[2] M. Zuo, Y. Huang, W. Ma, Z. Xue, J. Zhang, Y. Gong, et al., "Expert recommendations for tracheal intubation in critically ill patients with noval coronavirus disease 2019," *Chinese Medical Sciences Journal*, vol. 35, p. 105–109, 2020.

[3] D. Lewis, "Is the coronavirus airborne? Experts can't agree," *Nature*, vol. 580, no. 7802, p. 175, 2020.

[4] Population by Country – 2020, Countries in the world by population – 2020, Dataset of Tanu N Prabhu. Link: https://www.kaggle.com/tanuprabhu/population-by-country-2020.

[5] COVID-19 World Vaccination Progress, Daily and total vaccination for COVID-19 in the World, Dataset of Gabriel Preda. Link: https://www.kaggle.com/gpreda/covid-world-vaccination-progress.

[6] F. Ahmed, A. Q. Al Amin, M. Hasanuzzaman, and R. Saidur, "Alternative energy resources in Bangladesh and future prospect," *Renewable and Sustainable Energy Reviews*, vol. 25, pp. 698–707, 2013.

[7] M. D. Islam and A. Siddika, "Covid-19 and Bangladesh: A study of the public perception on the measures taken by the government," 2020.

[8] F. Rustam, A. A. Reshi, A. Mehmood, S. Ullah, B. On, W. Aslam, and G. S. Choi, "Covid-19 future forecasting using supervised machine learning models," *IEEE Access*, vol 8, pp. 101489–101499, 2020.

[9] R. Gupta, S. K. Pal, and G. Pandey, "A comprehensive analysis of covid-19 outbreak situation in India," medRxiv, 2020.

[10] R. Sujath, J. M. Chatterjee, and A. E. Hassanien, "A machine learning forecasting model for covid-19 pandemic in India," *Stochastic Environmental Research and Risk Assessment*, vol. 34, pp. 959–972, 2020.

[11] E. Dong, H. Du, and L. Gardner, "An interactive web-based dashboard to track covid-19 in real time," *The Lancet Infectious Diseases*, vol. 20, no. 5, pp. 533–534, 2020.

[12] K. Roosa, Y. Lee, R. Luo, A. Kirpich, R. Rothenberg, J.M. Hyman, P. Yan, G. Chowell, "Real-time forecasts of the covid-19 epidemic in China from February 5th to February 24th, 2020," *Infectious Disease Modelling*, vol. 5, pp. 256–263, 2020.

[13] Q. Li, W. Feng, and Y.-H. Quan, "Trend and forecasting of the covid-19 outbreak in China," *Journal of Infection*, vol. 80, no. 4, pp. 469–496, 2020.

[14] Z. Hu, Q. Ge, L. Jin, and M. Xiong, "Artificial intelligence forecasting of covid-19 in China," arXiv preprint arXiv:2002.07112, 2020.

[15] Z. Liu, P. Magal, O. Seydi, and G. Webb, "Predicting the cumulative number of cases for the covid-19 epidemic in China from early data," arXiv preprint arXiv:2002.12298, 2020.

[16] L. Peng, W. Yang, D. Zhang, C. Zhuge, and L. Hong, "Epidemic analysis of covid-19 in China by dynamical modeling," arXiv preprint arXiv:2002.06563, 2020.

[17] D. Fanelli and F. Piazza, "Analysis and forecast of covid-19 spreading in China, Italy and France," *Chaos, Solitons & Fractals*, vol. 134, p. 109761, 2020.

[18] G. Grasselli, A. Pesenti, and M. Cecconi, "Critical care utilization for the covid-19 outbreak in Lombardy, Italy: early experience and forecast during an emergency response," *JAMA*, vol. 323, no. 16, pp. 1545–1546, 2020.

[19] J. Wangping, H. Ke, S. Yang, C. Wenzhe, W. Shengshu, Y. Shanshan, W. Jianwei, K. Fuyin, T. Penggang, L. Jing, et al., "Extended sir prediction of the epidemics trend of covid-19 in Italy and compared with Hunan, China," *Frontiers in Medicine*, vol. 7, p. 169, 2020.

[20] C. Zhan, K. T. Chi, Z. Lai, T. Hao, and J. Su, "Prediction of covid-19 spreading profiles in South Korea, Italy and Iran by data-driven coding," medRxiv, 2020.

[21] C. Massonnaud, J. Roux, and P. Crépey, "Covid-19: Forecasting short term hospital needs in France," medRxiv, 2020.

[22] P. Liu, P. Beeler, and R. K. Chakrabarty, "Covid-19 progression timeline and effectiveness of response-to-spread interventions across the united states," medRxiv, 2020.

[23] A. A. Lover and T. McAndrew, "Sentinel event surveillance to estimate total sars-cov-2 infections, United States," medRxiv, 2020.

[24] T. Wise, T. D. Zbozinek, G. Michelini, C. C. Hagan, et al., "Changes in risk perception and protective behavior during the first week of the covid-19 pandemic in the united states," 2020.

[25] S.-K. Kim, "Aaedm: Theoretical dynamic epidemic diffusion model and covid-19 Korea pandemic cases," medRxiv, 2020.

[26] Y. Suzuki and A. Suzuki, "Machine learning model estimating number of covid-19 infection cases over coming 24 days in every province of South Korea (xgboost and multioutputregressor)," medRxiv, 2020.

9

Descriptive, Predictive, and Prescriptive Analytics in Healthcare

Kalimullah Lone and Shabir Ahmad Sofi

National Institute of Technology Srinagar

CONTENTS

9.1 Introduction

The most promising area of study in healthcare is the huge volume of patient health records accumulated in digital form. This data has grown in past years due to electronic health record (EHR) adoption, funded by Health Information Technology for Economic and Clinical Health Act [1]. The digital data revolution has led to the substantial growth of data in every field of healthcare. The process of analysing this data is called data analytics or simply analytics [2]. The building block in analytics is the machine learning which aims to develop algorithms and systems based on learning from data [3]. An important technique in machine learning is data mining which deals with the processing and modelling of huge amount of data to find unknown patterns and relationships. The huge amount of data is termed as Big Data in recent terminologies, which describe huge and always increasing data volume (Figure 9.1). The big data contains unstructured text data and is processed with a mining technique called text mining [4].

Clinical data in healthcare includes clinical narratives, patient reports, handwritten prescriptions, laboratory results and images. The data has both structured and unstructured nature [5]. Data in such formats is being used for finding hidden information and

DOI: 10.1201/9781003215981-9

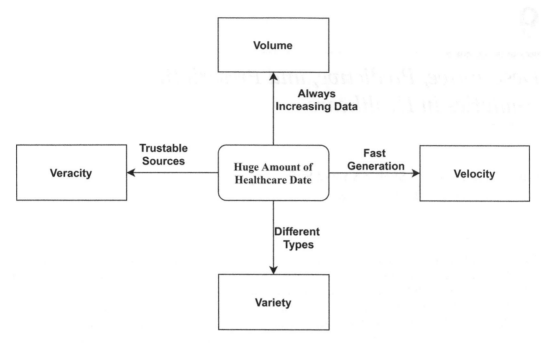

FIGURE 9.1
Big data attributes.

providing better decisions [6]. American Society for Clinical Oncology is developing a cancer learning intelligence network for quality (CancerLinQ) for comprehensive system for scholars and clinicians [7]. It consists of digital data generation, data collection, a digital support system, data mining techniques, graphical and pictorial representation [7]. Visual learning approaches are important in healthcare applications [8].

Big data analytics is like a pipeline with four different stages and the stages are shown in Figure 9.2. The process begins with the input data that comes from various sources, which in healthcare consists of clinical, financial, genomics, census and other related data. The next step is the feature extraction, which uses computational methods for organization and extraction of features from data. The process of normalization and pattern matching is performed with the help of natural language processing. The next step is to draw conclusions using machine learning and statistical methods, which we call it as statistical processing. Finally, we predict the outcome from the predictions.

9.2 Descriptive Analytics

The amount of data produced is increasing exponentially day by day. Such large datasets are described and quantized in terms of their main features, which try to reduce the datasets into human-usable form and actionable outcomes [1]. We call this descriptive analysis. Descriptive analytics collects historical data, organizes data and presents it in a way that can be understood. Two main techniques used in descriptive analytics are data aggregation and mining commonly known as data discovery. The process of descriptive analytics

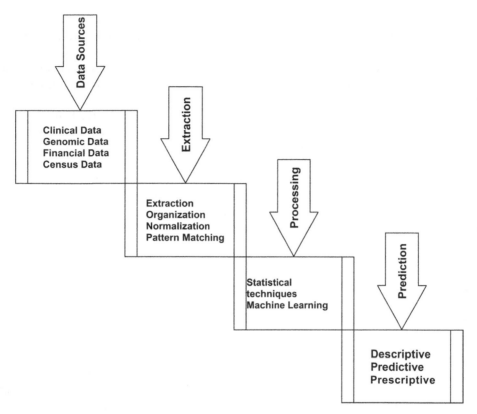

FIGURE 9.2
Analytics pipeline.

FIGURE 9.3
Descriptive analytics in healthcare.

has multiple stages and each stage has a specific role. Descriptive analytics can help in healthcare field by analysing various datasets and presenting that information in a more understandable format [9]. The stages of descriptive analytics are explained in Figure 9.3.

9.3 Predictive Analytics

Predictive analytics predicts and understands what could happen in future. Past data patterns and current situations are analysed to predict the future outcomes. It depends on learning algorithms so as to extract information from existing data for determining future [10]. These algorithms are of two types: unsupervised and supervised learning. Unsupervised learning is used for feature extraction to find structures in the data. An important method of such learning is clustering which groups data and data points on the basis of similarities. Supervised learning is used for classifications and mapping input with output [1].

Thus, prediction mechanisms are used in predicting pandemics, identification of areas or communities in need of healthcare facilities and weather forecasting. Chicago's public health department used analytics to screen mammography [10].

A lot of work has been done in healthcare with reference to predictive learning. Cancer detection in early stages is possible with clinical data using predictive-learning–based genetics and non-genetic factors. Recently, a model was developed to differentiate breast and non-breast cancers based on predictive diagnosis. Another research on oral cancer in Taiwan used logistic regression to predict survival rate among patients with 95.7% accuracy. Furthermore, research in Rice University predicted early warning signs for heart attacks. These examples show that predictive analytics have an important role in diagnosing and improving patient healthcare [11].

9.4 Prescriptive Analytics

Prescriptive learning is a predictive analytics method which also explains the set of rules through which the event has happened [5] (Figure 9.4). The set of rules is easy to act and interpret. Some algorithms such as artificial neural network (ANN) will not allow us to interpret why a decision or an outcome happened. We can simply say that prescriptive analytics is the combination of both descriptive and predictive analytics [7]. This type of analysis goes beyond predicting future events, since it can provide the best possible outcomes for the prevention of risks. Moreover, it determines the cause–effect relationship for finding the best performance that uses what-if scenarios [1].

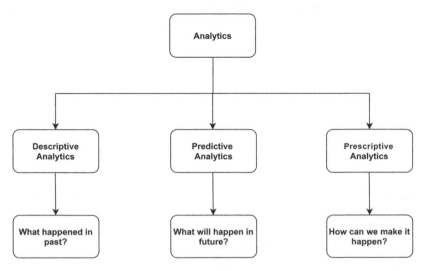

FIGURE 9.4
Types of analytics.

9.5 Analytics Techniques in Healthcare

Information can be represented visually or mathematically in a readable form. There are times when information is not sufficient to draw a conclusion from the existing knowledge bank [2]. There comes a need to analyse the existing knowledge and predict the future outcomes. A machine or computer readable form of knowledge is a set of rules or a mathematical model of a given problem. There are various ways such as data mining and machine learning to represent this knowledge and to analyse it [1]. Data mining extracts information from existing huge datasets in the form of patterns, trends and fruitful data. It allows organizations (healthcare) to mine huge datasets to take data-driven decisions [10]. Machine learning is a technique of analysing data through model building automatically in an analytical way. It allows systems to learn from existing data, find hidden patterns from that data and finally making a decision with minimum human efforts [11]. The process of machine learning can be either supervised or unsupervised.

9.5.1 Supervised Learning

It is a technique in which we have an input dataset and an output or a solution for every dataset [12]. Algorithms are applied to the input to find a predefined output from the dataset. This way a machine learns to produce an output that must resemble a predefined output. So, we can build a model that will make predictions for future inputs [1]. This process of learning is believed to be supervised under the guidance of a teacher. Learning and unlearning take place till the predictions on the training data match the predefined outcome [12]. Supervised learning uses techniques such as classification and regression.

9.5.1.1 Classification

Classification takes a dataset, processes it and provides an output in the form of category or a class. We can predict diagnosis of a patient based on body weight, height, young or old, blood sugar, blood pressure and many other measures [13]. These factors can be used to predict the probability of a heart attack in the recent future [1]. Classification techniques used in the analytics are shown in Figure 9.5. These techniques are explained briefly as follows.

9.5.1.1.1 Fuzzy Classification

It is a qualitative-reasoning–based method based on if-then rules which forms an expert system based on these rules. These if-then rules create a relation between the input and output. Various techniques such as heuristics, neuro-fuzzy methods and genetic algorithms are used to learn and generate fuzzy rules from existing datasets [13].

9.5.1.1.2 Random Forests

It is a machine learning technique that uses the concept of ensemble learning. It combines various classifiers in order to improve the performance of the model and to solve complex problems [6]. The datasets are partitioned into various subsets where each dataset has its own decision tree. These small trees are having a predictive accuracy and the average of these trees is predicted to find the best classifier. More the number of trees in the forest leads to higher accuracy [14].

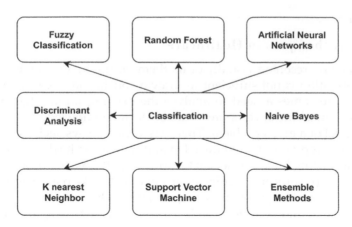

FIGURE 9.5
Classification techniques for analytics.

9.5.1.1.3 ANNs

ANN is a system that collects, extracts, processes and analyses information in a way similar to the human brain. It has a self-learning tendency through which decision-making becomes better with more and more learning. ANNs are guided by a set of learning rules called back propagation. Its structure is simply similar to a human brain with a lot of neurons connected to each other like a web. It is applied in healthcare in many fields of cancer prediction, diagnosis of myocardial infraction with the help of automatic electrocardiographic interpretation, clinical diagnosis and non-clinical applications for better management [15].

9.5.1.1.4 Discriminant Analysis

It is a process by which we remove higher dimensional space features to a space with lower dimensions by removing redundant and useless features. We take class labels into consideration while dealing with discriminant analysis [13]. It is used for early disease detection with the help of EHRs. The predictions are made by finding the probabilities of each input set and then placing it in a suitable class. The class with the highest probability will be the output class and the predictions will be made [15].

9.5.1.1.5 Naive Bayes

It is a classification method in which problem instances are assigned as class labels and are represented as vectors of feature values. It has a family of algorithms for training these classifiers in which one feature is independent of the other feature. It can be used to find out positive and negative sentiments of a patient by finding data correlation from patient data [13,14].

9.5.1.1.6 K-Nearest Neighbour

The technique relies on the distance classification in which a constant k is user-defined and an unlabelled vector. The classification is done by assigning the label to a point and finding its nearest neighbour. It mostly uses Euclidean distance for continuous variables and hamming distance for discrete variables. It can be used in gene expression microarray data and can be used for disease classification to diagnose a disease [14]. In K-Nearest Neighbour (KNN), we represent instances through attribute vectors. An attribute vector for an instance x is { $a_1(x)$, $a_2(x)$,..., $a_n(x)$ }, where $a_i(x)$ is the value of ith attribute A_i of x. C denotes a class variable and c denotes a value corresponding to that class. $c(x)$ is the class of the instance c. KNN uses distance function to measure similarity or difference between two instances. Standard Euclidean distance $d(x,y)$ between x and y is usually used as a distance function.

$$d(x,y) = \sqrt{\sum_{n=1}^{n}\left(a_i(x) - a_i(y)\right)^2} \tag{9.1}$$

When we have an instance x, the most common class of x's KNN is assigned to x.

$$c(x) = arg\,max \sum_{n=1}^{k} \delta(c, c(yi)) \tag{9.2}$$

where $c \in C$, y_i's are the KNNs of x and k is the number of neighbours and $\delta(c, c(y_i)) = 1$ if $c = c(y_i)$ and $\delta(c, c(y_i)) = 0$ otherwise [16].

9.5.1.1.7 Support Vector Machine

The distinct classification of data points is done in N-dimensional space in order to find a hyper plane. Support vectors represent data points close to hyper plane and have an impact on the position and orientation of hyper plane [1]. The hyperplane determines the most possible label for unseen data. The training process of support vector machine finds a hyperplane that has a maximum distance between vectors coming from both class labels. Thus, a hyperplane maximizes the distance or margin between the classes. It can be both linear and non-linear. If the data points are separated by a hyperplane through a straight line, we call it a linear hyperplane. If the data points can't be separated with a straight line, we call it a non-linear hyperplane. Moreover, the complexity of a support vector machine depends on the number of features used. A hypothetical example with two features will show its hyperplane as a line. Figure 9.6 explains a hyperplane with two features represented by a line. The analysis of support vector machine essentially has three stages. The stages are feature selection, training and testing the classifier and performance evaluation. The essential and mandatory for training is transformation of raw and original data into a set of features, which act as an input to support vector machine. There are various methods to select features such as embedded, filter and wrapper. In embedded method, the process of feature selection is performed automatically during the construction of learning algorithm. In filter method, feature selection is performed as a pre-processing step before classification in order to remove elements of least importance. It is a faster method in terms of computation and is preferable for large datasets. In wrapper method, all the possibilities are checked and the classifier is trained continuously with the help of feedback. Feedbacks are used to find a subset of features for next iteration. Training and testing the classifier makes use of practical observations. Training and testing a support vector machine sets up parameters in the decision function in order to orient hyperplane in such a way that the resulting projections separate the two classes at maximum. Performance is usually described by accuracy, specificity and sensitivity [17].

9.5.1.1.8 Ensemble Learning

It is a technique in which output accuracy is increased by combining various models instead of a single model. The three main classes of ensemble learning are bagging, stacking and boosting. Bagging uses various samples from a dataset and fits many decision

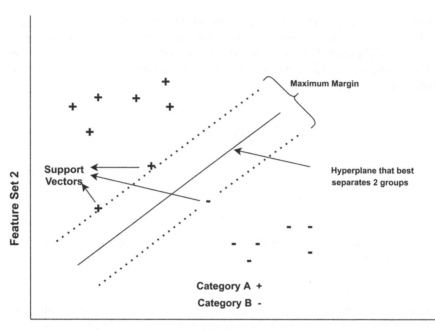

FIGURE 9.6
Hyperplane that maximally separates the support vectors.

trees to find the average of predictions. Stacking fits various model types on the same data-set and uses another model for best predictions. Boosting learns from previous mistakes to perform better predictions in the future [15].

9.5.1.2 Regression

When the predicted output of a particular problem is a real value, we call it regression. The analysis of dependent and independent variable is described through a relationship [18]. Curve fitting or a straight-line curve is performed on a number of data points. This fitting is done in such a way that the distance between the point and the curve is minimal. It is widely used for prediction and forecasting [19].

9.5.1.2.1 Linear Regression

It is a relationship between a dependent and one or many variables which can be dependent as well as independent using a simple straight fit curve. It helps in finding the relation of one disease symptom on another. Polynomial regression finds a relation between dependent and other independent variables of nth-degree polynomial. The mathematical equation for linear regression is $(y = bx + c)$; the equation describes a best fit line for the relationship between dependent variable y and an independent variable x, where m is the slope and c is the intercept [18].

9.5.1.2.2 Logistic Regression

It is a regression technique in which the dependent variable has a binary behaviour (dichotomous). It explains the nature of data and the relation of dichotomous variable and other independent variables [19].

9.5.1.2.3 Ridge Regression

When the independent variables are highly correlated, the influence of one variable on other cannot be differentiated. Such a condition is called multicollinearity. This gives rise to unstable regression coefficients having very high variance. This problem is addressed by ridge regression. It estimates the coefficients of multiple regression models in situations when there is a high correlation between independent variables. Ridge regression can be used in the diagnosis of a disease, when there are different independent variables and a dependent variable. There is a very high correlation among the independent variables (symptoms of a disease) and the dependent variable (disease itself) [18,19].

9.5.1.2.4 Lasso Regression

It is a linear regression type in which data values are shrunk towards the central point similar to mean having simple models with fever parameters. It is well suited for models with high multicollinearity. It can be used in datasets with hundreds of variables of independent nature to select a variable. It can be used in cost prediction for the improvement of risk adjustment and health management [18].

9.5.2 Unsupervised Learning

It is a technique in which we have an input dataset with no idea about the output solution. Algorithms are applied to the input data to find the hidden patterns and solutions needed in future. We do not have any predefined output available with us [1]. The machine learns from every output or a new solution. It is an independent learning technique. The process of learning is believed to be unsupervised as there is no guidance of a teacher [4]. The system learns from its previous solutions and new solutions are compared with previous solutions in order to find the best solution among all [12]. Two main techniques used in unsupervised learning are clustering and dimension reduction.

9.5.2.1 Clustering

Clustering is a technique in which an input dataset is partitioned into clusters to find the hidden patterns and groupings in the data. These clusters divide various data points of a dataset into groups. The groups are formed in such a way that same groups have similar data points and different to data points of other groups. It actually groups points on the basis of similarity and dissimilarity. It can be used in healthcare to identify patients with similar symptoms and diseases. Thus, it can be partitioned into groups based on similar symptoms [20]. Various techniques of clustering are as follows.

9.5.2.1.1 K-means Clustering

K-means clustering is a technique to group unlabelled data into different clusters. K defines the number of clusters which are predefined. K=2 means two clusters, K=3 means three clusters and so on. It groups data into clusters and allows us to conveniently discover categories of groups without any training [21].

9.5.2.1.2 Hierarchical Clustering

Hierarchical clustering treats each point as a separate cluster, followed by the identification of two closest clusters and merging of these similar clusters. The process is repeated until all the clusters are merged [20].

9.5.2.1.3 Genetic Algorithms

It is a search-based technique based on genetics and natural selection. It uses the concept of survival for the fittest to select individuals for the next generation. It works with an initial population, its fitness function, selection, crossover and mutation. It has a wide range of applications in medical and healthcare [21].

9.5.2.1.4 ANNs

The technique already discussed in classification is also applied in regression.

9.5.2.1.5 Hidden Markov Model

It is an approach to deal with hidden biological problems. It identifies events on the basis of observation and hidden events that are important for probabilistic modelling [21].

9.5.2.2 Dimension Reduction

It is a technique to reduce the number of attributes, features and variables required to represent input data. The outcome of the technique is a dataset with fewer dimensions. The reduction of the dimensions will allow data to be represented in a simple way and faster in terms of processing time [22]. Various techniques used in dimension reduction are as follows.

9.5.2.2.1 Principal Component Analysis

We have datasets with a number of features or attributes that make the data understandable. If there are a number of attributes or features, the datasets will become difficult to understand and interpret. Its application in machine learning will be much more difficult. To overcome this challenge, we will find the features with very high variance [22]. The features with high variance will contribute more to the outcome and will have a high power of explanation. Principle component analysis is the most popular dimension reduction method currently used. It finds principal components from the data through the identification of a hyperplane which is close to the data points and projecting the data on it [1].

9.5.2.2.2 Linear Discriminant Analysis

It is a dimension reduction technique which actually pre-processes the classification of patterns. Its aim is to place a dataset into a moderate dimension class of understandable features that are able to minimize overfitting and costs. It performs the classification of objects into two or more groups that express objects based on a set of parameters. The main aim of the technique is to find a group of parameters with their association with reference to objects and separate the groups with a best classification model [23].

9.5.2.2.3 Multidimensional Statistics

It is a branch in mathematics that tries to find an optimal design to collect, process and systematize multivariate data. It tries to find out the behaviour and structure of the correlations between various components to get practical and scientific assumption [24].

9.5.2.2.4 Random Projection

It is a decomposition technique used to reduce high-dimensional data. This technique is mostly preferred because of its simplicity and power to produce low error rates. It uses Johnson–Lindenstrauss Lemma to reduce higher dimensions to lower dimensions with little to no distortion. Gaussian and sparse are the two techniques of random projection for dimension reduction [25].

9.6 Healthcare Analytics Life Cycle

Descriptive and predictive analysis deals with the discovery of knowledge for a support system, whereas the prescriptive analysis uses what-if questions to find the cause–effect relationships for finding the best possible solutions for automatic decision-making [1]. In Figure 9.7, prescriptive analytics performs a proactive decision using the outcome of predictive analytics. Thus, timely decisions of event indication and event prediction are important to understand the behaviour of healthcare [5].

Descriptive analytics discovers insights of the event root causes and answers of what happened and why it happened. The Figure 9.7 shows decision-making at various analytical stages. Figure 9.8 shows the system diagram that locates data in the initial phase and

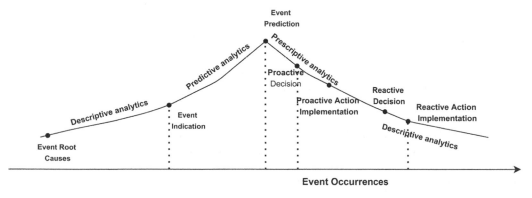

FIGURE 9.7
Prescriptive analytics decision stages.

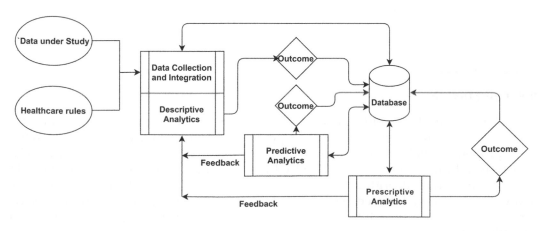

FIGURE 9.8
System design of analytics techniques.

understands the rules of healthcare [2]. The located data is collected and integrated in the system database. All the analytical techniques are used one after the other with a full connectivity with the database [3]. The outcomes of all the analytical techniques are collected in the database for future supervised and unsupervised learning [10].

9.7 Proposed Architecture for Healthcare Analytics

The architecture of fog in Figure 9.9 has Internet of Things devices at the bottom for the generation of data. The data has least chances of processing at this layer. Mostly, the processing is done at fog and cloud layers. We have devised a model which processes data at various layers, with some powerful tools. The data can be of any nature; it may be structured, semi-structured and unstructured. This data needs processing in terms of parallel processing, data import/export, script language, massive parallel processing, distributed applications and message passing. We have various tools, which can handle these operations. Parallel processing and data management are done by Hadoop. Hadoop has some applications such as Pig and Hive to handle queries and scripts. It also has Sqoop, which handles Relational Database Management System (RDBMS) data and Hadoop data. HBase is stored on top of Hadoop Distributed File System and is a much faster distributed database. There are occasions when we need massive parallel processing and distributed application, where we use tools such as Impala and Cassendra. Zookeeper also handles distributed applications. We have a proper communication mechanism to handle message passing through a message broker called Kafka. The processing is done by all these tools, the data is now ready to be visualized in another layer. The layer has Tableau, R and Python which can visualize data. Machine learning applications are implemented on some tools such as Mahout, Weka, RapidMiner and KNIME. The data items are visualized through Charts, Graphs, Reports and Heat maps. Machine learning algorithms implemented on these tools help us to analyse data processed by other layers. If the data is not visualized through these in-built algorithms, then we can use R/ Python to build a source code for the required problems. The algorithms used for analytics are easily implemented in Weka, Python, R language, Tableau, Mahout, KNIME and Rapid Miner.

9.8 Conclusion

The chapter tried to simplify the concepts of analysis with a proper explanation for understanding it thoroughly. Descriptive, predictive and prescriptive learning analytics were properly explained. All the analytical techniques were discussed at full in relation to healthcare. The uses of supervised and unsupervised learning with the help of their supporting algorithms were categorized in their proper domains. Healthcare analytics life cycle addressed the use of all analytical methods at their proper place. Finally, we proposed an architecture for complete analysis from data generation to result visualization.

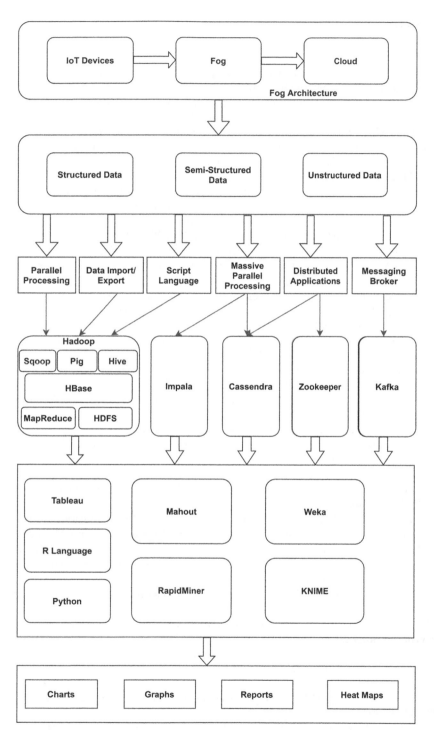

FIGURE 9.9
Proposed architecture for analytics.

References

1. El Morr, C., and Hossam, A.-H. "Descriptive, predictive, and prescriptive analytics." *Analytics in Healthcare* (pp. 31–55). Springer, Cham, 2019.
2. Fahl, J., *Data Analytics: A Practical Guide to Data Analytics for Business, Beginner to Expert.* CreateSpace Independent Publishing Platform, 2017.
3. Hersh, W.R., Hoyt, R.E., and Yoshihashi, A.K. "Healthcare data analytics." *Health Informatics: Practical Guide for Healthcare and Information Technology Professionals.* Lulu.com (2014): 1–14.
4. Hassan, S., Dhali, M., Zaman, F., and Tanveer, M. "Big data and predictive analytics in healthcare in Bangladesh: Regulatory challenges." *Heliyon* 7, no. 6 (2021): e07179.
5. Lepenioti, K., et al. "Prescriptive analytics: a survey of approaches and methods." *International Conference on Business Information Systems*. Springer, Cham. 2018.
6. Mosavi, N.S., and Santos, M.F. "How prescriptive analytics influences decision making in precision medicine." *Procedia Computer Science* 177 (2020): 528–533.
7. Sappelli, M., et al. "A vision on prescriptive analytics." *ALLDATA* 2017 (2017): 54.
8. Khanday, N.Y., and Sofi, S.A. "Taxonomy, state-of-the-art, challenges and applications of visual understanding: A review." *Computer Science Review* 40 (2021): 100374.
9. Oleg, M. "Descriptive metaphysics, descriptive analytics, descriptive aesthetics. The structure of cognition in kants critique of pure reason." *Studies in Transcendental Philosophy* 1(1), 2020. doi: 10.18254/S271326680009383-2.
10. Lopes, J., Guimarães, T., and Santos, M.F. "Predictive and prescriptive analytics in healthcare: a survey." *Procedia Computer Science* 170 (2020): 1029–1034.
11. Leung, C.K., et al. "Data science for healthcare predictive analytics." *Proceedings of the 24th Symposium on International Database Engineering & Applications*. 2020.
12. Van Engelen, J.E., and Hoos, H.H. "A survey on semi-supervised learning." *Machine Learning* 109, no. 2 (2020): 373–440.
13. Panicker, S. "Use of machine learning techniques in healthcare: a brief review of cardiovascular disease classification." *2nd International Conference on Communication & Information Processing (ICCIP)*. 2020.
14. Sujitha, R., and Seenivasagam, V. "Classification of lung cancer stages with machine learning over big data healthcare framework." *Journal of Ambient Intelligence and Humanized Computing* 12 (2021): 5639–5649.
15. Char, D.S., Abràmoff, M.D., and Feudtner, C. "Identifying ethical considerations for machine learning healthcare applications." *The American Journal of Bioethics* 20, no. 11 (2020): 7–17.
16. Jiang, L., Cai, Z., Wang, D., and Jiang, S. "Survey of improving k-nearest-neighbor for classification." *Fourth International Conference on Fuzzy Systems and Knowledge Discovery (FSKD 2007)* (Vol. 1, pp. 679–683). IEEE, 2007, August.
17. Pisner, D.A. and Schnyer, D.M. 2020. "Support vector machine." *Machine Learning* (pp. 101–121). Academic Press.
18. Montgomery, D.C., Peck, E.A., and Geoffrey Vining, G. *Introduction to Linear Regression Analysis*. John Wiley & Sons, 2021.
19. Ali, B.J., and Anwar, G. "The effect of marketing culture aspects of healthcare care on marketing creativity." *International Journal of English Literature and Social Sciences* 6, no. 2 (2021): 171–182.
20. Sinaga, K.P., and Yang, M-S. "Unsupervised K-means clustering algorithm." *IEEE Access* 8 (2020): 80716–8072.
21. Gesicho, M.B., Were, M.C., and Babic, A. "Evaluating performance of health care facilities at meeting HIV-indicator reporting requirements in Kenya: an application of K-means clustering algorithm." *BMC Medical Informatics and Decision Making* 21, no. 1 (2021): 1–18.

22. Boquet, G., et al. "A variational autoencoder solution for road traffic forecasting systems: Missing data imputation, dimension reduction, model selection and anomaly detection." *Transportation Research Part C: Emerging Technologies* 115 (2020): 102622.

23. Nie, F., et al. "Adaptive local linear discriminant analysis." *ACM Transactions on Knowledge Discovery from Data (TKDD)* 14, no. 1 (2020): 1–19.

24. Chen, C.-M., et al. "A computer-aided diagnosis system for differentiation and delineation of malignant regions on whole-slide prostate histopathology image using spatial statistics and multidimensional DenseNet." *Medical Physics* 47, no. 3 (2020): 1021–1033.

25. Wan, S., Kim, J., and Won, K.J. "SHARP: hyperfast and accurate processing of single-cell RNA-seq data via ensemble random projection." *Genome Research* 30, no. 2 (2020): 205–213.

10

IoT Enabled Worker Health, Safety Monitoring and Visual Data Analytics

Selvaraj Kesavan, Subhash Almel, and B.S. Muralidhar

DXC Technology

CONTENTS

10.1 Introduction

Mineral Mining is one of the oldest activities known to human beings and has evolved over centuries. The process of mining has been evolving by leveraging on available technology and will continue to evolve using emerging technologies. Reckless mining can lead to drying out the minerals and creating a huge vacuum. Hence, it is important to adopt and innovate to sustain mining for longer duration. To achieve sustainability in mining, it is important that the mining companies adopt emerging technologies and embark on a Digital Transformation.

Researchers are working in numerous areas of the connected mining such as worker safety [1], including fall detection [2, 3], vehicle routing and scheduling, plant operation, pollution and hazardous gas detection[4], emergency handling[5], centralized command and control. Internet of Things (IoT) is one of the key enablers in connected mining; it actively helps in many areas to leverage advanced sensor along with connectivity networks

DOI: 10.1201/9781003215981-10

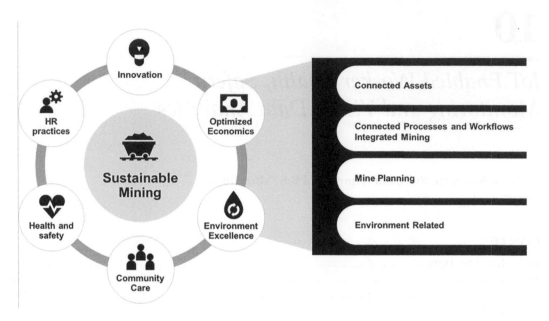

FIGURE 10.1
Sustainable mining.

and edge computing capability [6]. It is inevitable to bring all the elements in the mining together and generate visibility. Our focus is on building a Smart Connected Platform that addresses all the aspects of Connected Smart Mining. It is recommended that the Connected Smart Mining platform is built in a phased manner. Four phases are safety and security of personnel, maintenance of equipment and vehicles, mine planning and environment-related (Figure 10.1). This chapter mainly focuses on the connected mining framework as an end-to-end solution for mining health and safety.

10.2 Connected Assets

The concept of Connected Assets includes Human Resources, Machines and Vehicles that help the mining company achieve their goals.

10.2.1 Connected People

All over the world, thousands of miners get affected due to gas explosion, intoxication, increasing temperature and sudden change in the individual's health vitals. It is essential to have safety and security mechanism in place all the time and alert supervisor or operation center executives in real time to reduce delay in emergency response and action. It is highly critical to demarcate zones within the mining area to provide authorized entry and to restrict the access to the common workers to eliminate potential health risks. The combination of different IoT sensors and intelligent processing of the sensor data will provide the best insight on what is happening in the environment to generate optimal responses [7]. An integrated system is required, which facilitates features such as access control, track and trace while inside the mines, geofence, track health vital and environmental gas detection. Real-time reporting helps for better decision making and operational excellence. Provision of emergency alert to the supervisor or concerned people in case of any critical issues.

10.2.2 Connected Vehicles

To improve operational efficiency and worker safety, the operators need to be aware of the health equipment in real time.

There are two broadly classified types of vehicles used in mining, namely mining-specific vehicles and utility vehicles. Mining specific vehicles are loaders, dumpers, drillers, bolters and trucks.

The parameters to be monitored for all kinds of vehicles are hydraulics, oil levels, breaks, fuel efficiency and heat. The utility-like transport vehicles need to be monitored for oil levels, breaks, weight (in case of trucks) and fuel efficiency.

10.3 Protection of the Environment and Conservation of Water

Since the mines use a lot of water, there is a lot of contamination in the groundwater. Hence, it is important that the groundwater is treated properly and consumed in an efficient manner.

There is lot of dust in the atmosphere due to mining. To ensure that this dust does not escape into surrounding areas, grass and other vegetation are grown, and sprinklers are deployed so that the dust settles down. To manage grass and other vegetation, there is a need for water. It is hence critical that the water usage is monitored. Sensors are put at various locations along the water pipelines to alert any leakages. Based on the data collection over a period, mine operators can plan their water requirements and store water as per their requirements.

10.4 Mine Planning

Mine planning is important as natural resources are limited and can get exhausted fast if mined without any planning. The mine planning is typically done for three terms, namely short term, mid-term and long term. Short-term planning typically is done for the duration of less than 1 year. This involves planning to meet immediate demand from the market and hence plans laid out for workforce requirements and logistics on transport vehicles. Mid-term planning typically is done for the durationbetween1 and 3 years. This helps miners to plan based on the demand trends in the market. It gives an opportunity to the miners to identify areas in the immediate surrounding to mine and any additional equipment required. Long-term planning helps the miners to identify locations/areas that can be potentially explored to mine. Adoption of newer technologies can be planned and implemented. There are many challenges and drawbacks in the existing systems. The aim is to provide comprehensive solution to address all the problems and improve the safety and security aspects of the mining ecosystem.

10.5 Proposed Connected Mining Solution

To connect people, equipment and vehicles, devices are designed to be small, rugged and can communicate with each other and other systems in the ecosystem. Typical technologies used by devices in mining are IoT, network and wireless protocols such as Bluetooth Low Energy (BLE) [8], Wi-Fi and 4G/LTE/5G [9]. Evolution of technologies and cloud infrastructure brings innovation and real-time connectivity into mining industries [10]. Wireless sensor networks play a critical role in implementing connected, smart solutions for mining safety [11]. The aim of connected mining is to use capabilities of digital technologies to automate, monitor and track actionable intelligence through data-driven analytics and artificial intelligence. This will help to realize the true potential of the assets, improve the performance and reduce the capital and operating expenses. To address the issues faced in mining, it is necessary to have framework to integrate and interconnect multiple mining elements, subsystems and external systems (Figure 10.2).

The high-level architecture of connected mining system is presented in Figure 10.3. A connected mining system should monitor and detect equipment's data, the environment, worker's health vitals, access parameters, visitor data, etc. through various sensors and devices. This data is streamed to a centralized server using appropriate communication

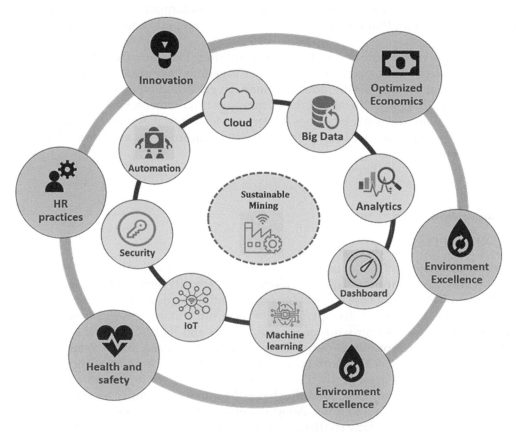

FIGURE 10.2
Connect mining ecosystem and enablers.

channels and protocols. The real-time events generated from the data help to take quick action. The architecture framework consists of four major layers, namely Application and Visualization, Core Platform Services, IoT Platform/Services, and Devices and Sensors.

The framework comprises components to connect end-to-end health sensors and receive the real-time data. The services and data analytics in the core platform help to identify critical mining insights and alerts in case of drastic change in the measured values. The received values can also be directly interpreted in real time.

10.5.1 Application and Visualization

The application layer caters to different functionality to visually represent the insights for better interpretation and decisions. The third-party systems such as emergency handling and health service can be also integrated and invoked as on when required. The key functionalities are user management, access management, health monitoring and location tracking, alerts and notifications, and emergency response (Figure 10.3).

10.5.2 Core Platform and Services

Core platform provides data storage, services to get data from IoT platform, validate the rules and generate alerts. It is highly critical to implement proper authentication and authorization mechanism in mining [12]. Authentication service in core platform helps to validate the login user identity. The external systems can be integrated and accessed from platform to provide certain functionalities. The services periodically receive data from respective IoT platforms, run the validation as per the defined rules and store the data in the database. Application posts the request to the service via Application Programming Interface (API) management layer and access the required information.

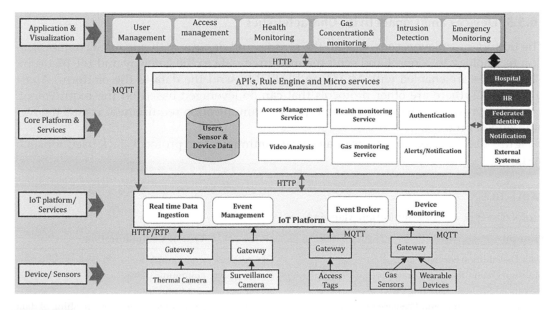

FIGURE 10.3
Proposed connected mining solution.

10.5.3 IoT Platform and Services

IoT platform has the ability to centrally manage multiple devices at scale and provide remote configuration, monitoring and decommissioning. It facilitates seamless connection between device to platform, platform to device and direct connectivity between sensors and platform. It also provides infrastructure and tools to manage, store, and process real-time analysis of data. Multiple IoT platforms used by the vendors can receive data from respective devices. The applications can subscribe to the IoT platform to receive real-time events. Whenever IoT platform receives data from specific topic, the subscribers are posted with an event. The key components of IoT platforms are Data Ingestion, Event Broker, Event Management and Device Monitoring.

10.5.4 Communication Network and Protocols

Protocols and communication channels enable edge devices/sensors that receive real-time data from readers and device gateway. Device gateway collects data from multiple edge devices and filter aggregators and ingests data to the platform for further processing and analyses. Various application and network protocols can be leveraged based on the use case, power requirement, connectivity, cost, processing constraint and distance. The sensors, readers and gateways are powered by BLE to send and receive data. Communication between Bluetooth devices happens over short-range and adhoc networks. When a network is established, one device takes the role of the master while all the other devices act as slaves. Piconets are established dynamically and automatically as Bluetooth devices enter and leave radio proximity.

Gateways use application protocol over available network (LAN, WLAN, LPWAN, etc.) to send or receive data to platform. Message Queuing Telemetry Transport (MQTT) is specially designed for Machine-to-machine (M2M)communication and IoT connectivity which helps transfer application data from/to gateway to the platform.

10.5.5 Devices and Connectivity Characteristics

The bottom-most layers consist of all the sensors and devices with adequate communication technology to connect and send the measured data to the gateway and IoT platform. The devices are enabled with MQTT and HTTP to send the data to the platform. Apart from MQTT, there are other protocols that can be leveraged based on the requirement. Table 10.1 provides a mapping on the type of communication requirement versus the recommended protocol.

Figure 10.4 describes six layers of a typical communication protocol stack used for such systems.

TABLE 10.1

Protocol – Type of Communication Mapping

Protocol	Type of Communication
Data Distribution Service	Device–device communication
Message Queue Telemetry Transport	Device–server communication
Advanced Message Queuing Protocol	Server–server communication
Extensible Messaging and Presence Protocol	Device–server protocol for continuous pushing of data
Constrained Application Protocol	Device–server communication

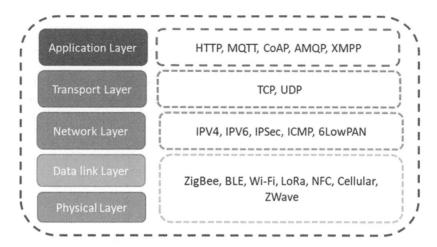

FIGURE 10.4
Communication protocol stack.

TABLE 10.2

Topology – Technology Mapping

Topology	Bluetooth LE	ANT+	ZigBee	Wi-Fi HaLow
Broadcast	√	√		
Peer-to-peer	√	√	√	√
Star	√	√	√	√
Scanning	√	√	√	
Mesh	√	√	√	

Table 10.2 provides recommendation of wireless technologies that can be used for various topology requirements.

The list of sensors, platforms and tools used to implement connected mining framework are captured in Table 10.3.

10.6 Development and Deployment

The main intention of this work is to prove the concept of connected mining and monitoring system which combined with IoT could be used for enhancing and optimizing the existing mining ventilation, worker safety and real-time monitoring. The data obtained from the sensors and devices can be analyzed and utilized for the improvement of health monitoring and for planning emergency rescue response. Real-time access management readers and tags help to monitor workers' entry, exit and zone access management. Health and environmental sensors collect sensor data and compile it to provide a broader and more accurate picture of what that worker is experiencing. The comprehensive dashboard displays the holistic view of the employee access, violations, health and safety parameters giving plant managers or incident commanders information they can use to anticipate unsafe

TABLE 10.3

Connected Mining Implementation– Hardware/Software

Module	Component	Specification
Device and sensors	Access cards	BLE 5.0 tags, battery operated, up to 20 m range
	Access readers	BLE 5.0 readers, battery operated, up to 20 m range
	Access readers with buzzers	BLE 5.0 reader, battery operated, up to 20 m range, sound and vibration sensor in-built
	Gas sensors	BLE 5.0, battery operated, up to 20 m range CO, NH_3, Temperature, C_6H_6
	Personal health care sensor	BLE 5.0, battery operated SpO_2, pulse rate, heart rate, body temperature
	Gateway	ARM Cortex IEEE 802.11a/b/g/n Ethernet BLE 5.0, up to 20 m range
Protocols	Gateway to platform connectivity	Message Queue Telemetry Transport (MQTT), ethernet
Front-end application	Angular stack	Angular 8
Back end	Platform services and business logic	Spring Boot Microservices
	Database	MySQL
Platform and services	Device connectivity and management	AWS IoT
Hosting	Object storage (application deployment)	AWS S3
	Content distribution and caching	AWS CloudFront
Protocols and standards	Application to back end	MQTT over WebSocket (Publish-subscribe), HTTP

conditions, access violations and respond to or prevent dangerous scenarios. The data from the sensors and devices are collected on the mining floor, analyzed at the edge location to detect real-time anomaly and later transferred to the platform data lake for further analysis and to derive insights. The dashboard analytics helps the administrators, operators and business owners to visualize data, to derive insights in real time and take quick action.

Alerts are classified and displayed as Intrusion, Pulse Rate (High/Low) and CO Detection. It is further explained that these alerts would go to an emergency response system for the emergency teams to respond. The access, gas and health sensors are activated and data from gas sensors (CO, temperature, NH_3, C_6H_6), health sensors (SpO_2, blood pressure, pulse rate, body temperature) and access information are sent to the gateway through readers. As part of the implementation, the firmware, algorithm and application are developed and deployed in sensors, readers and gateway by the authors. The algorithm in a gateway helps to analyze data in real time. For example, if there is a sudden increase in gas level in underground, the gateway immediately alerts with sound. Due to rising temperature, CO may provide an indication of potential danger in the mining at the given time. The supervisor or engineers can detect and act to mitigate the risk. The individual mining worker's health vitals and access data are also captured in real time which help to monitor the individual worker, know the exact location and monitor health parameters to avoid any health emergency. The data are aggregated in IoT platform and stored in a database with timestamp. The dashboard displays the data in real time and alerts the administrators. The data collection interval can be configured at the reader and gateway

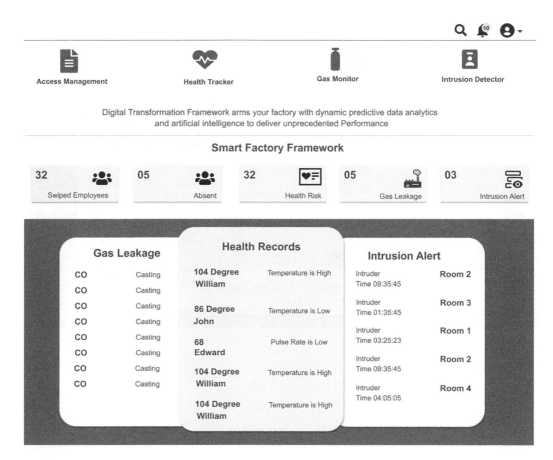

FIGURE 10.5
Connected mining application dashboard.

level. However, it is recommended that the data interval is configured at a 5-second sampling interval to get appropriate results.

10.6.1 Application Dashboard

The comprehensive connected mining dashboard (Figure 10.5) captures real-time information about worker access details, gas, health and intrusion alerts. Whenever violation in the health, gas threshold and intrusion detected, the alerts are generated. In the underground mining, the buzzer will create sound to alert the supervisor and workers. The alerts can also be visualized in the application dashboard.

10.6.2 Intrusion Detection and Worker's Health Dashboard

A sample dashboard of intrusion detection is shown in Figure 10.6. This dashboard provides information of any intrusion that occurred in the given area that is monitored.

The historic information of individual workers' health vitals was captured and shown in Figure 10.7. The dashboard provides information of various vitals such as SpO_2, temperature and heartbeat rate for a given employee/worker.

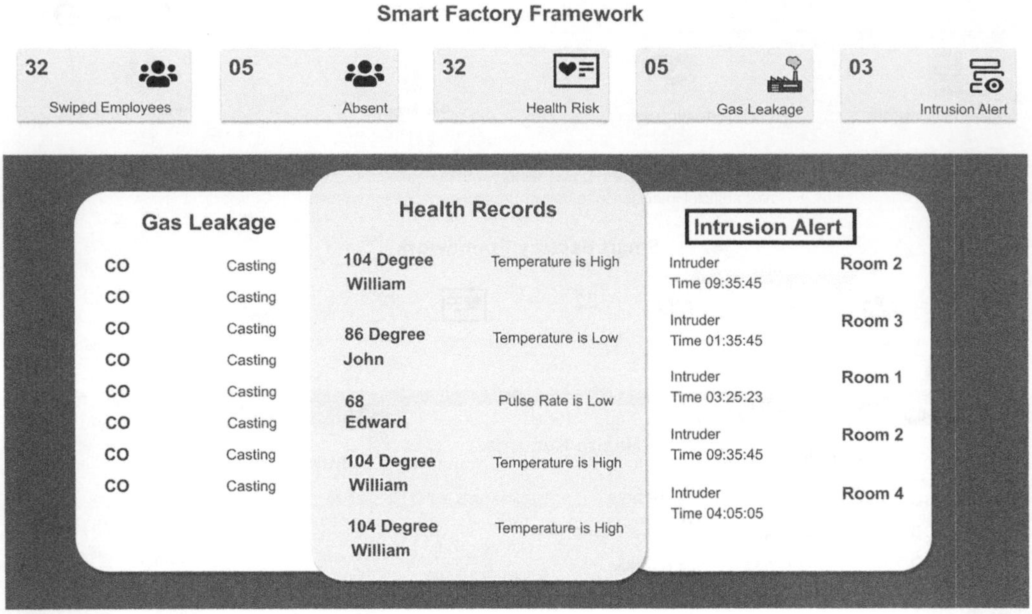

Smart Factory Framework

32		05		32		05		03	
Swiped Employees			Absent		Health Risk		Gas Leakage		Intrusion Alert

Gas Leakage

CO	Casting
CO	Casting
CO	Casting
CO	Casting
CO	Casting
CO	Casting
CO	Casting
CO	Casting

Health Records

104 Degree William	Temperature is High
86 Degree John	Temperature is Low
68 Edward	Pulse Rate is Low
104 Degree William	Temperature is High
104 Degree William	Temperature is High

Intrusion Alert

Intruder Time 09:35:45	Room 2
Intruder Time 01:35:45	Room 3
Intruder Time 03:25:23	Room 1
Intruder Time 09:35:45	Room 2
Intruder Time 04:05:05	Room 4

FIGURE 10.6
Intrusion detection alert.

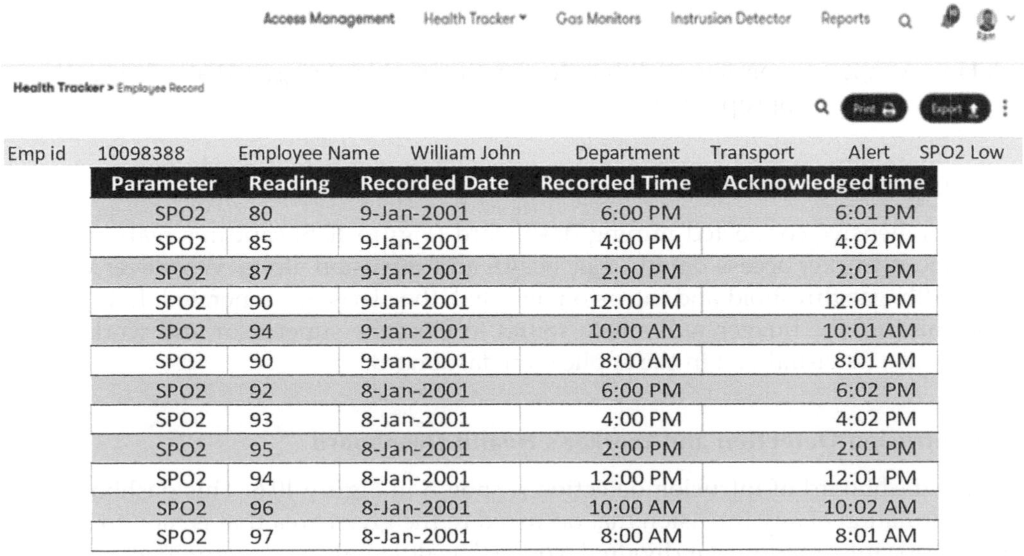

Access Management   Health Tracker ▾   Gas Monitors   Instrusion Detector   Reports   Q

Health Tracker > Employee Record

Emp id	10098388	Employee Name	William John	Department	Transport	Alert	SPO2 Low

Parameter	Reading	Recorded Date	Recorded Time	Acknowledged time
SPO2	80	9-Jan-2001	6:00 PM	6:01 PM
SPO2	85	9-Jan-2001	4:00 PM	4:02 PM
SPO2	87	9-Jan-2001	2:00 PM	2:01 PM
SPO2	90	9-Jan-2001	12:00 PM	12:01 PM
SPO2	94	9-Jan-2001	10:00 AM	10:01 AM
SPO2	90	9-Jan-2001	8:00 AM	8:01 AM
SPO2	92	8-Jan-2001	6:00 PM	6:02 PM
SPO2	93	8-Jan-2001	4:00 PM	4:02 PM
SPO2	95	8-Jan-2001	2:00 PM	2:01 PM
SPO2	94	8-Jan-2001	12:00 PM	12:01 PM
SPO2	96	8-Jan-2001	10:00 AM	10:02 AM
SPO2	97	8-Jan-2001	8:00 AM	8:01 AM

FIGURE 10.7
Workers' health dashboard.

10.7 Conclusion

A real-time monitoring system is developed to provide clearer and more point-to-point perspective of the underground mine. Connected mining framework concept was developed for real-time sensor-based data collection and monitoring system for underground mining, deriving key insights by integrating data and analysis, monitoring, access from centralized command and control center. It provides seamless access management, zone-based access restrictions, intruder detection, health vitals, underground mining environment pollution data and gas detection. The comprehensive, unified command and control center was developed to visualize worker details of the entire department and act based on the violations/conditions. The connected mining helps workers for their safety and security, and management to reduce manual effort, downtime and meet time to market. In future, we will improvise the solution by adding additional sensors such as dust, vibration and water leakage to cover all possible scenarios in underground mining system to improve safety and security.

References

1. P. Hazarika, "Implementation of safety helmet for coal mine workers", 1st IEEE International Conference on Power Electronics Intelligent Control and Energy Systems, pp. 1–3, 2016.
2. Z. Fu, T. Delbruck, P. Lichtsteiner, and E. Culurciello. June 2008. "An address-event fall detector for assisted living applications". *IEEE Transactions on Biomedical Circuits and Systems*, Vol. 2, Issue 2, pp. 88–96.
3. T. Shany, S. J. Redmond, M. R. Narayanan, and N. H. Lovell. March 2012. "Sensors based wearable systems for monitoring of human movement and falls". *IEEE Sensors Journal*, Vol. 12, Issue 3, pp. 658–670.
4. D.-D. Lee, D.-S. Lee. October 2001. "Environmental gas sensors". *Sensors Journal, IEEE*, Vol. 1, pp. 214–224.
5. W. Bing, X. Zhengdong, Z. Yao, and Y. Zhenjiang. Nov. 2014. "Study on coal mine safety management system based on 'hazard, latent danger and emergency responses". *Procedia Engineering*, Vol. 84, pp. 172–177.
6. S. Kesavan and G. K. Kalambettu, "IOT enabled comprehensive, plug and play gateway framework for smart health", 2018 Second International Conference on Advances in Electronics, Computers and Communications (ICAECC), Bangalore, pp. 1–5, 2018.
7. X. Xia, Z. Chen, and W. Wei, "Research on monitoring and prewarning system of accident in the coal mine based on big data". *Scientific Programming*, Vol. 2018, pp. 1–10, 2018.
8. Y. Wu and G. Feng, "The study on coal mine monitoring using the Bluetooth wireless transmission system", 2014 IEEE Workshop on Electronics, Computer and Applications, pp. 1016–1018, 2014.
9. J. Song, Y. Zhu and F. DongK, "Automatic monitoring system for coal mine safety based on wireless sensor network", IEEE Radio Science and Wireless Technology Conference, pp. 933–936, 2011.
10. S. Kesavan, "State-of-art, modular, cloud enabled video collaboration solution for next generation manufacturing industries", 2019 Global Conference for Advancement in Technology (GCAT), Bangalore, India, pp. 1–6, 2019.
11. V. Henriques, R. Malekian. Jun. 2016. "Mine safety system using wireless sensor network", *IEEE Access*, Vol. 4, pp. 3511–3521.
12. N. Ye, Y. Zhu, R.-C. Wang, R. Malekian, and L. Qiao-Min, "An efficient authentication and access control scheme for perception layer of Internet of Things," *Application Mathematics Information Sciences*, Vol. 8, Issue 4, pp. 1617–1624, 2014.

11

Prevalence of Nomophobia and Its Association with Text Neck Syndrome and Insomnia in Young Adults during COVID-19

Richa Hirendra Rai
Delhi Pharmaceutical Sciences and Research University

Vishal Mehta
Acharya Narendra Deva University of Agriculture and Technology (ANDUAT)

Pallavi
Delhi Pharmaceutical Sciences and Research University

Sachindra Pratap Singh
Indian Institute of Technology (IIT) Delhi

CONTENTS

DOI: 10.1201/9781003215981-11

11.1 Introduction

Since the invention of smartphones back in 1992, smartphones have become almost an indispensable part of our lives. As per the report of "Internet and Mobile Association of India (2019), there were 451 million active internet users in India during the first quarter of 2019 (January–March, 2019) of which 99% of the users both in urban and rural areas used smartphones to access the internet". The spread of COVID-19 has made work or study from home quotidian nowadays making it the new normal. According to the BARC India-Nielsen report, the amount of time spent on mobile phone usage had risen by 16% until week 6 of the lockdown in January 2020 when compared to pre-COVID period (January, 2020).

Davey and Davey (2014) rightfully said that, "Advancement of the technology is not what is frightening, but the misuse and excessive indulgence of people in their smartphone is!" As Zhuang et al. (2021) propounded in his study that the smartphone users generally were the young adults of the age 18–29 years and approximately 52.9% of them were over users. Also, this was seconded by Sood and Butt (2020) in their study conducted on Indians above 18 years of age, where they found 43% of them were addicted to this gadget.

Nomophobia has emerged as a disorder caused due to overuse of smartphones (González-Cabrera et al. 2017). No-mo-phobia, an abbreviation of "no mobile phone phobia", and it is suggestive of "the discomfort, nervousness or anxiety caused by being out of contact with a mobile phone" (Bragazzi and del Puente 2014).

Rodríguez-García et al. (2020) also described nomophobia as a public health issue distinctive of the digital age. The overuse of mobile phones has been associated with a myriad of musculoskeletal and psychological symptoms. Heavy smartphone usage has been associated with musculoskeletal symptoms or pain most commonly reported in the neck region, less in upper back and then the shoulders along with anxiety, insomnia, depression and psychological distress in combination with an unhealthy lifestyle (Park et al. 2015).

Samani et al. (2018) believe that Text Neck Syndrome (TNS) has recently surfaced as a global epidemic affecting a considerable number of people using mobile phones irrespective of their age. "Text neck" is used to describe "neck pain incurred due to prolonged use of devices such as smartphones with an incorrect body posture" (Dolah, Yie, and Gee 2020). Alzarea and Patil (2015) found that 71.2% subjects complained of pain in the cervical region due to excessive use of mobile phones, this overuse leads to the modification of the body's attitude and mechanics which then passes on to the neck leading to TNS.

Sleep deprivation has a very deep and extensive impact on health. *Diagnostic and Statistical Manual of Mental Disorders (DSM-5*; 2013) has defined insomnia as, "dissatisfaction with sleep quantity or quality, associated with one (or more) of the following symptoms: difficulty initiating sleep, difficulty maintaining sleep, characterized by frequent awakenings or problems returning to sleep after awakenings". According to many studies conducted worldwide, insomnia was found to be "the most commonly encountered sleep disorder and occurs in 10%–50% of the population!" (Bhaskar, Hemavathy, and Prasad 2016). In India, the percentage of insomnia in adults was found to be as high as 33% (Akhtar and Mallick 2019).

The emerging phenomenon of smartphone addiction has been associated with challenges related to physical and social well-being (Alsalameh et al., 2019). In the present situation of COVID-19, the condition is likely to exacerbate with people getting a lot more dependent on their smartphones due to forced lockdown, it being the most compatible source of edutainment, leading to a concurrent increase in the related health concerns. Thus, this study was taken up to assess the prevalence of nomophobia and its association with TNS and insomnia in young adults during COVID-19.

11.2 Aim of the Study

The purpose of this study is to find an association between nomophobia with TNS and insomnia in young adults during COVID-19. The secondary objective was also to find the prevalence of nomophobia in young adults during COVID-19 and to report any association between TNS and insomnia.

11.3 Hypotheses

H_1: There is a statistically significant association between nomophobia with TNS and insomnia during COVID-19

H_2: There is a statistically significant association between TNS and insomnia during COVID-19

H_0: There is no association between nomophobia with TNS and insomnia during COVID-19

11.4 Review of Literature: Nomophobia

Akulwar-Tajane et al. (2020) conducted a "Cross-sectional survey during COVID-19 lockdown period (April to June 2020)"on a sample of 150 physiotherapy students to assess their quality of sleep and usage of technology and its impact on the sleep and physical as well as mental well-being through a self-reported questionnaire. An alarming 52% of students reported excessive time spent on phone affected their sleep pattern, 48% of the them reported that it affected their physical well-being and 28.7% of students admitted negative effects on their mental well-being. This study thus highlighted the impact of smartphone usage on the health of young generation during the pandemic situation.

Yildirim and Correia (2015) conducted a research for the development and validation of self-reported questionnaire titled "Exploring the dimensions of nomophobia". In this two-phased, exploratory sequential mixed methods design study conducted on the U.S. undergraduate students, the initial phase consisted of "qualitative exploration of nomophobia" via interviews and the various dimensions of no-mobile-phobia were identified. The second phase leads to the development of the "20-item nomophobia questionnaire (NMP-Q)" which was then further validated on 301 students to have a good internal consistency with Cronbach's α reliability coefficient of 0.945, thus found to be a good tool for the evaluation of the severity of nomophobia.

11.5 Review of Literature: TNS

Aliberti and his colleagues (2020) studied the postural abnormalities and skeletal muscle pain and disorders due to the use of smartphones. Both qualitative and quantitative aspects were evaluated using a questionnaire recruiting 334 university students of the age 18–26 years. The result of the study found excessive daily smartphone usage in 36.8% of students with female dominance (42.6%) as compared to men (24.0%). Both groups used mobile phone for more than 5 hours/day while only 3.6% of students used smartphones for less than 2 hours. The neck in 45°C of flexion induces abnormal changes not only in the cervical but also in the lumbar and dorsal curvatures thus affecting the entire posture.

Evgene et al. (2020) studied the "Phenomenon of text neck in higher education students". Having studied the responses of 60 females and 30 males of 18–28 years of age through a self-reported questionnaire administered through Google docs for the awareness of this syndrome which is called "Text neck", the results of the study showed 66% participants were suffering from shoulder pain or discomfort in different degrees, headache in 56% and 50% suffered from neck pain or discomfort. The study concluded that young people are unaware about "the devastating impact of the gadgets on the health condition, in particular musculoskeletal system".

Alfaitouri and Altaboli (2019) conducted their study on "The Effect of Posture and Duration of Smartphone Usage on Neck Flexion Angle". Healthy young adult participants (ten females and ten males) reported with more than 1 year of smartphone usage and for more than an hour per day were included in the study. Photographic analysis procedures were undertaken to assess the neck flexion angle for each participant first in standing, then sitting without arms rested and later that with arms rested on a table at a time starting from zero, 5, 10, 15 and 20 minutes. The results indicated that neck flexion angle was affected by both posture and the number of hours spent on the smartphone ($p < 0.001$) but there was no significant interaction between them ($p = 0.906$). The study concluded that both posture and time spent on the smartphone had significant effects on neck posture which was affected the least in standing and increased subsequently as the usage of smartphone crossed over a period of 20 minutes in all the postures assessed.

Vijayakumar and his colleagues (2018) conducted an analytical study on 59 confirmed cases of TNS on young subjects of the age 18–25 years titled, "Assessment of Co-Morbid Factors Associated with Text Neck Syndrome among Mobile Phone Users". The participants who were recruited for the study spent a minimum of 3 or more hours on phone in a day and had at least three of the six symptoms of a condition called Text Neck. The symptoms of the syndrome include pain in the neck region, upper thoracic back, shoulder pain, headache, loss of sleep, tingling and numbness in hands. The head posture was assessed using Image Meter application, grip strength by Hand-grip Dynamometer, active cervical joint range assessed with Goniometer and Pressure Biofeedback was used to assess neck muscle strength. The results of the study found ailments of the neck and cervical spine in all subjects while 94.91% were having pain in the upper thoracic back region, 89.83% reported pain in the head and grip strength was also affected and 59.32% had pain in the shoulder. The study concluded that TNS leads to a serious comorbidity called Forward Head Posture and other chronic disorders which are progressive in nature, and the condition is reversible if it is timely diagnosed and subsequent postural modifications are assumed, which can also abate the symptoms and development of the disorder.

Kim and Koo (2016) studied the "Effect of duration of smartphone use on muscle fatigue and pain caused by Forward Head Posture" in 34 adults. Groups were made according to the usage of smartphone for 10, 20 and 30 minutes each. The fatigue in erector spinae and upper trapezius muscles was assessed using Electromyography (EMG) worsened with the prolonged use of smartphone and the subjects demonstrated higher scores on the Visual Analogue Scale. The results of the study concluded that postural corrections and a break after every 20 minutes of usage of digital device are recommended to avoid any musculoskeletal disorders (MSD) and pain.

11.6 Review of Literature: Insomnia

Enomoto et al. (2018) explored the "Reliability and validity of the Athens Insomnia Scale (AIS) in chronic pain patients". Overall, 144 chronic pain patients were assessed on questionnaires for assessing the reliability and validity of AIS-8 and AIS-5. The result found that "AIS had adequate internal consistency and test–retest reliability, and a higher AIS score was obtained for patients with insomnia than those without insomnia. The cut-off value for detecting insomnia was estimated at 4 points in the AIS-5".

Wei and his colleagues (2018) conducted a study titled "Insomnia Really Hurts: Effect of a Bad Night's Sleep on Pain Increases with Insomnia Severity". The study analysed data entered in the Netherlands Sleep Registry between January 2011 and October 2017 by 3,508 participants. The measures used in the study were "Insomnia Severity Index" (ISI) for insomnia, "Four-Dimensional Symptom Questionnaire" (4-DSQ) and "Chronic Pain Grade" (CPG) for pain intensity. The result of the study showed that "Habitual ISI correlated with the somatization subscale of the 4-DSQ (Spearman correlation coefficient=0.47, $p<0.001$) and with the pain intensity score from the CPG (Spearman correlation coefficient=0.33, $p<0.001$)". Pain was seen to become worse particularly after sleep was affected in the night and showed improvement after a quality night's sleep.

Artner et al. (2013) evaluated 1,016 patients for the "prevalence of sleep deprivation". The subjects with "Chronic Neck Pain" (CNP) and "Chronic Low Back Pain" (CLBP) who consulted an orthopaedic department were assessed for gender, age, sleep quality, pain, grade of chronicity and migration of pain, and a diagnosis was established. Pearson's chi-squared test demonstrated increased prevalence of insomnia (42.22%) in patients with CNP and CLBP, even along with the administration of analgesics. About 19.88% of the patients reported serious sleep quality issues with less than 4 hours of sleep at night and thus concluded that this parameter should also be assessed while treating patients with chronic MSD.

11.7 Methodology

A web-questionnaire-based observational survey design was adopted for this study. Assuming a power of 0.8 at $\alpha=0.05$ and an effect size of 0.32, the estimated sample size was determined as $N \approx 330$. Participants from Delhi NCR region were distributed the questionnaire by Google form through online platforms such as Email and WhatsApp. The link for the Google form is https://forms.gle/8QsWBKfeuF2TorKY8. Young adults of the age group 18–24 years using a smartphone for a minimum duration of 1 year, with a minimum smartphone usage duration of 2 hours in a day were included in the study. Subjects with a

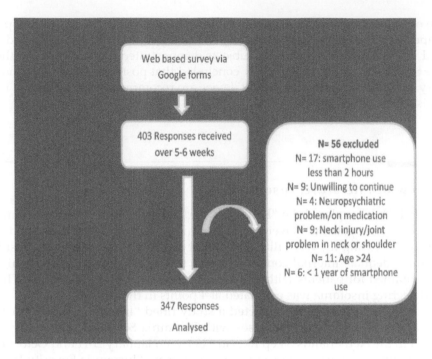

FIGURE 11.1
Data retrieval process.

history of any orthopaedic problem reported in the last 1 month, or any mental ailment or neuropsychiatric problem, on any kind of medications, those who could not comprehend the questionnaire due to language barrier and unwilling to participate were excluded from the study. Outcome measurement included assessment of TNS using self-reported symptoms. Other than this, outcome measures of scores of NMP-Q (Cronbach's alpha reliability coefficient=0.945 and Construct validity $r=0.710$, $p<0.01$) and AIS-5 (Cronbach's alpha reliability coefficient=0.89 and Construct validity r=0.80, $p<0.001$) were also assessed.

The study questionnaire consisted of four sections including (1) demographic data and data related to smartphone use; (2) assessment of smartphone addiction through NMP-Q; (3) assessment of TNS through self-reported symptoms and (4) insomnia assessment through AIS-5. The data was collected over a period of 5–6 weeks (Figure 11.1). Data was analysed using IBM SPSS version 20.

11.8 Result

Data was analysed using IBM SPSS version 20.
Formula Used (Abdulqader 2017)
By taking the case of one explanatory variable X with one binary outcome variable Y, the logistic model predicts the logit of Y from X which represents a natural logarithm of odds of Y.

$$In \frac{\pi}{1-\pi} = \alpha + \beta x \tag{11.1}$$

The left-hand side is called the log-odds or logit. The Logistic Regression (LR) model has a logit that is linear in X. Hence,

$$\pi(x) = E\left[\frac{Y}{X}\right] = \frac{e^{\alpha+\beta x}}{1+e^{\alpha+\beta x}} \tag{11.2}$$

where π is the probability of the outcome of interest given that $X = x$, α is a parameter which represents the Y-intercept, and β is a parameter of the slope, X can be qualitative (categorical) or quantitative variable, and Y is always qualitative or categorical. The formula (11.1) can be expressed and extended from simple to multiple linear regression as follows:

$$In\ \frac{\pi}{1-\pi} = \alpha + \sum_{i=1}^{k} \beta_i x_i \tag{11.3}$$

Therefore,

$$\pi(x) = E\left[\frac{Y}{X}\right] = \frac{e^{\alpha+\sum_{i=1}^{k}\beta_i x_i}}{1+e^{\alpha+\sum_{i=1}^{k}\beta_i x_i}}, \tag{11.4}$$

where π is the event probability, α is the Y-intercept, βs are the parameters of the slope and Xs are the combinations of explanatory variables. α and βs are estimated by the maximum likelihood estimator approach. Table 11.1 presents the demographic characteristics of subjects.

11.8.1 Part I: Demographic Characteristics of Subjects

TABLE 11.1

Demographic Characteristics of Subjects

		Age	Height (in cm)	Weight (in kg)	BMI
N	Valid	347	347	347	347
	Missing	0	0	0	0
Mean		21.29	166.94	63.21	22.69
Std. error of mean		0.091	0.517	0.686	0.235
Std. deviation		1.696	9.634	12.773	4.384
Variance		2.875	92.805	163.149	19.222
Range		6	80	83	37
Minimum		18	120	37	12
Maximum		24	200	120	49

11.8.2 Part II: Hypothesis Testing

11.8.2.1 TNS v/s Nomophobia

H_O = There is no significant impact of nomophobia on TNS
H_a = There is a significant impact.

11.8.2.1.1 Model Validation

The chi-square statistic with a value of 30.449 ($p < 0.05$) shows that nomophobia has a significant impact on TNS. Pseudo R-square value of 0.117 (Nagelkerke R-square) and 0.084 (Cox & Snell R-square) shows correlation between independent variables.

11.8.2.1.2 Model Effectiveness

According to the classification table, independent and dependent variable matrix was able to form a binary logistic model which shows TNS Yes prediction 99.1% of times and No prediction 10.4% of times with overall correct prediction 69.7%.

11.8.2.1.3 Model Output

With nomophobia as ordinal categorical variable and TNS as a binary variable, the model output shows the following:

1. log-odds ratio of a person suffering with TNS if a person has severe nomophobia with respect to a person does not having nomophobia is 20.250 [95% CI 4.099–100.051] with ($p < 0.05$).
2. log-odds ratio of a person suffering with TNS if a person has moderate nomophobia with respect to a person does not having nomophobia is 3.276 [95% CI 1.570–6.833] with ($p < 0.05$).
3. log-odds ratio of a person suffering with TNS if a person has mild nomophobia with respect to a person does not having nomophobia is 1.283 [95% CI 0.677–2.434] with ($p > 0.05$).

11.8.2.2 AIS v/s Nomophobia

H_O = There is no significant impact of nomophobia on AIS
H_a = There is a significant impact.

11.8.2.2.1 Model Validation

The chi-square statistic with a value of 25.104 ($p < 0.05$) shows that nomophobia has a significant impact on AIS. Pseudo R-square value of 0.093 (Nagelkerke R-square) and 0.070 (Cox & Snell R-square) shows correlation between independent variables.

11.8.2.2.2 Model Effectiveness

According to the classification table, independent and dependent variable matrix was able to form a binary logistic model which shows AIS Yes prediction 28.8% of times and No prediction 86.9% of times with overall correct prediction 60.8%.

11.8.2.2.3 Model Output

With nomophobia as ordinal categorical variable and AIS as binary variable, the model output shows the following:

1. log-odds ratio of a person suffering with AIS if a person has severe nomophobia with respect to a person does not having nomophobia is 6.600 [95% CI 1.682–25.896] with ($p < 0.05$).

2. log-odds ratio of a person suffering with AIS if a person has moderate nomophobia with respect to a person does not having nomophobia is 2.536 [95% CI 2.536–11.053] with ($p < 0.05$).

3. log-odds ratio of person suffering with AIS if a person has mild nomophobia with respect to a person does not having nomophobia is 2.077 [95% CI 1.182–3.650] with ($p > 0.05$).

11.8.2.3 AIS v/s TNS

H_O=There is no significant impact of AIS on TNS
H_a=There is a significant impact.

11.8.2.3.1 Model Validation

The chi-square statistic with a value of 49.231 ($p < 0.05$) shows that AIS has a significant impact on TNS. Pseudo R-square value of 0.117 (Nagelkerke R-square) and 0.132 (Cox & Snell R-square) shows correlation between independent variables.

11.8.2.3.2 Model Effectiveness

According to the classification table, independent and dependent variable matrix was able to form a binary logistic model which shows AIS Yes prediction 85.9% of times and No prediction 48.7% of times with overall correct prediction 65.4%.

11.8.2.3.3 Model Output

With TNS and AIS as a binary variable, the model output shows the following:

1. log-odds ratio of a person suffering with AIS if a person has TNS with respect to a person does not having TNS is 5.780 [95% CI 3.393–9.847] with ($p < 0.05$).

11.8.3 Part III: Odds Ratio and Relative Risk Ratio Analysis

Formula Used (Zhang and Yu 1998)

$$\text{Odd} - \text{Ratio(OR)} = \frac{P_1}{1 - P_1} \bigg/ \frac{P_0}{1 - P_0} \tag{11.5}$$

$$\text{Relative Risk(RR)} = \frac{P_1}{P_0} \tag{11.6}$$

Here, P_0 indicates the incidence of the outcome of interest in the nonexposed group and P_1 in the exposed group.

11.8.3.1 AIS v/s Nomophobia

See Tables 11.2 and 11.3.

Thus, odds are 3.1 times more that someone with nomophobia will develop insomnia (AIS) [95% CI 0.854–11.375]. An individual with nomophobia is relatively at 2.1 times more risk of developing insomnia (AIS) [95% CI 0.781–5.886].

TABLE 11.2

AIS v/s Nomophobia

			Nomophobia1 * AIS Cross Tabulation		
			AIS		
			Yes	No	Total
Nomophobia	Yes	Count	153	180	333
		% within nomophobia	45.9%	54.1%	100.0%
	No	Count	3	11	14
		% within nomophobia	21.4%	78.6%	100.0%
Total		Count	156	191	347
		% within nomophobia	45.0%	55.0%	100.0%

TABLE 11.3

Risk Estimate

		95% Confidence Interval	
	Value	Lower	Upper
Odds ratio for nomophobia (Yes/No)	3.117	0.854	11.375
For cohort AIS=Yes	2.144	0.781	5.886
For cohort AIS=No	0.688	0.514	0.920
N of valid cases	347		

TABLE 11.4

TNS v/s Nomophobia

			Nomophobia1 * TNS Cross Tabulation		
			TNS		
			Yes	No	Total
Nomophobia	Yes	Count	230	103	333
		% within nomophobia	69.1%	30.9%	100.0%
	No	Count	2	12	14
		% within nomophobia	14.3%	85.7%	100.0%
Total		Count	232	115	347
		% within nomophobia	66.9%	33.1%	100.0%

11.8.3.2 AIS v/s Nomophobia

See Tables 11.4 and 11.5.

Thus, odds are 13.4 times more that someone with nomophobia will develop TNS [95% CI 2.945–60.946]. An individual with nomophobia is relatively at 4.8 times more risk of developing TNS [95% CI 1.337–17.478].

11.8.3.3 AIS v/s TNS

See Tables 11.6 and 11.7.

TABLE 11.5

Risk Estimate

	Value	95% Confidence Interval	
		Lower	Upper
Odds ratio for nomophobia (Yes/No)	13.398	2.945	60.946
For cohort TNS=Yes	4.835	1.337	17.478
For cohort TNS=No	0.361	0.276	0.471
N of valid cases	347		

TABLE 11.6

AIS v/s TNS

TNS * AIS Cross Tabulation					
			AIS		
			Yes	No	Total
TNS	Yes	Count	134	98	232
		% within TNS	57.8%	42.2%	100.0%
	No	Count	22	93	115
		% within TNS	19.1%	80.9%	100.0%
Total		Count	156	191	347
		% within TNS	45.0%	55.0%	100.0%

TABLE 11.7

Risk Estimate

	Value	95% Confidence Interval	
		Lower	Upper
Odds ratio for TNS (Yes/No)	5.780	3.393	9.847
For cohort AIS=Yes	3.019	2.041	4.466
For cohort AIS=No	0.522	0.439	0.622
N of valid cases	347		

Thus, odds are 5.8 times more that someone with TNS will develop insomnia (AIS) [95% CI 3.393–9.847]. An individual with TNS is relatively at 3 times more risk of developing insomnia (AIS) [95% CI 2.041–4.466].

11.9 Discussion

The results of this study show that there is a statistically significant impact of nomophobia on TNS with chi-square statistic value of 30.449 ($p<0.05$) and insomnia with a chi-square statistic value of 25.104 ($p<0.05$). Odds are 3.1 times more that someone with nomophobia will develop insomnia (AIS) [95% CI 0.854–11.375] and 13.4 times more that someone with nomophobia will develop TNS [95% CI 2.945–60.946].

Excessive use of smartphone has not yet been included as a clinical disorder in the "DSM-5" or "International Classification of Diseases-10"; but as per the study of Ting et al. (2020), several aspects of this addictive behaviour appear to have similarities with other recognized behavioural addictions (Bragazzi and del Puente 2014).

According to the results of the present study and also a great matter of concern, 86.7% of subjects agreed that their smartphone usage had increased during the COVID-19 pandemic, and 58.5% of the subjects accepted being warned by someone about their excessive use of smartphone. This is as per the study of Olson et al. (2020) which demonstrated that problematic smartphone use had grown between 2014 and 2020, and the trend was expected to continue during the COVID-19 pandemic.

Kaviani and his colleagues (2020) in their study listed young age adults (18–25 years) and duration on smartphone usage per day (more than 3 hours) to significantly increase "problematic dependency, prohibited use and dangerous use of smartphones". In the current study, only 4.03% of the young adult population (18–24 years) was found to be non-nomophobic. Kanmani et al. (2017) found a similar trend of smartphone addiction with less than 2% of their subjects coming out to be non-nomophobics.

Of the 95.97% subjects falling in the nomophobia category according to the NMP-Q scores, 56.48% of the subjects are found to be moderately nomophobic with the scores between 60 and 99, followed by 20.17% severely nomophobic subjects with the scores between 100 and 140 and 19.3% with a mild level of nomophobia with scores between 21 and 59.

The result of the current study found the presence of TNS in 232 (66.9%) subjects based on the presence of reported symptoms of pain in the cervical region, shoulder and arms, including wrist joint and hands along with numbness. The reported symptoms of pain were found to be maximum in the upper shoulder/neck (68%), followed by pain in the wrists/hands (60.80%), pain in the shoulders (56.48%) and pain in the arms (50.72%). The feeling of numbness and tingling in the hands or fingers was the least reported symptom present in 92 subjects (26.51%). Similar results and occurrence of pain were reported in the upper thoracic back (70.3%), cervical (65.9%), wrist joint and hands (68.7%), and shoulders (56.6%) by the subjects also in other studies (Mustafaoglu et al. 2021).

The incidence of MSD has also been associated with the repetitive and prolonged use of smartphones by other authors. They have also studied the forceful and low amplitude use of smartphones for longer duration and its association with pain in cervical and upper extremity (Shah and Sheth 2018). The presence of pain in the neck in 68% subjects and in the shoulders in 56.48% of the subjects can be attributed to the reason cited in the study done by Gustafsson and colleagues (2017) who explained that constant sitting with the head in flexion while using a smartphone without arm support leads to a constant load on the cervical and shoulder muscles which ultimately leads to pain.

A significant impact of nomophobia severity was found on the occurrence of TNS with chi-square statistic value of 30.449 ($p < 0.05$), i.e. odds are 13.4 times more that someone with nomophobia will develop TNS [95% CI 2.945–60.946]. Lau et al. (2010) correlated the presence of chronic cervical pain to the abnormal posture of the head and neck. The probable cause of CNP can be attributed to the reduction of lordosis of the cervical spine and that of the pain threshold of the muscles therein (Park et al., 2015).

According to the scores of AIS-5, 156 (44.96%) participants were found to be insomniacs, with a score of ≥4 and 78.1% of the participants accepted checking their phones as soon as they wake up. Rozgonjuk et al. (2016) found a positive relationship between excessive digital

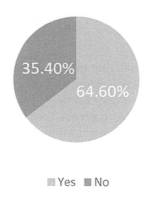

Yes ■ No

FIGURE 11.2
Participants finding difficulty in falling asleep due to smartphone usage.

device usage and anxiety, sleep quality and disorders, stress and depression. Alsalameh et al. (2019) in their study also found a significant correlation ($p < 0.001$) between duration of smartphone usage and time taken to sleep with their subjects taking more than an hour to sleep after using their smartphones at night.

A significant impact of severity of nomophobia was found on the occurrence of insomnia with a chi-square statistic value of 25.104 ($p < 0.05$) (Figure 11.2). Odds are 3.1 times more that someone with nomophobia will develop insomnia (AIS) [95% CI 0.854–11.375]. This association can be attributed to the exposure to blue light emitted by the smartphone which stimulates vigilance behaviour (Ting and Chen 2020). Farooq et al. (2019) in their study found that most of their subjects took more than 2 hours to fall asleep attributing it to the blue light emission and the consequent disturbance in melatonin production leading to an impairment in the sleep–wake cycle.

Female dominance is seen for both the conditions, i.e. TNS and insomnia with 37.46% of female subjects having TNS and 24.50% having insomnia. Whereas the percentage of male subjects having TNS is found to be 29.39% and that of insomnia is 20.17%.

According to the results of the current study, insomnia was found to have a significant impact on the presence of TNS with a chi-square statistic value of 49.231($p < 0.05$) and an odds ratio of 5.780 [95% CI 3.393–9.847]. The occurrence of neck pain due to insomnia can be explained with help of the study done by Scarabottolo et al. (2020) who attributed the increase in cervical pain to the activation of the autonomic sympathetic nervous system due to a decrease in sleep duration leading to inhibition of muscle relaxation and thus increasing the tone of the muscle.

11.10 Conclusion

The results of the study demonstrate increased prevalence of nomophobia during COVID-19 pandemic in the young adult population and thus the risk of clinical MSD. Due to the significant association of nomophobia with TNS and insomnia, the delirious effects of these conditions are most likely to be increased as well.

11.11 Future Scope

The future scope of the study includes that this study could be performed on different age groups, such as adolescents, middle age group and older age group, as the harmful dependency of smartphone is not restricted only to the young adult population. The sample size can be increased to make the study more generalized. This study could be performed as a blind or double-blind study with random sampling to reduce the chances of any bias. The self-reported symptoms of the participants can be assessed individually to yield better and more reliable results and also to remove any chances of disparity. Moreover, the lengthier version 30 of AIS-8 can be used to include the quality and quantity of daytime sleep to better assess the features of insomnia. Further association can also be found between pain in different joints and mobile usage hours.

References

Abdulqader, Q.M. 2017. "Applying the binary logistic regression analysis on the medical data." *Science Journal of University of Zakho* 5 (4): 330. doi: 10.25271/2017.5.4.388.

Akhtar, Nasreen, and Hrudananda Mallick. 2019. "Recommendations for a National Sleep Policy in India." *National Medical Journal of India*. doi: 10.4103/0970-258X.272131.

Akulwar-Tajane, Isha, Kashish K. Parmar, Palak H. Naik, and Ayushi V. Shah. 2020. "Rethinking screen time during COVID-19: Impact on psychological well-being in physiotherapy students." *International Journal of Clinical and Experimental Medicine Research* 4 (4): 201–16. doi: 10.26855/ijcemr.2020.10.014.

Alfaitouri, Sundus, and Ahamed Altaboli. 2019. "The effect of posture and duration of smartphone usage on neck flexion angle." *Proceedings of the Human Factors and Ergonomics Society Annual Meeting* 63 (1): 962–66. doi: 10.1177/1071181319631137.

Aliberti, Sara, Piero Luigi Invernizzi, Raffaele Scurati, and Tiziana D'isanto. 2020. "Posture and skeletal muscle disorders of the neck due to the use of smartphones." *Journal of Human Sport and Exercise* 15: S586–98. doi: 10.14198/jhse.2020.15.Proc3.11.

Alsalameh, Abdullah M, Mohammad J Harisi, Muath A Alduayji, Abdullah A Almutham, and Farid M Mahmood. 2019. "Evaluating the relationship between smartphone addiction/overuse and musculoskeletal pain among medical students at Qassim University." *Journal of Family Medicine and Primary Care* 8 (9): 2953. doi:10.4103/jfmpc.jfmpc_665_19.

Alzarea, Bader K, and Santosh R Patil. 2015. "Mobile phone head and neck pain syndrome: Proposal of a new entity." *Ohdm* 14 (5): 313–17.

Artner, Juraj, Balkan Cakir, Jane Anna Spiekermann, Stephan Kurz, Frank Leucht, Heiko Reichel, and Friederike Lattig. 2013. "Prevalence of sleep deprivation in patients with chronic neck and back pain: A retrospective evaluation of 1016 patients." *Journal of Pain Research* 6: 1–6. doi: 10.2147/JPR.S36386.

Bhaskar, Swapna, D. Hemavathy, and Shankar Prasad. 2016. "Prevalence of chronic insomnia in adult patients and its correlation with medical comorbidities." *Journal of Family Medicine and Primary Care* 5 (4): 780. doi: 10.4103/2249-4863.201153.

Bragazzi, Nicola Luigi, and Giovanni del Puente. 2014. "A proposal for including nomophobia in the new DSM-V." *Psychology Research and Behavior Management* 7 (May): 155–60. doi: 10.2147/PRBM.S41386.

Davey, Sanjeev, and Anuradha Davey. 2014. "Assessment of smartphone addiction in Indian adolescents: A mixed method study by systematic-review and meta-analysis approach." *International Journal of Preventive Medicine* 5(12): 1500–1511.

Dolah, Jasni, Joey Loh Jo Yie, and Lilian Lee Shiau Gee. 2020. "Improving knowledge of text neck and neck pain using interactive smartphone application for undergraduate students in Universiti Sains Malaysia." *Jurnal Gendang Alam (GA)*. https://doi.org/10.51200/ga.vi.2522

Enomoto, K, T Adachi, K Yamada, D Inoue, M Nakanishi, T Nishigami, and M Shibata. 2018. "Reliability and validity of the Athens insomnia scale in chronic pain patients." *Journal of Pain Research* 11: 793–801.

Evgene, Nikolenko, Adamovych Iryna, and Vovk Kira. 2020. "Phenomenon of Text Neck in Higher Education Students." *Actual Problems of Modern Medicine*, no. 6: 20–25. doi:10.26565/2617-409x-2020-6-03.

Farooq, Lubna, Akhtar Ali, Sehrish Mahmood, Mahnoor Farzand, Hina Masood, and Sumreen Mujahid. 2019. "Association between excessive use of mobile phone and insomnia among pakistani teenagers cross sectional study." *American International Journal of Multidisciplinary Scientific Research* 5 (4): 10–15.

González-Cabrera, Joaquín, Ana León-Mejía, Carlota Pérez-Sancho, and Esther Calvete. 2017. "Erratum: Adaptation of the nomophobia questionnaire (NMP-Q) to Spanish in a sample of adolescents (ActasEspanolas de Psiquiatria (2017) 45:4 (137–144))." *ActasEspañolas de Psiquiatría* 45 (5): 256.

Gustafsson, Ewa, Sara Thomée, Anna Grimby-Ekman, and Mats Hagberg. 2017. "Texting on mobile phones and musculoskeletal disorders in young adults: A five-year cohort study." *Applied Ergonomics* 58: 208–14. doi: 10.1016/j.apergo.2016.06.012.

Kanmani, Aparna, U Bhavani, and R Maragatham. 2017. "NOMOPHOBIA – An insight into its psychological aspects in India." *The International Journal of Indian Psychology* 4 (2): 2349–3429.

Kaviani, Fareed, Brady Robards, Kristie L. Young, and Sjaan Koppel. 2020. "Nomophobia: Is the fear of being without a smartphone associated with problematic use?" *International Journal of Environmental Research and Public Health* 17 (17): 1–19. doi: 10.3390/ijerph17176024.

Kim, Seong-Yeol, and Sung-Ja Koo. 2016. "Effect of duration of smartphone use on muscle fatigue and pain caused by forward head posture in adults." *Journal of Physical Therapy Science* 28 (6): 1669–72.

Lau, Kwok Tung, Ka Yuen Cheung, kwok Bun Chan, Man Him Chan, King Yuen Lo, and Thomas Tai Wing Chiu. 2010. "Relationships between sagittal postures of thoracic and cervical spine, presence of neck pain, neck pain severity and disability." *Manual Therapy* 15 (5): 457–62. doi: 10.1016/j.math.2010.03.009.

Mustafaoglu, Rustem, Zeynal Yasaci, Emrah Zirek, Mark D. Griffiths, and Arzu Razak Ozdincler. 2021. "The relationship between smartphone addiction and musculoskeletal pain prevalence among young population: A cross-sectional study." *Korean Journal of Pain* 34 (1): 72–81. doi: 10.3344/KJP.2021.34.1.72.

Olson, Jay A., Dasha A. Sandra, and Élissa S Colucci. 2020. "Smartphone addiction is increasing across the world : A meta-analysis of 24 countries." *Computers in Human Behaviour* no. December: 1–21.

Park, Junhyuk, Jinhong Kim, Jonggun Kim, Kwangho Kim, Namkang Kim, Inwon Choi, Sujung Lee, and Jongeun Yim. 2015. "The effects of heavy smartphone use on the cervical angle, pain threshold of neck muscles and depression." *Advanced Science and Technology Letters* 91: 12–17. doi: 10.14257/astl.2015.91.03.

Rodríguez-García, Antonio Manuel, Jesús López Belmonte, and Antonio José Moreno-Guerrero. 2020. "Nomophobia: An individual's growing fear of being without a smartphone—A systematic literature review." *International Journal of Environmental Research and Public Health*. doi:10.3390/ijerph17020580.

Rozgonjuk, Dmitri, Valdur Rosenvald, Sven Janno, and Karin Täht. 2016. "Developing a shorter version of the Estonian smartphone addiction proneness scale (E-SAPS18)." *Cyberpsychology* 10 (4). doi: 10.5817/CP2016-4-4.

Samani, Pankti P., Neeraj A. Athavale, Ashok Shyam, and Parag K. Sancheti. 2018. "Awareness of text neck syndrome in young-adult population." *International Journal of Community Medicine and Public Health* 5 (8): 3335. doi: 10.18203/2394-6040.ijcmph20183057.

Scarabottolo, Catarina Covolo, Rafael Zambelli Pinto, Crystian Bitencourt Oliveira, William Rodrigues Tebar, Bruna Thamyres Ciccotti Saraiva, Priscila Kalil Morelhão, Leandro Delfino Dragueta, Gustavo Santos Druzian, and Diego Giulliano Destro Christofaro. 2020. "Back and neck pain and poor sleep quality in adolescents are associated even after controlling for confounding factors: An epidemiological study." *Sleep Science* 13 (2): 107–12. doi:10.5935/1984-0063.20190138.

Shah, Priyal P., and Megha S. Sheth. 2018. "Correlation of smartphone use addiction with text neck syndrome and SMS thumb in physiotherapy students." *International Journal of Community Medicine and Public Health* 5 (6): 2512. doi:10.18203/2394-6040.ijcmph20182187.

Sood, Ritu Sanjeev, and Aaqib Anwaar Butt. 2020. "Nomo phobia: Review on smartphone addiction in indian perspective." *Journal of Critical Reviews*. doi:10.31838/jcr.07.03.135.

Ting, Chuong Hock, and Yoke Yong Chen. 2020. *Smartphone Addiction. Adolescent Addiction*. Second Edition. Elsevier Inc. doi:10.1016/b978-0-12-818626-8.00008-6.

Vijayakumar, M, Sanika Mujumdar, and Aishwarya Dehadrai. 2018. "Assessment of co-morbid factors associated with text-neck syndrome among mobile phone users." *IJSRST* 4 (9): 38–46.

Wei, Yishul, Tessa F. Blanken, and Eus J.W. Van Someren. 2018. "Insomnia really hurts: Effect of a bad night's sleep on pain increases with insomnia severity." *Frontiers in Psychiatry* 9 (AUG): 46155. doi:10.3389/fpsyt.2018.00377.

Yildirim, Caglar, and Ana Paula Correia. 2015. "Exploring the dimensions of nomophobia: Development and validation of a self-reported questionnaire." *Computers in Human Behavior* 49: 130–37. doi:10.1016/j.chb.2015.02.059.

Zhang, Jun, and Kai F. Yu. 1998. "What's the relative risk? A method of correcting the odds ratio in cohort studies of common outcomes." *Journal of the American Medical Association* 280 (19): 1690–91. doi:10.1001/jama.280.19.1690.

Zhuang, Linbo, Lisheng Wang, Dongming Xu, Zhiyong Wang, and Renzheng Liang. 2021. "Association between excessive smartphone use and cervical disc degeneration in young patients suffering from chronic neck pain." *Journal of Orthopaedic Science* 26 (1): 110–15. doi:10.1016/j.jos.2020.02.009.

12

The Role of AI, Fuzzy Logic System in Computational Biology and Bioinformatics

A.H.M. Shahariar Parvez and Sadiq Iqbal
Bangladesh University

Subrato Bharati and Prajoy Podder
Bangladesh University of Engineering and Technology (BUET)

Pinto Kumar Paul
Ranada Prasad Shaha University

Aditya Khamparia
Babasaheb Bhimrao Ambedkar University

CONTENTS

12.1 Introduction

With the advancement of bioinformatics, it is easy to know how the human body works, how complex molecules interact, and how evaluation happened [1–3]. The effect of bioinformatics is growing rapidly and researchers not only use it to read about human beings but also it is recently used to know about other species. The interest in their habitat and

DOI: 10.1201/9781003215981-12

adoption and their interaction with nature is increasing. This study may help to discover new species but with that, it has become a problem to deal with the dataset as the dataset is growing day by day. Therefore, bioinformatics leads us to the future where a better lifestyle may wait for the human beings.

12.1.1 Bioinformatics

Bioinformatics is a superset of different scientific fields such as biology, computer science, mathematics, information technology, and statistics [2,4–7]. Bioinformatics gathers biological data, such as regulations of cells, functions of genes and drug design, and analyzes these data using different types of complex algorithms. Without the study of bioinformatics, new medicine could not be possible and it becomes a modern field of biology.

In order to overcome complexity in analysing large datasets and to minimize human error in calculations, the bioinformatics sector depends on Artificial Intelligence (AI). All biological studies are capable of producing the datasets used in computational intelligence and they are humongous in size. The key purposes of bioinformatics field are (1) to manage large datasets, (2) develop and test tools in order to remove the complexity in computations, (3) provide support in silicon simulation in structural biology, and (4) model genomic data and proteomic data so that researchers can clearly understand the concept of crucial molecular interactions [4]. Though the bioinformatics concept came out into view recently, the concept was conceived over 50 years ago. Combining computation and information processing with biology was realized first in 1970 [4]. However, computation systems are developed by time with the advancement of computer software and technology. Those machines are widely adopted to handle bioinformatics calculations and to accelerate the process and reduce error.

12.1.2 Challenges in Bioinformatics

Typically, genetic information of a cell lies in the DNA. That information is coded with four nucleobases, i.e. Cytosine (C), Adenine (A), Thymine (T), and Guanine (G). Nucleobases or nitrogenous bases usually are nitrogen-containing biological compounds. These form nucleosides. There are 3 billion nucleobases present in the human genome [8]. Therefore, genes are capable of producing proteins and proteins are the most essential particles that form structure. Besides, proteins are formed using 20 letters string with an amino acid as a base.

Bioinformatics deals with raw data consisting of protein sequence, nucleic acid, genome interactions, etc. The trillions of sequence are stored which means trillions of information are waiting to be turned into knowledge. The data of different beings are different and the data of the same beings are also different. Information flows from DNA to RNA in order to synthesize protein in a cell [9]. So, efficiently storing data is the first challenge in bioinformatics.

The second foremost challenge is the mining of knowledge and it is a part of computational biology. Complex algorithms such as genetic algorithm (GA), Basic Local Alignment Search Tool (BLAST) algorithm, and many more are used to solve the problem. However, this type of challenge requires software and techniques which is responsible for converting heterogeneous data into biological knowledge [9]. The software and methods are helpful to study the data and produce knowledge in a manner that can be tested.

TABLE 12.1

Comparison between Computational Biology and Bioinformatics

Category	Computational Biology	Bioinformatics
Definitions	Computational biology is the combination of biology and mathematics, which works for developing methods for solving biology-based problems	Bioinformatics is used to develop or test software tools based on some characteristics and check whether the tools can solve a class of problems or not
Type	Only computational	Computational, but also includes collecting and storing data
Result output	Mathematical equations	Statistical analysis
Main focus	Computational techniques for understanding the biology	Engineering side and biological aspects

12.2 Computational Biology and Bioinformatics: A Comparison

Computational biology can be considered as a super class of different subfields. It is more than just gathering information or knowledge about biology. Nevertheless, it also includes mathematical calculations, ordinary or partial differential equations to develop new algorithms or validate existing algorithms. However, bioinformatics considers a computational method/tool to solve a class of similar problems and write papers about this method [10–15]. Table 12.1 provides the comparison with respect to some categories.

12.3 Machine Learning Approach

Machine learning (ML) approaches are well known for prediction, classification, and feature extraction. The ML algorithms are highly preferable to use in applications for picking out relevant features from the high-dimensional biological data [1,16–19]. Recently, ML methods are used in many major applications in bioinformatics such as to find out gene features, classify biological sequences, predict the outcomes accurately, and cluster biological data. ML can be applied in six different areas: proteomics, systems biology, genomics, microarrays, evolution, and text mining [20]. There are some challenges or difficulties in applying ML techniques in bioinformatics [18,21,22].

There are a variety of methods of ML in bioinformatics as follows:

- Knowledge Discovery:

    Discovering knowledge from information is the reason for learning and that knowledge is used to improve skill set and performance [20,23]. Knowledge discovery is the method of acquiring useful data from the database and analysing them to utilize effectively as knowledge-based ML techniques. Analysing data is important to find out significant hidden knowledge that is mixed up with various types of necessary data.

- Decision Tree (DT):

    A DT, also known as a regression tree or classification tree, is a simple and effective ML method that is applied to classify datasets using a discrete-valued function. This method constructs a tree using a divide-and-conquer technique [20]. The intelligent agent of the tree takes the dataset with its properties and returns true or false decision.

- Genetic Algorithm:

  GA is a very popular and simple algorithm that is capable to solve high-dimensional problems [24]. This algorithm uses a population which is a bit string. The population which is selected for the test will go through different phases of evolutions and a better surviving candidate will be selected at every phase. This method helps to cut off a weak candidate and accept a new one.

- Clustering:

  Clustering is one kind of ML approach used to identify similarities and classify them. Clustering algorithms are used to identify the subtypes of some serious diseases where the degree of variations is high. Clustering algorithms are two types – k-clustering and hierarchical clustering. In k-clustering algorithms, collected input data are classified according to their features and organize them to a group, whereas in hierarchical clustering algorithm, input data are represented hierarchically like a top-down tree where the same groups of data are placed together [20,25,26].

12.4 Artificial Neural Network Approach

Artificial Neural Network (ANN) is effective in bioinformatics, as it is capable to solve complex problems even with the noisy training data [22,27]. The ANN is flexible but it is a black-box approach. It is hard to validate and interpret as it contains complex mathematical equations and statistics. Besides interpreting each node, it seems too hard in the neural network approach. Figure 12.1 summarizes the process of integrating AI with bioinformatics. Despite having many complexities, ANN is capable of comparing and aligning the sequences, analysing the regulation of genes, drug design and docking and predicting and classifying the arrangement of proteins.

12.5 BLAST Algorithm

The BLAST algorithm is employed to compare sequences where, for example, the similarity search of nucleic acid sequences can be found with a single query sequence. BLAST can be used as an effective technique to compare similarities, alignments, and annotations between protein/gene sequences [28]. BLAST has different kinds of algorithms that depend on databases and query types. BLAST is faster as it adopted many heuristic techniques to locate and match substrings of two sequences [29]. Figure 12.2 illustrates the framework of the BLAST algorithm.

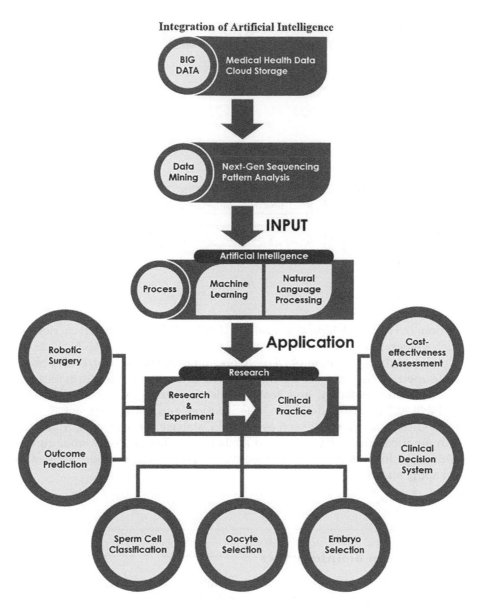

FIGURE 12.1
Integration of AI and bioinformatics.

12.6 Advancement of Deep Learning Architectures in Bioinformatics

The fundamental models and concepts of various deep learning (DL) architectures have been executed from ANN [22,26,30–32]. Though DL has recently adopted from the subfield of an ML system, it has likely massive deployments extending from the topics of computer vision, machine vision, signal processing, voice, computational biology and sequence, and

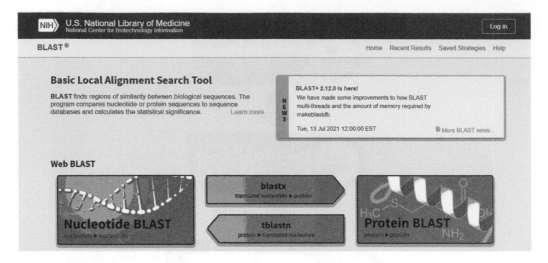

FIGURE 12.2
Framework of BLAST algorithm.

text prediction, overall modelling the creative AI fields [13,21,33–39]. DL carries out some models such as hierarchical learning, deep structured learning, and ANN [10,23,40–57].

Table 12.2 shows the application of DL networks on genomic dataset. It also offers some performance metrics that are varied on different datasets of bioinformatics research. Prediction, data augmentation, and feature selection are summarized in Table 12.2. Moreover, Table 12.3 describes detection, classification, and image segmentation methods applied in medical image dataset such as Digital Database for Screening Mammography (DDSM), Traumatic brain injury (TBI), and Alzheimer's Disease Neuroimaging Initiative (ADNI). Table 12.4 focuses on DL technique with a performance report applied in some biomedical applications.

12.7 Fuzzy Logic in Bioinformatics

Bioinformatics handles an enormous amount of biomedical data to analyse where, most of the time, data are fuzzy and imprecise. New technologies and robust-integrated systems are required to handle these fuzzy data. Bioinformatics already adopted some fuzzy logic and fuzzy technology. For example,

a. Protein motifs can be extracted using neuro-fuzzy applications [76]. It is a 3D structure of proteins or amino acid. Fuzzy logic helps to improve the flexibility of motifs. Also, the fuzzy clustering techniques are used to classify the amino acid sequences into several super families.

b. Fuzzy technologies are capable of analysing polynucleotides and differentiate between them [77].

c. Gene expression data can be analysed using this adaptive logic approach [78]. Besides, fuzzy technologies are used in exploring and deciphering genetic networks and analysing the relationships between genes.

TABLE 12.2

DL Technique on Genome Datasets

Data Type	Application	DL Model	Dataset	Performance Metrics	References
Sequences	Feature selection of MiRNA/Gene	DBN	MLL GE, prostate tumour, and SRBCT	F1-score: 84.7%, Recall: 84.1%, Precision: 85.3%	[58]
	Target prediction of micro-RNA	LSTM	Pairing data of miRNA–mRNA	Accuracy: 96.4%, F1-score: 91.1%, Sensitivity: 93.9%, PPV: 88.5%	[59]
	Prediction of micro-RNA	RNN	miRBoost	F-score: 93%, SP: 99%, g-mean: 94%	[60]
	Prediction of splice junctions	DBN	UCSC and GWH	Accuracy: 88.8%	[61]
	Reconstruction of protein structure	DA	Protein data	GDT-TS score: 99.52%	[62]
	DNA-binding protein prediction	CNN	JASPAR database	AUC: 80%	[63]
	Data augmentation of gene expression	GAN	GEO database	AUC: 65%	[64]
	Prediction of RNA/DNA sequence	CNN	DREAM	AUC: 93% and ROC evaluation	[33]
	Noncoding variation of gene prediction	CNN	ENCODE DGF	AUC evaluation	[65]

TABLE 12.3

DL Technique on Medical Imaging Datasets

Data Type	Application	DL Model	Dataset	Performance Metrics	References
Image	Segmentation of brain lesion	CNN	TBI dataset	Sensitivity: 60%, Precision: 68%, DSC: 59%	[66]
	Classification of biomedical images	CNN	PACS	Accuracy: 97.25%	[67]
	Breast cancer diagnosis	Hybrid MVGG16 ImageNet	DDSM	Accuracy: 94.3%, F1-score: 93.6%, Recall: 93.7%, Precision: 93.5%	[13]
	Segmentation process of retinal blood	GAN	STARE, DRIVE datasets	AUC PR: 92%, AUC ROC: 98%	[67]
	MCI/AD diagnosis	DBN	ADNI dataset	Accuracy: 91.4%	[68]
	MCI/AD diagnosis	DBM	ADNI dataset	Accuracy: 93.52%	[69]
	Autism disorder recognition	DNN	ABIDE	Specificity: 63%, Accuracy: 70%, Sensitivity: 74%	[70]
	Neuronal membranes segmentation	CNN	Challenging dataset of EM segmentation	-	[71]
	COVID-19 diagnosis	NASNet	CT dataset of COVID-19	Accuracy: 82.4%, F1-score: 84.59%, Precision: 92.16%	[25]

TABLE 12.4

DL Technique on Biomedical Signals Datasets

Data Type	Application	DL Model	Dataset	Performance Metrics	References
Signals	Seizure prediction	CNN	Freiburg dataset	Sensitivity: 71%	[72]
	Emotion classification	CNN	DEAP	Accuracy: 66.8%	[73]
	Emotion recognition	DA	MAHNOB-HCI	Accuracy: 53.4%	[74]
	Classification ECG arrhythmia	DBN	MIT-BIH arrhythmia	Specificity: 96.5%, Accuracy: 98.83%, Sensitivity: 99.83%	[75]

d. It is necessary to align multiple sequences to get optimal alignment and it is possible by applying a dynamic programming algorithm [79].

e. DNA sequencing and gene clustering from microarray data can be achievable using fuzzy genetic systems [80].

f. Using the k-nearest neighbours algorithm, subcellular locations in protein can be predicted from their dipeptide composition [81].

g. In pedigreed populations, simulations of complex traits are possible with fuzzy-valued effects, which are influenced by genes [82].

h. Fuzzy C-means, a partitioning method, applies to get the attribute cluster membership values.

i. Using a fuzzy alignment model, the sequence patterns can be mapped to putative function classes. Besides, functional and ancestral relationships between proteins can be unravelled by alignment methods, or fuzzy classification rules can be developed using the neural network approach of a radial basis function [83].

j. Complementary deoxyribonucleic acid (cDNA) can be processed automatically from microarray images using a fuzzy vector filtering framework.

"If x and y, then z" – this simple rule-based approach is adopted by fuzzy logic for solving control problems. Besides, it also provides different types of features to make a good selection for different modelling and control applications. Some features are so prominent that they accept imprecise and noisy inputs and programmed nicely to fail safely. Also, some features of fuzzy systems can take any rational number of inputs and produce many outputs. It is also possible for the system to model a nonlinear system where modelling mathematically is impossible. The three following steps are required to do modelling and control systems based on fuzzy logic: fuzzification, inference rule, and defuzzification.

12.8 Bioinformatics in COVID-19

Since SARS-CoV-2 infections have increased rapidly and become a pandemic, almost every country is suffering from this. Therefore, efforts are immediately required in order to develop an efficacious corona virus vaccine. Multiple structural (spike, envelope, membrane, nucleocapsid) and non-structural proteins are encoded in coronaviruses. With SARS-CoV-2 being lately found, there's presently depleted information regarding immunogenic epitopes eliciting protein or T cell reactions. Introductory studies counsel that SARS-CoV-2 is very similar to SARS-CoV-1, supported organic process study, complete ordering, and likeness within the mechanism of cell entry and connecting in the human cell receptor [2,6,11,19,21,24,25,53,84,85].

On the basis of a whole-genome sequence alignment, SARS-CoV-2 shared 89 identities, 82 with SARS-CoV and 96.3% with bat CoV RaTG13, with the SARS-like CoVZXC21 [85,86]. Arrangement of the expected macromolecule sequences of SARS-CoV-2 to those of SARS-like or SARS-CoV coronaviruses unconcealed a complete of 380 amino alkanoic acid substitutions between these viruses [53,86]. These amino alkanoic acid changeovers were allocated as follows: 348 mutations in non-functional proteins (ORF1ab, 3a, 3b, 7a, 7b, 9b, and ORF14), 27 in S macromolecule, and 5 in N macromolecule. No amino alkanoic acid substitutions were recognized in M or E proteins, representing that M and E proteins are extremely preserved among these viruses.

Research additionally has shown that the protein responses produced against the S super molecule, the foremost exposed super molecule of SARS-CoV, may be protective against infection in animal models [87]. What is more, varied researches have presented that antibodies are created against the SARS-CoV super molecule N, an extremely immunogenic super molecule, and widely expressed throughout the infection [54]. Furthermore, studies have in contestable that SARS-CoV-2 elicits a sturdy lymph cell response and this body substance reaction causes the clearance of SARS-CoV-2. T cells similarly play an essential role in infectious agent infections, for instance, CD4 T cells offer B cell help for protein production that results in long-lasting protection. Hence, the progress of vaccines against SARS-CoV-2, which will stimulate T and B cells, is constructive [18,19].

Mishra et al. attempt to deploy the bioinformatics method to validate and identify anti-inflammatory drug to beat the impact of COVID-19 and take a look at to seek out the operating impact and inhibition of Hydroxychloroquine drug and the way it beats coronavirus 6Y84 and 7buy proteinase and then it operates in the body and fight against COVID-19. The anti-inflammatory drug binds and frees over proteinase 6y84 and 7buy and manages their action in the body [88].

T and B cells square measure two vital arms of the scheme against pathogens, together with viruses. Activation of those cells plays a vital role within the body's defences. These cells square measure activated in each vaccine (artificial active) and pathogen entry (natural active) forms [55,84,85].

12.9 Fuzzy Rough Set Theory on Cancer Diagnosis

In our offered procedure, we have developed Fuzzy-Preference-Based Rough Set (FPRS) concept that has been deployed in the proposed system to select the important features (genes). Discovering informative and useful genes with the help of Fuzzy Set (FS) algorithms is a significant characteristic of diagnosing and recognizing cancer. Not only computational cost but also noise can be reduced by applying FS to improve the prediction accuracy [89,90].

In this experiment, the most relevant features are achieved using two fuzzy models of the FPRS method. One is Fuzzy Upward Consistency (FUC) and the other is Fuzzy Downward Consistency. Then the DT classifier is applied on each partition of the datasets used here inspecting the genes. Sample size of the datasets used in these experiments is

TABLE 12.5

Brief Summaries of the Datasets for the Experiments in this Work

Dataset	Number of Samples	Number of Features	Number of Classes
Leukaemia	72	5147	2
Breast cancer Wisconsin (BCW)	699	9	2

TABLE 12.6

Classification Accuracy with the Variations of Training and Testing Set

Dataset	Fuzzy Model	Number of Genes	Accuracy After DT Classifier Is Applied		
			Train 90%, Test 10%	Train 80%, Test 20%	Train 70%, Test 30%
WBC	FUC	3	99.96	99.02	98.78
	FLC	5	98.91	97.58	97.44
Leukaemia	FUC	9	96.85	96.52	92.38
	FLC	16	93.12	92.20	89.04

small and there is a huge number of attributes. This scenario has also been summarized in Table 12.5. The rough set concept includes an operational tool for dealing with such type of datasets having huge inconsistency due to the redundant and noisy data.

12.9.1 Dataset Description

The datasets used in this work are accessible in (http://www.biolab.si/supp/bi-cancer/projections/). The description of datasets has been summarized in Table 12.5.

12.9.2 Result and Analysis

The accuracy obtained by FUC is higher than Fuzzy Downward Consistency (FLC) for not only White Blood Cell (WBC) datasets but also for Leukaemia dataset. It is also shown that 90% training data and 10% testing data provide good accuracy in FUC and FLC methods among the three data-partitioning cases. DT classifier has been applied in this experiment. The highest classification accuracy of 99.96% has been achieved with three genes applying the proposed method (FUC and DT) for the WBC dataset. The highest classification accuracy of 96.85% has been achieved with nine genes applying the proposed method (FUC and DT) for Leukaemia dataset. C1, C2 and C3 have been found as informative genes in WBC dataset applying the proposed model (FPRS+DT). MPO, DNTT, CST3, CD79A, CCND3, DC19, TCF3, ZYX, and CD33 have been found as informative genes. Table 12.6 depicts the validation set of training and testing.

12.10 Conclusion with Future Opportunity

This paper is divided into two sections. First part is mainly a short review of computational biology and bioinformatics. Second part is the application of fuzzy theory and ML for gene classification of WBC and Leukaemia dataset. To combat COVID-19, the crucial factor of ML, DL, and bioinformatics are escalating progressively. The challenges of ML applications on bioinformatics are creating an impact on COVID-19. For these purposes, ANN such as ML, DL with its applications, has created knowledge on the detection of COVID-19. This review can offer a summary of bioinformatics, challenges, accenting on the ML approaches, and illustrations of some effective algorithms to utilize in bioinformatics. Next, this chapter has also provided a brief review of the fuzzy logic system for bioinformatics applications where the Gene Regulatory Network (GRN) interface has shown the three basic steps such as fuzzification, inference rule, and defuzzification. It will be integrated into a powerful technology. In the application section, FUC and FLC models have been deployed as a gene-selection method. With the combination of FPRS and ML, the proposed technique can play a significant role to collect necessary information and define some important criteria for selecting informative and unwanted genes.

Along with multidimensional data, software packages enable the incorporation of systems biology methods. Protein–protein datasets continue to grow in size as human interactive connections are identified and understanding these pathways in molecular may and should be included into genomics research. The biological process might be best represented as a series of independent structures, rather than as a component of a larger system. With the growing availability of datasets and the decreasing cost of sequencing, genomic analysis is no longer limited to a particular genome, an evaluation of two isolated samples of cancer genome, or bigger. Present-day technology can investigate individual samples and compare databases one at a time. Rather than that, it is an advanced technology that enables the simultaneous examination of many genomes at a scale similar to genome-wide association research. The datasets applied in genomics research will certainly continue to increase in depth and sample size. Bioinformatics, more than ever, will be critical in detecting the data flood. While the gains achieved by this flood will be significant and beneficial, academics should also anticipate the unforeseeable paradigm shifts on the horizon.

DL as an inference method powered by large data necessitates high-performance parallel computing capabilities. Combined with additional algorithmic advances and rapid accumulation of varied perceptual data, it is gaining widespread success in a wide range of areas and applications. It has seen significant improvements in its research techniques, particularly in computational biology and bioinformatics, which are both data-intensive fields. Finally, because of the tremendous creativity and accomplishments achieved by broad learning in a variety of subfields, some have said that deep knowledge may spark another internet-like wave. In the long term, DL technology has the ability to influence the whole destiny of our lives and civilizations. However, DL in academia or in the AI industry should not be misinterpreted or exaggerated since it presents many technical difficulties. Overall, we anticipate that this assessment will offer our researcher with a pertinent perspective that will enable him or her to get a thorough knowledge of and progress in this more rapidly developing field.

References

1. K. A. Shastry and H. A. Sanjay, "Machine learning for bioinformatics," in *Statistical Modelling and Machine Learning Principles for Bioinformatics Techniques, Tools, and Applications*, K. G. Srinivasa, G. M. Siddesh, and S. R. Manisekhar (eds). Springer: Berlin, Germany, 2020, pp. 25–39.

2. S. Bharati, P. Podder, M. R. H. Mondal, and V. B. Prasath, "CO-ResNet: Optimized ResNet model for COVID-19 diagnosis from X-ray images," *International Journal of Hybrid Intelligent Systems,* vol. 17, pp. 71–85, 2021.

3. P. K. Paul, S. Bharati, P. Podder, and M. R. Hossain Mondal, "10 The role of IoMT during pandemics" in: *Computational Intelligence for Managing Pandemics,* A. Khamparia, R. Hossain Mondal, P. Podder, B. Bhushan, V. H. C. D. Albuquerque, and S. Kumar (eds). De Gruyter: Berlin, Germany, 2021, pp. 169–186.

4. S. R. Manisekhar, G. M. Siddesh, and S. S. Manvi, "Introduction to bioinformatics," in: *Statistical Modelling and Machine Learning Principles for Bioinformatics Techniques, Tools, and Applications,* K. G. Srinivasa, G. M. Siddesh, and S. R. Manisekhar (eds). Springer: Berlin, Germany, 2020, pp. 3–9.

5. P. Podder, S. Bharati, M. R. H. Mondal, P. K. Paul, and U. Kose, "Artificial neural network for cybersecurity: A comprehensive review," *Journal of Information Assurance and Security,* vol. 16, no. 1, pp. 010–023, 2021.

6. P. Podder, A. Khamparia, M. R. H. Mondal, M. A. Rahman, and S. Bharati, "Forecasting the spread of COVID-19 and ICU requirements," *International Journal of Online and Biomedical Engineering (iJOE),* vol. 17, no. 5, p. 81, 2021.

7. S. Bharati and M. R. Hossain Mondal, "12 Applications and challenges of AI-driven IoHT for combating pandemics: A review" in: *Computational Intelligence for Managing Pandemics,* A. Khamparia, R. Hossain Mondal, P. Podder, B. Bhushan, V. H. C. D. Albuquerque, and S. Kumar (eds). De Gruyter: Berlin, Germany, 2021, pp. 213–230.

8. S. Bharati, P. Podder, and M. R. H. Mondal, "Diagnosis of polycystic ovary syndrome using machine learning algorithms," in *2020 IEEE Region 10 Symposium (TENSYMP),* Dhaka, Bangladesh, IEEE, 2020, pp. 1486–1489.

9. P. Larranaga et al., "Machine learning in bioinformatics," *Briefings in Bioinformatics,* vol. 7, no. 1, pp. 86–112, 2006.

10. M. R. A. Robel, S. Bharati, P. Podder, and M. R. H. Mondal, "IoT driven healthcare monitoring system," in: *Fog, Edge, and Pervasive Computing in Intelligent IoT Driven Applications,* D. Gupta and A. Khamparia (eds). Wiley: Hoboken, NJ, 2020, pp. 161–176.

11. S. Bharati, "How artificial intelligence impacts businesses in the period of pandemics?" *Journal of the International Academy for Case Studies,* vol. 26, no. 5, pp. 1–2, 2020.

12. S. Bharati, M. R. A. Robel, M. A. Rahman, P. Podder, and N. Gandhi, "Comparative performance exploration and prediction of fibrosis, malign lymph, metastases, normal lymphogram using machine learning method," in *International Conference on Innovations in Bio-Inspired Computing and Applications.* Springer: Berlin, Germany, 2019, pp. 66–77.

13. A. Khamparia et al., "Diagnosis of breast cancer based on modern mammography using hybrid transfer learning," *Multidimensional Systems and Signal Processing,* vol. 32, pp. 747–765, 2020.

14. P. Podder, S. Bharati, and M. R. H. Mondal, "10 Automated gastric cancer detection and classification using machine learning," in: *Artificial Intelligence for Data-Driven Medical Diagnosis,* D. Gupta, U. Kose, B. L. Nguyen, and S. Bhattacharyya (eds). De Gruyter: Berlin, Germany, 2021, pp. 207–224.

15. S. Bharati and P. Podder, "1 Performance of CNN for predicting cancerous lung nodules using LightGBM," in: *Artificial Intelligence for Data-Driven Medical Diagnosis,* , D. Gupta, U. Kose, B. L. Nguyen, and S. Bhattacharyya (eds). De Gruyter: Berlin, Germany, 2021, pp. 1–18.

16. S. Bharati, M. A. Rahman, and P. Podder, "Breast cancer prediction applying different classification algorithm with comparative analysis using WEKA," in *2018 4th International Conference on Electrical Engineering and Information & Communication Technology (iCEEiCT),* Dhaka, Bangladesh, IEEE, 2018, pp. 581–584.

17. S. Bharati, P. Podder, R. Mondal, A. Mahmood, and M. Raihan-Al-Masud, "Comparative performance analysis of different classification algorithm for the purpose of prediction of lung cancer," in *International Conference on Intelligent Systems Design and Applications,* Auburn, WA, Springer, 2018, vol. 941, pp. 447–457.

18. P. Podder, S. Bharati, M. R. H. Mondal, and U. Kose, "Application of machine learning for the diagnosis of COVID-19," in: *Data Science for COVID-19*, U. Kose et al. (eds). Elsevier: Amsterdam, 2021, pp. 175–194.
19. M. R. H. Mondal, S. Bharati, and P. Podder, "Diagnosis of COVID-19 using machine learning and deep learning: A review," *Current Medical Imaging*, vol. 17, no. 12, pp. 1403–1418, 2021.
20. E. Naresh, B. P. V. Kumar, and S. P. Shankar, "Impact of machine learning in bioinformatics research," in *Statistical Modelling and Machine Learning Principles for Bioinformatics Techniques, Tools, and Applications*, K. G. Srinivasa, G. M. Siddesh, and S. R. Manisekhar (eds). Springer: Berlin, Germany, 2020, pp. 41–62.
21. S. Bharati, P. Podder, and M. R. H. Mondal, "Hybrid deep learning for detecting lung diseases from X-ray images," *Informatics in Medicine Unlocked*, vol. 20, p. 100391, 2020.
22. S. Bharati, P. Podder, and M. R. H. Mondal, "Artificial neural network based breast cancer screening: A comprehensive review," *International Journal of Computer Information Systems and Industrial Management Applications*, vol. 12, pp. 125–137, 2020.
23. P. Podder, S. Bharati, M. A. Rahman, and U. Kose, "Transfer learning for classification of brain tumor," in *Deep Learning for Biomedical Applications*, U. Kose, O. Deperlioglu, and D. Jude Hemanth (eds). CRC Press, Boca Raton, FL, 2021, pp. 315–328.
24. S. Bharati, P. Podder, M. Mondal, and V. B. Prasath, "Medical imaging with deep learning for COVID-19 diagnosis: A comprehensive review," *International Journal of Computer Information Systems and Industrial Management Applications*, vol. 13, pp. 91–112, 2021.
25. S. Bharati, P. Podder, M. R. H. Mondal, and N. Gandhi, "Optimized NASNet for diagnosis of COVID-19 from lung CT images," *Presented at the 20th International Conference on Intelligent Systems Design and Applications (ISDA 2020)*, 2020. https://doi.org/10.1007/978-3-030-71187-0_59
26. A. Ahmad and L. Dey, "A k-mean clustering algorithm for mixed numeric and categorical data," *Data & Knowledge Engineering*, vol. 63, no. 2, pp. 503–527, 2007.
27. S. Bharati, T. Z. Khan, P. Podder, and N. Q. Hung, "A comparative analysis of image denoising problem: Noise models, denoising filters and applications," *Cognitive Internet of Medical Things for Smart Healthcare*, vol. 311, pp. 49–66, 2020.
28. P. Lakshmi and D. Ramyachitra, "Review about bioinformatics, databases, sequence alignment, docking, and drug discovery," in: *Statistical Modelling and Machine Learning Principles for Bioinformatics Techniques, Tools, and Applications*, K. G. Srinivasa, G. M. Siddesh, and S. R. Manisekhar (eds). Springer: Berlin, Germany, 2020, pp. 11–23.
29. S. F. Altschul, "BLAST algorithm," *e LS*, 2001.
30. V. Mnih et al., "Human-level control through deep reinforcement learning," *Nature*, vol. 518, no. 7540, pp. 529–533, 2015.
31. J. Schmidhuber, "Deep learning in neural networks: An overview," *Neural Networks*, vol. 61, pp. 85–117, 2015.
32. P. Mamoshina, A. Vieira, E. Putin, and A. Zhavoronkov, "Applications of deep learning in biomedicine," *Molecular Pharmaceutics*, vol. 13, no. 5, pp. 1445–1454, 2016.
33. B. Alipanahi, A. Delong, M. T. Weirauch, and B. J. Frey, "Predicting the sequence specificities of DNA-and RNA-binding proteins by deep learning," *Nature Biotechnology*, vol. 33, no. 8, pp. 831–838, 2015.
34. M. W. Libbrecht and W. S. Noble, "Machine learning applications in genetics and genomics," *Nature Reviews Genetics*, vol. 16, no. 6, pp. 321–332, 2015.
35. S. Zhang et al., "A deep learning framework for modeling structural features of RNA-binding protein targets," *Nucleic Acids Research*, vol. 44, no. 4, p. e32, 2016.
36. A. Esteva et al., "Dermatologist-level classification of skin cancer with deep neural networks," *Nature*, vol. 542, no. 7639, pp. 115–118, 2017.
37. S. Bharati, P. Podder, and P. K. Paul, "Lung cancer recognition and prediction according to random forest ensemble and RUSBoost algorithm using LIDC data," *International Journal of Hybrid Intelligent Systems*, vol. 15, no. 2, pp. 91–100, 2019.

38. M. V. Madhavan, D. N. H. Thanh, A. Khamparia, S. Pande, R. Malik, and D. Gupta, "Recognition and classification of pomegranate leaves diseases by image processing and machine learning techniques," *CMC-Computers Materials & Continua,* vol. 66, no. 3, pp. 2939–2955, 2021.

39. U. Erkan and D. N. H. Thanh, "Autism spectrum disorder detection with machine learning methods," *Current Psychiatry Research and Reviews Formerly: Current Psychiatry Reviews,* vol. 15, no. 4, pp. 297–308, 2019.

40. G. Ditzler, R. Polikar, and G. Rosen, "Multi-layer and recursive neural networks for metagenomic classification," *IEEE Transactions on Nano Bioscience,* vol. 14, no. 6, pp. 608–616, 2015.

41. M. Liang, Z. Li, T. Chen, and J. Zeng, "Integrative data analysis of multi-platform cancer data with a multimodal deep learning approach," *IEEE/ACM Transactions on Computational Biology and Bioinformatics,* vol. 12, no. 4, pp. 928–937, 2014.

42. J. Xu et al., "Stacked sparse autoencoder (SSAE) for nuclei detection on breast cancer histopathology images," *IEEE Transactions on Medical Imaging,* vol. 35, no. 1, pp. 119–130, 2015.

43. I. Goodfellow, Y. Bengio, A. Courville, and Y. Bengio, *Deep Learning.* MIT Press Cambridge, MA, 2016.

44. Y. Hu and X. Lu, "Learning spatial-temporal features for video copy detection by the combination of CNN and RNN," *Journal of Visual Communication and Image Representation,* vol. 55, pp. 21–29, 2018.

45. C. Angermueller, H. J. Lee, W. Reik, and O. Stegle, "DeepCpG: Accurate prediction of single-cell DNA methylation states using deep learning," *Genome Biology,* vol. 18, no. 1, pp. 1–13, 2017.

46. Q. Pan, O. Shai, L. J. Lee, B. J. Frey, and B. J. Blencowe, "Deep surveying of alternative splicing complexity in the human transcriptome by high-throughput sequencing," *Nature Genetics,* vol. 40, no. 12, pp. 1413–1415, 2008.

47. D. Ray et al., "Rapid and systematic analysis of the RNA recognition specificities of RNA-binding proteins," *Nature Biotechnology,* vol. 27, no. 7, pp. 667–670, 2009.

48. A. Jolma et al., "DNA-binding specificities of human transcription factors," *Cell,* vol. 152, no. 1–2, pp. 327–339, 2013.

49. T. I. Lee and R. A. Young, "Transcriptional regulation and its misregulation in disease," *Cell,* vol. 152, no. 6, pp. 1237–1251, 2013.

50. A. Krizhevsky, I. Sutskever, and G. E. Hinton, "Imagenet classification with deep convolutional neural networks," *Advances in Neural Information Processing Systems,* vol. 25, pp. 1097–1105, 2012.

51. S. Chilamkurthy et al., "Deep learning algorithms for detection of critical findings in head CT scans: A retrospective study," *The Lancet,* vol. 392, no. 10162, pp. 2388–2396, 2018.

52. F. Dubost et al., "3D regression neural network for the quantification of enlarged perivascular spaces in brain MRI," *Medical Image Analysis,* vol. 51, pp. 89–100, 2019.

53. M. R. H. Mondal, S. Bharati, P. Podder, and P. Podder, "Data analytics for novel coronavirus disease," *Informatics in Medicine Unlocked,* vol. 20, p. 100374, 2020.

54. P. Zhou et al., "A pneumonia outbreak associated with a new coronavirus of probable bat origin," *Nature,* vol. 579, no. 7798, pp. 270–273, 2020.

55. L. Wu et al., "Trispecific antibodies enhance the therapeutic efficacy of tumor-directed T cells through T cell receptor co-stimulation," *Nature Cancer,* vol. 1, no. 1, pp. 86–98, 2020.

56. B. Tang, Z. Pan, K. Yin, and A. Khateeb, "Recent advances of deep learning in bioinformatics and computational biology," *Frontiers in Genetics,* vol. 10, p. 214, 2019.

57. S. Bharati, P. Podder, M. R. H. Mondal, and P. K. Paul, "Applications and challenges of cloud integrated IoMT," in: *Cognitive Internet of Medical Things for Smart Healthcare,* A. E. Hassanien, A. Khamparia, D. Gupta, K. Shankar, and A. Slowik (eds). Springer: Berlin, Germany, 2021, pp. 67–85.

58. R. Ibrahim, N. A. Yousri, M. A. Ismail, and N. M. El-Makky, "Multi-level gene/MiRNA feature selection using deep belief nets and active learning," *Presented at the 36th Annual International Conference of the IEEE Engineering in Medicine and Biology Society,* Chicago, IL, 2014.

59. B. Lee, J. Baek, S. Park, and S. Yoon, "deepTarget: End-to-end learning framework for microRNA target prediction using deep recurrent neural networks," *Presented at the Proceedings of the 7th ACM International Conference on Bioinformatics, Computational Biology, and Health Informatics,* Seattle, WA, 2016.

60. S. Park, S. Min, H. Choi, and S. Yoon, "deepMiRGene: Deep neural network based precursor microrna prediction," arXiv preprint arXiv:1605.00017, 2016.

61. T. Lee and S. Yoon, "Boosted categorical restricted Boltzmann machine for computational prediction of splice junctions," *Presented at the International Conference on Machine Learning*, Lille, 2015.

62. H. Li, Q. Lyu, and J. Cheng, "A template-based protein structure reconstruction method using deep autoencoder learning," *Journal of Proteomics & Bioinformatics*, vol. 9, no. 12, p. 306, 2016.

63. H. Zeng, M. D. Edwards, G. Liu, and D. K. Gifford, "Convolutional neural network architectures for predicting DNA–protein binding," *Bioinformatics*, vol. 32, no. 12, pp. i121–i127, 2016.

64. M. Marouf et al., "Realistic in silico generation and augmentation of single-cell RNA-seq data using generative adversarial networks," *Nature Communications*, vol. 11, no. 1, pp. 1–12, 2020.

65. J. Zhou and O. G. Troyanskaya, "Predicting effects of noncoding variants with deep learning–based sequence model," *Nature Methods*, vol. 12, no. 10, pp. 931–934, 2015.

66. K. Kamnitsas et al., "Efficient multi-scale 3D CNN with fully connected CRF for accurate brain lesion segmentation," *Medical Image Analysis*, vol. 36, pp. 61–78, 2017.

67. J. Cho, K. Lee, E. Shin, G. Choy, and S. Do, "Medical image deep learning with hospital PACS dataset," arXiv preprint arXiv:1511.06348, 2015.

68. F. Li, L. Tran, K.-H. Thung, S. Ji, D. Shen, and J. Li, "Robust deep learning for improved classification of AD/MCI patients," *Presented at the International Workshop on Machine Learning in Medical Imaging*, Boston, MA, 2014. https://doi.org/10.1007/978-3-319-10581-9_30

69. H.-I. Suk, S.-W. Lee, D. Shen, and Alzheimer's Disease Neuroimaging Initiative, "Hierarchical feature representation and multimodal fusion with deep learning for AD/MCI diagnosis," *Neuro Image*, vol. 101, pp. 569–582, 2014.

70. A. S. Heinsfeld, A. R. Franco, R. C. Craddock, A. Buchweitz, and F. Meneguzzi, "Identification of autism spectrum disorder using deep learning and the ABIDE dataset," *Neuro Image: Clinical*, vol. 17, pp. 16–23, 2018.

71. D. Ciresan, A. Giusti, L. Gambardella, and J. Schmidhuber, "Deep neural networks segment neuronal membranes in electron microscopy images," *Advances in Neural Information Processing Systems*, vol. 25, pp. 2843–2851, 2012.

72. P. Mirowski, D. Madhavan, Y. LeCun, and R. Kuzniecky, "Classification of patterns of EEG synchronization for seizure prediction," *Clinical Neurophysiology*, vol. 120, no. 11, pp. 1927–1940, 2009.

73. S. Tripathi, S. Acharya, R. D. Sharma, S. Mittal, and S. Bhattacharya, "Using deep and convolutional neural networks for accurate emotion classification on DEAP dataset," *Presented at the Twenty-Ninth IAAI Conference*, San Francisco CA, 2017.

74. S. Jirayucharoensak, S. Pan-Ngum, and P. Israsena, "EEG-based emotion recognition using deep learning network with principal component based covariate shift adaptation," *The Scientific World Journal*, vol. 2014, pp. 1–10, 2014.

75. Y. Yan, X. Qin, Y. Wu, N. Zhang, J. Fan, and L. Wang, "A restricted Boltzmann machine based two-lead electrocardiography classification," *Presented at the 2015 IEEE 12th International Conference on Wearable and Implantable Body Sensor Networks (BSN)*, Cambridge, MA, 2015. https://doi.org/10.1109/BSN.2015.7299399

76. B. C. H. Chang and S. K. Halgamuge, "Protein motif extraction with neuro-fuzzy optimization," *Bioinformatics*, vol. 18, no. 8, pp. 1084–1090, 2002.

77. A. Torres and J. J. Nieto, "The fuzzy polynucleotide space: Basic properties," *Bioinformatics*, vol. 19, no. 5, pp. 587–592, 2003.

78. S. Tomida, T. Hanai, H. Honda, and T. Kobayashi, "Analysis of expression profile using fuzzy adaptive resonance theory," *Bioinformatics*, vol. 18, no. 8, pp. 1073–1083, 2002.

79. M. Schlosshauer and M. Ohlsson, "A novel approach to local reliability of sequence alignments," *Bioinformatics*, vol. 18, no. 6, pp. 847–854, 2002.

80. N. Belacel, M. Čuperlović-Culf, M. Laflamme, and R. Ouellette, "Fuzzy J-Means and VNS methods for clustering genes from microarray data," *Bioinformatics*, vol. 20, no. 11, pp. 1690–1701, 2004.

81. Y. Huang and Y. Li, "Prediction of protein subcellular locations using fuzzy k-NN method," *Bioinformatics*, vol. 20, no. 1, pp. 21–28, 2004.
82. C. Carleos, F. Rodriguez, H. Lamelas, and J. A. Baro, "Simulating complex traits influenced by genes with fuzzy-valued effects in pedigreed populations," *Bioinformatics*, vol. 19, no. 1, pp. 144–148, 2003.
83. A. Torres and J. J. Nieto, "Fuzzy logic in medicine and bioinformatics," *Journal of Biomedicine and Biotechnology*, vol. 2006, pp. 1–7, 2006.
84. Z. Noorimotlagh, C. Karami, S. A. Mirzaee, M. Kaffashian, S. Mami, and M. Azizi, "Immune and bioinformatics identification of T cell and B cell epitopes in the protein structure of SARS-CoV-2: A systematic review," *International Immunopharmacology*, vol. 86, p. 106738, 2020.
85. D. Paraskevis, E. G. Kostaki, G. Magiorkinis, G. Panayiotakopoulos, G. Sourvinos, and S. Tsiodras, "Full-genome evolutionary analysis of the novel corona virus (2019-nCoV) rejects the hypothesis of emergence as a result of a recent recombination event," *Infection, Genetics and Evolution*, vol. 79, p. 104212, 2020.
86. J. F.-W. Chan et al., "Genomic characterization of the 2019 novel human-pathogenic coronavirus isolated from a patient with atypical pneumonia after visiting Wuhan," *Emerging Microbes & Infections*, vol. 9, no. 1, pp. 221–236, 2020.
87. L. I. N. Ying et al., "Identification of an epitope of SARS-coronavirus nucleocapsid protein," *Cell Research*, vol. 13, no. 3, pp. 141–145, 2003.
88. S. Mishra, P. A. Jain, S. Ahmad, and S. Mishra, "Bioinformatics approach for COVID-19 (coronavirus) disease prevention treatment and drug validation," *EJMO*, vol. 4, no. 3, pp. 234–238, 2020.
89. D. Chakraborty and U. Maulik, "Identifying cancer biomarkers from microarray data using feature selection and semisupervised learning," *IEEE Journal of Translational Engineering in Health and Medicine*, vol. 2, pp. 1–11, 2014.
90. A. Houari, W. Ayadi, and S. B. Yahia, "A new FCA-based method for identifying biclusters in gene expression data," *International Journal of Machine Learning and Cybernetics*, vol. 9, no. 11, pp. 1879–1893, 2018.

13

Analysis for Early Prediction of Diabetes in Healthcare Using Classification Techniques

Navneet Verma
DCRUST

Sukhdip Singh
DCRUST

Devendra Prasad
Chitkara University

CONTENTS

13.1 Introduction

Diabetes is also called Diabetes Mellitus. When the glucose level in the blood is high it is called Diabetes. In our body, an organ named 'pancreas' releases a hormone called insulin, and with the help of this hormone, our blood carries glucose and provides it to different body cells. Glucose stays in our blood when our body does not produce enough amount of insulin (Kavakiotis et al. 2017). This increased amount of glucose in the blood causes Diabetes or called Type 1 Diabetes. Whereas in Type 2 Diabetes, the reason is the same for its occurrence; as this is the early stage, it can be cured using diabetes medicines, healthy food, and physical activities. In many developing and developed countries, this chronic disease is increasing rapidly, especially in rural areas and the reason is lack of awareness. Three types of diabetes – Type-1, Type-2, and Type-3 – have been explored (Pranto et al.

DOI: 10.1201/9781003215981-13

2020). This research work is mainly focused on the detection of diabetes as early as possible, by taking into account the severity level of this disease. For the experimental purpose, we collect 768 female patients' diagnostic datasets from Kaggle having nine attributes, such as the number of Glucose, Pregnancies, Blood Pressure, Insulin, Skin Thickness, Diabetes Pedigree Function, body mass index (BMI), age, and outcome. Based on these attributes, we construct a prediction model using different machine learning (ML) classification techniques to predict diabetes mellitus. Through the support of ML classification techniques, a predictive model can be created in which we can label the data of a particular class from the input dataset. There are many techniques in ML for predicting diabetes mellitus on the basis of extracting valuable knowledge from the recorded dataset (Kononenko 2001). Despite the existence of various ML algorithms, predicting best results is difficult. Therefore, we are using five different algorithms of ML using Python language which are Support Vector Machine (SVM), Random Forest, K-Nearest Neighbor (KNN), Naive Bayes, and Logistic Regression.

13.2 Literature Survey

Important attributes that contribute maximum in early detection of Diabetes Mellitus using predictive analysis have been discussed (Sneha and Gangil 2019). ML-based Synthetic Minority Over Sampling Technique (SMOTE) algorithm uses excessive process and feature selection to classify and predict diabetes from a new balanced dataset. SVM, Decision Tree, AdaBoost, and Bagging are used for modeling and prediction (Li, Li, and Yao 2018). The experimental results showed that the AdaBoost algorithm performs better in case of classification and decision trees perform comparatively lower than SVM and ensemble method. Various ML algorithms, such as random forest, XGBoost algorithm, SVM, linear regression, and decision tree, are used to predict whether a person is suffering from diabetes or not. In another paper, logistic regression is used for predicting diabetes (Vizhi and Dash 2020).

13.3 Materials and Methods

13.3.1 Data Preprocessing

The dataset contains various attributes that have been represented with the help of a table with the type and range value of each attribute (Table 13.1). To make the dataset more effective, all 0s are replaced with the corresponding mean value of those attributes.

(a) Correlation and Heat Map: Data Correlation is a method by which we can recognize the relationship between various variables and attributes in a dataset. Figure 13.1 shows the heat map of the diabetes dataset.

To check the correctness of the dataset values, a scatter plot is generated (Figure 13.2) by taking 20 samples of glucose attributes.

(b) Normalization: After the data cleaning process, the normalization process brings all the attributes under the same level.

TABLE 13.1

Structure of Dataset

S. No.	Attributes	Type	Values
1	Pregnancies	Integer	{0–17}
2	Glucose	Integer	{44–199}
3	Blood pressure	Integer	{24–122}
4	Skin thickness	Integer	{7–99}
5	Insulin	Integer	{0–846}
6	BMI	Floating	{18.2–67.1}
7	Diabetes pedigree function	Floating	{0.078–2.42}
8	Age	Integer	{21–81}
9	Outcome	Binary	{0–1}

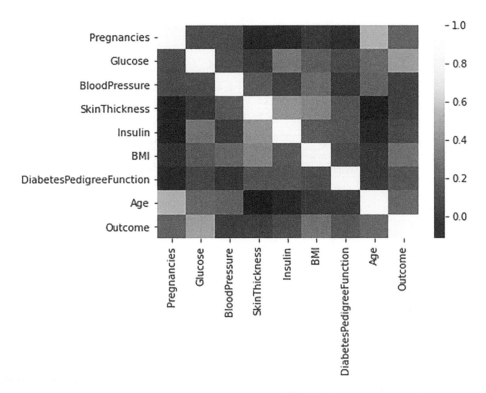

FIGURE 13.1
Heatmap.

13.4 ML Techniques

ML provides efficient techniques to extract knowledge from diagnostic medical datasets (Verma, Singh, and Prasad 2021). Supervised learning is divided into two types of problems, i.e. classification and regression (Kavakiotis et al. 2017). In this analysis, the classification problem of supervised ML is used. Common classification algorithms such

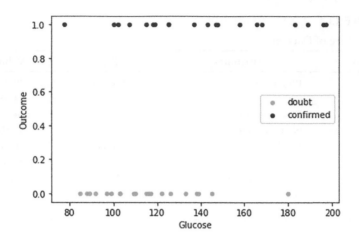

FIGURE 13.2
Scattered graph.

Classification Testimony for SVM

	precision	recall	f1-score	support
0	0.83	0.87	0.85	102
1	0.72	0.65	0.69	52

accuracy			0.80	154
macro avg	0.78	0.76	0,77	154
weighted avg	0.80	0.80	0.80	154

Confusion Matrix: $\begin{bmatrix} 89 & 13 \\ 18 & 34 \end{bmatrix}$

FIGURE 13.3
Classification testimony for SVM.

as SVMs, KNN, Logistic Regression, Ensemble Methods (Random Forest), and Gaussian Naïve Bayes are used.

13.4.1 SVM

SVM generates a hyperplane that divides the data into two classes (Faruque, Asaduzzaman, and Sarker 2019). SVM can differentiate instances into specific classes and the entities which are not supported by data can also be classified. It is shown in Figure 13.3.

13.4.2 KNN

Similarity measure KNN makes classification on the basis of its nearby neighbors. (Muhammad, Algehyne, and Usman 2020). Here k is all the time a positive integer value which is the number of nearby neighbors. Neighbor's value is chosen from the class set and proximity between two points which is defined by Euclidean distance. Euclidean distance, equation 13.1, is the distance or the length of a segment connecting the two points either in the plane or three-dimensional space. It is also shown in Figure 13.4.

Classification Testimony for kNN

	precision	recall	f1-score	support
0	0.78	0.83	0.81	102
1	0.62	0.54	0.58	52

accuracy			0.73	154
macro avg	0.70	0.69	0.69	154
weighted avg	0.73	0.73	0.73	154

Confusion Matrix: $\begin{bmatrix} 85 & 17 \\ 24 & 28 \end{bmatrix}$

FIGURE 13.4
Classification testimony for KNN.

Classification Testimony for Logistic Regression

	precision	recall	f1-score	support
0	0.84	0.88	0.86	102
1	0.74	0.67	0.71	52

accuracy			0.81	154
macro avg	0.79	0.78	0.78	154
weighted avg	0.81	0.81	0.81	154

Confusion Matrix: $\begin{bmatrix} 90 & 12 \\ 17 & 35 \end{bmatrix}$

FIGURE 13.5
Classification testimony for logistic regression.

$$\text{Euclidean distance: } \sqrt{\sum_{i=0}^{n} (x_i - y_i)^2} \tag{13.1}$$

Here, x, y are the two points in the Euclidean space (n), and x_i, y_i are the Euclidean vectors starting from the origin of the space.

13.4.3 Logistic Regression

Logistic regression is used to classify the probability of a binary response, positive or negative for diabetes, on one or more predictors (Muhammad, Algehyne, and Usman 2020). It uses sigmoid function according to equation 13.2. It is also shown in Figure 13.5.

Sigmoid function:

$$S(x) = \frac{1}{1 + e^{-x}} \tag{13.2}$$

13.4.4 Ensemble Method (Random Forest)

The ensemble method provides a better prediction and it uses many learning algorithms together for solving a particular problem (Chaki et al. 2020). Here, a random forest of

Classification Testimony for Random Forest

	precision	recall	f1-score	support
0	0.78	0.84	0.81	102
1	0.64	0.54	0.58	52

accuracy			0.74	154
macro avg	0.71	0.69	0.70	154
weighted avg	0.73	0.74	0.73	154

Confusion Matrix: $\begin{bmatrix} 86 & 16 \\ 24 & 28 \end{bmatrix}$

FIGURE 13.6
Classification testimony for random forest.

Classification Testimony for Gaussian NB

	precision	recall	f1-score	Support
0	0.82	0.81	0.82	102
1	0.64	0.65	0.65	52

accuracy			0.76	154
macro avg	0.73	0.73	0.73	154
weighted avg	0.76	0.76	0.76	154

Confusion Matrix: $\begin{bmatrix} 83 & 19 \\ 18 & 34 \end{bmatrix}$

FIGURE 13.7
Classification testimony for Gaussian Naive Bayes.

bagging ensemble method reduces variance and improves the performance for predicting diabetes. It operates by constructing a large number of decision trees at training time and outputs the class that is the mode of the classes or classification or mean prediction, i.e. regression of the individual trees. It is shown in Figure 13.6.

13.4.5 Gaussian Naive Bayes

Bayes Theorem is the foundation of Gaussian Naive Bayes classifiers. It classifies outputs assuming that the classification does not depend on any other input feature (Sneha and Gangil 2019). Naive Bayes classifiers require small training data for the approximation of the parameters required for classification. It is based on simple design and execution and can apply to several real-life situations. As the data is continuous here, the continuous values related to each class are distributed according to a normal distribution. The likelihood function of the features is represented with equation 13.3.

$$P\left(X_i|y\right) = \frac{1}{\sqrt{2\pi\sigma_y^2}} \exp\left(-\frac{\left(x_i - \mu_y\right)^2}{2\sigma_y^2}\right) \tag{13.3}$$

Only continuous-valued features and models are supported by Gaussian Naive Bayes but conforming to a Gaussian (normal) distribution. It is shown in Figure 13.7.

13.5 Results and Discussion

Overall, the execution process of this work is presented by flow chart in Figure 13.8. In each classification algorithm of this work, we used a few common parameters to measure the performance like in SVM kernel value is linear, gamma set to auto and the value of c is 2, in Random Forest classifier n_estimators value is 10 and random_state is 4, in KNN method n_neighbors parameter (k) is set on value 5. Evaluation of all the classification algorithms is done under particular statistical ability aspects which are explained from equations 13.7–13.11, such as accuracy, recall, specificity, precision, and f1-score, to check their performance. True Positive (TP), True Negative (TN), False Positive (FP), and False Negative (FN) are the measures that are calculated by these classifications.

Here, TP means when the patient has diabetes, and prediction results are also yes. TN means when the patient does not have diabetes and prediction results are also no. FP means when the patient does not have diabetes and but the prediction results are yes. FN means when the patient has diabetes and prediction results are no.

The calculation methods for measuring these factors are as follows.

In classification methods, accuracy is the ratio of true predictions calculated by the model divided by all kinds of suitable predictions either false or true.

$$\text{Accuracy} = \frac{TP + TN}{TP + FP + FN + TN} \tag{13.4}$$

Recall, TP rate, or sensitivity is used to compute the ratio of positive instances that have diabetes with the actual positive instances, i.e. patients having diabetes are TP and FN.

$$\text{Recall} = TPR = \text{Sensitivity} = \frac{TP}{TP + FN} \tag{13.5}$$

The patients who do not have diabetes (TN) value divided by the non-diabetes patients who are predicted by the model will tell us the Specificity or TN rate and specificity is the opposite of recall.

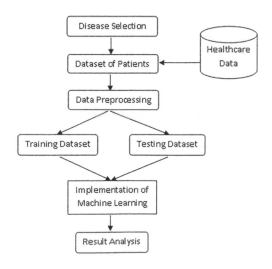

FIGURE 13.8
Overall process flow.

$$\text{Specificity} = \text{TNR} = \frac{\text{TN}}{\text{TN} + \text{FP}} \tag{13.6}$$

Predicted by the classification algorithm, the number of TP scores divided by the number of positive (True and False) values gives us a positive predictive value or precision.

$$\text{Precision} = \frac{\text{TP}}{\text{TP} + \text{FP}} \tag{13.7}$$

The weighted average of the recall and precision is called the F1 measure. When a classification algorithm performs well then it should be one and it will be zero if the performance is not well.

$$\text{F1} = \frac{2 * (\text{Recall} * \text{Precision})}{\text{Recall} + \text{Precision}} \tag{13.8}$$

TABLE 13.2

Results of ML Methods

MLA Name	MLA Train Accuracy	MLA Test Accuracy	MLA Precision	MLA Recall	MLA AUC
Logistic regression CV	0.7736	0.8052	0.729167	0.673077	0.772813
Random forest classifier	1.0000	0.7792	0.673077	0.673077	0.753205
SVC	0.8355	0.7662	0.666667	0.615385	0.729261
Gaussian Naive Bayes	0.7590	0.7597	0.641509	0.653846	0.733786
k-neighbors classifier	0.8176	0.7338	0.622222	0.538462	0.685897

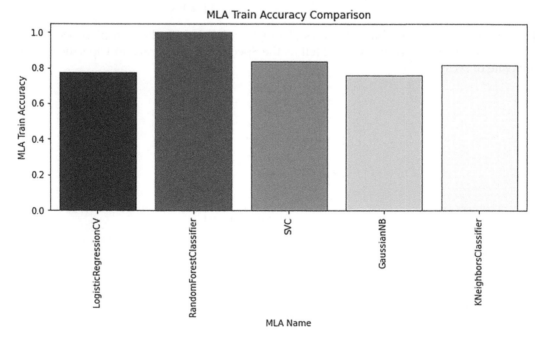

FIGURE 13.9
Accuracy result of training dataset.

This work is implemented in Python language with the help of various supporting library files. The results of the used classification algorithms are shown in Table 13.2 and Figures 13.9 and 13.10. It can be seen that the random forest classifier shows improved results as compared to others on the training dataset and Logistic Regression performs better compared to others on the testing dataset. The prediction features played an important role and the importance of each feature playing the main role in diabetes prediction value has been plotted in Figure 13.11, where *x*-axis is the name of the features and the

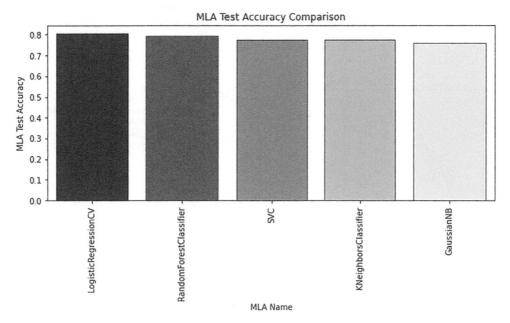

FIGURE 13.10
Accuracy result of testing dataset.

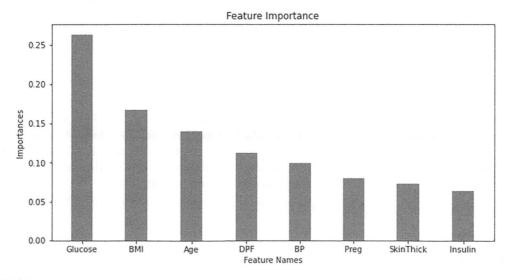

FIGURE 13.11
Graph based on feature importance.

TABLE 13.3

Feature Importance

Glucose	0.263146
BMI	0.167385
Age	0.140298
Diabetes pedigree function	0.113084
Blood pressure	0.099685
Pregnancies	0.080358
Skin thickness	0.072520
Insulin	0.063524

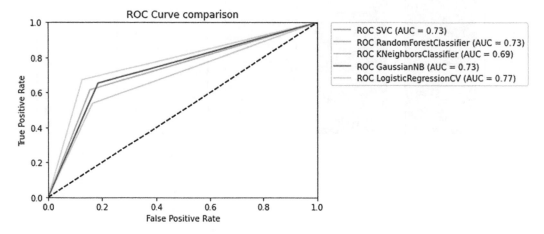

FIGURE 13.12
ROC curve.

y-axis represents the importance of each feature. It is also shown in Table 13.3 and the receiver operating characteristic curve is shown in Figure 13.12.

13.6 Conclusion

The early and effective prediction of diabetes in healthcare using ML classification techniques has been discussed. Various classification algorithms are used here such as SVM, KNN, Logistic Regression, Ensemble (Random Forest), and Gaussian Naive Bayes classifiers. The experimental results could be an asset of healthcare to early prediction and decide as per the severity level of diabetes which can save more human lives.

References

Badiuzzaman Pranto, Sk Maliha Mehnaz, Esha Bintee Mahid, Imran Mahmud Sadman, Ahsanur Rahman, and Sifat Momen. 2020. "Evaluating machine learning methods for predicting diabetes among female patients in Bangladesh." *Information (Switzerland)* 11 (8). doi: 10.3390/INFO11080374.

Ioannis Kavakiotis, Olga Tsave, Athanasios Salifoglou, Nicos Maglaveras, Ioannis Vlahavas, and Ioanna Chouvarda. 2017. "Machine learning and data mining methods in diabetes research." *Computational and Structural Biotechnology Journal* 15. The Authors: 104–116. doi: 10.1016/j.csbj.2016.12.005.

Igor Kononenko. 2001. "Machine learning for medical diagnosis: history, state of the art and perspective." *Artificial Intelligence in Medicine* 23 (1): 89–109. doi: 10.1016/S0933-3657(01)00077-X.

Jyotismita Chaki, S. Thillai Ganesh, S. K. Cidham, and S. Ananda Theertan. 2020. "Machine learning and artificial intelligence based diabetes mellitus detection and self-management: A systematic review." *Journal of King Saud University - Computer and Information Sciences*, no. xxxx. The Authors. doi: 10.1016/j.jksuci.2020.06.013.

Kayal Vizhi, and Aman Dash. 2020. "Diabetes prediction using machine learning." *International Journal of Advanced Science and Technology* 29 (6): 2842–2852. doi: 10.32628/cseit206463.

Lawan Jibril Muhammad, Ebrahem A. Algehyne, and Sani Sharif Usman. 2020. "Predictive supervised machine learning models for diabetes mellitus." *SN Computer Science* 1 (5). Springer Singapore: 1–10. doi: 10.1007/s42979-020-00250-8.

Md Faisal Faruque, F. Asaduzzaman, and Iqbal H. Sarker. 2019. "Performance Analysis of Machine Learning Techniques to Predict Diabetes Mellitus." *ArXiv. International Conference on Electrical, Computer and Communication Engineering (ECCE)*, 7–9 February, 2019.

N. Sneha, and Tarun Gangil. 2019. "Analysis of diabetes mellitus for early prediction using optimal features selection." *Journal of Big Data* 6 (1). Springer International Publishing. doi: 10.1186/s40537-019-0175-6.

Navneet Verma, Sukhdip Singh, and Devendra Prasad. 2021. "A review on existing IoT architecture and communication protocols used in healthcare monitoring system." *Journal of the Institution of Engineers (India): Series B*. Springer India. doi: 10.1007/s40031-021-00632-3.

Yukai Li, Huling Li, and Hua Yao. 2018. "Analysis and study of diabetes follow-up data using a data-mining-based approach in New Urban Area of Urumqi, Xinjiang, China, 2016–2017." *Computational and Mathematical Methods in Medicine* 2018. doi: 10.1155/2018/7207151.

14

Nomenclature of Machine Learning Algorithms and Their Applications

Ritu Aggarwal and Suneet Kumar

Maharishi Markandeshwar Engineering College

CONTENTS

14.1 Introduction

Machine learning (ML) is a type of self-learning technique in which a machine learns on its own without explicit programming. It can simply be trained from the data, and a breakthrough comes with the generation of accurate outcomes. ML provides machines with the ability to learn automatically [1]. Machines can also learn from experience [2]. ML is a combination of data and a statistical tool that produces output-based prediction. The proposal for ML data is relevant to data extraction and Bayesian prognostic model. Data taken by machines are accepted as an input, and by applying an algorithm on that data, output or results are produced [3]. ML provides different kinds of applications such as predictive maintenance, fraud detection, and portfolio optimization. In ML, the work becomes easier because the programmers do not write codes and new rules every single time; once it is written, it could be reused anywhere when required [4]. In response to the adaption of this algorithm, new experiences and new data provide efficiency over time [5–7]. The following points will explain the importance of ML.

Heart disease is a reason for earlier death in humans. It occurs due to blockage in heart vessels when the supply of blood and oxygen in the heart is stopped. Two types of cholesterols are responsible for the heart disease – high-density lipoprotein and low-density lipoprotein [5]; with the help of proper tests and early predictions, we can easily predict the heart disease. Some of the ML techniques could be used for the prediction of heart disease at early stages. The best statistical tool (like MATLAB and WEKA) can be used to study, recognize, and classify an outline from the information concept and to train the dataset by the computer to mechanize the tasks that are very difficult for human beings. Human beings forget things easily, but machines do not [8]. A machine could store millions of data. It gives better accuracy and results with large datasets. The rest of this chapter is as follows: In Section 14.1, Introduction, we discuss the ML prediction of the heart disease at early stages.

In Section 14.2, Related Work Study, we discuss various models used by existing researchers for disease prediction.

In Section 14.3, a brief overview of the five ML algorithms used in this chapter is given, such as support vector machine (SVM), K-nearest neighbor (KNN), naive Bayes (NB), decision tree (DT), and logistic regression (LR), and their features are studied.

In Section 14.4, with the help the heart disease dataset and its attributes and calculate the accuracy of the ML techniques using the tool Python Jupyter Notebook.

In Section 14.5, the results are discussed along with how the heart dataset gives the best outcomes in terms of accuracy.

In Section 14.6, we conclude the chapter.

14.2 Related Work

In this section, studies and survey conducted on various ML techniques by various researchers are discussed. The existing ML techniques and their accuracy. When implementing the same classifiers on the heart disease dataset, different results in terms of accuracy were obtained.

Reddy et al. [1] proposed a model for heart disease prediction using ML techniques on the Cleveland dataset and obtained results in terms of accuracy as 70% using the LR classifier. Mohan et al. [6] studied the HD prediction using random forest classifier using the Hybrid Random Forest with Linear Model (HRFLM) method. They used the Cleveland dataset and depicted an accuracy rate of SVM of 88.7%. Jabbar [9] presented data mining techniques that are frequently used to predict whether a patient is normal or having coronary illness. Naïve Bayes is an ML classifier that unwinds the conventional Naïve Bayes suspicion. In the proposed model cases, the hidden naive Bayes (HNB) can be applied to coronary illness prediction (expectation). Our exploratory outcomes on coronary illness in sensitivity performance metrics show that the HNB records 100%. Data mining techniques are often used to classify whether a patient is normal or having heart disease. HNB is a data mining model that relaxes the traditional NB's conditional independence assumption. Our proposed model claims that the HNB can be applied to heart disease classification (prediction). Our experimental results on heart disease dataset show that the HNB records 100% in terms of accuracy and outperforms NB.

Thaiparnit et al. [10] started from the collection of data on heart disease. Data preparation and selection is a prerequisite for data mining. To identify people with heart disease, the data were then analyzed using vertical Hoeffding decision tree (VHDT). It is a technique used to extract data. The experiments showed that the data extraction by VHDT shows an accuracy of 85.43%. Jabbar et al. [11] proposed a model using Genetic Algorithm

(GA) and KNN and achieved an accuracy of 89% on AR dataset and KNN+GA achieved an accuracy of 100%.

14.3 A Brief Overview of the Five ML Algorithms

A brief introduction to ML algorithms is in the following.

14.3.1 Support Vector Machine (SVM)

Support vector machine is used for the ramification linear and nonlinear data. The support vector machine is also known as SVM. It can transfer linear data into higher dimension data by the linear mapping method. SVM works by finding an optimal line that performs the partitioning of the dataset into two classes. This line is called a hyperplane. It uses a variable space containing two classes for 0 and 1. The hyperplane acts as a boundary between the two classes. SVM model will place the data across one side of the hyperplane producing classification. The distance between the nearest data points of the class is known as margin [5]. The hyperplane should be chosen such that the margin should be maximum [5]. If the margin is larger, then it means the hyperplane can distinguish between two classes in a better way [12]. In the SVM, the SVM kernel uses SVM and ML algorithms. The SVM kernel has two parts (RBF and POLY); they are used to distinguish between the similarity of vectors in the feature space by the ML algorithm of SVM that allows only the nonlinear models [13].

14.3.2 KNN

In this algorithm, the class of input data can be predicted based on the class of similar data in the training data. The classification of input data is done using the class of their neighbor. For finding out the neighbor, we use different distance measures [14]. It is a very lazy method in which functions are optimizing locally and computation is not done at the same time or postponed until the final classification is obtained. The class of data in test data is found by the class of k-nearest neighbors of that input data. If the dataset contains continuous variables, we can use the Euclidean distance to find out neighbors. If the dataset contains categorical variables, we use the hamming distance. If the dataset contains both continuous variables and categorical variables, then continuous variables are converted into categorical variables [15]. After finding the k-nearest neighbors, the class of data is predicted based on majority class. Suppose we use six nearest neighbors and the class of four neighbors is 1 and the class of two neighbors is 0, then the class of input data will be 1. K-mean algorithm is used for measuring the accuracy for dimensionality reduction that is conscientious for the attributes for the heart condition prediction, and the class label is not affected by them [13].

14.3.3 NB

NB algorithm is used for prediction modeling. By the exploitation of the Bayesian theorem, the Bayesian method is used as a classification method, taking the probability of each class and calculating the value of x for each class with conditional probability. According to Bayes' theorem, $P(A|B)=P(A)*P(B|A)/A(B)$, where $P(B|A)=P(A \cap B/P(B))$, so that the Bayesian classifier is used to estimate the conditional probability data and their instances of a class are classified as the higher conditional probability [16]. Probabilities in the probabilistic model to make predictions with new data implementation is called the NB theorem. This algorithm assumes the attribute value for a particular class, and other attributes take independent values [17,18].

14.3.4 DT

It is a type of SL that uses the method of categorical and continuous input and output variables [19]. It is the graphical representation of modules using the decision matrix analysis [20]. It is also an ensemble learning, which has some methods of classification, regression, and others. It has three nodes: decision nodes, fortuity nodes, and terminating nodes [12,21]. In the tree model, the leaves represent the class labels and branches represent conjunctions of features that lead to those class labels. The higher cognitive process unit evaluates the decision, and all class labels or external nodes are operated by this. Some of the child nodes are on the opposite side of external nodes [5]. A DT model is shown in Figure 14.1.

14.3.5 Logistic Regression

It is a model or method of ML. Data are taken as the field of statistics. This model can be used on the datasets having a binary classification. It analyzes the dataset by the values having one or more independent variables that distinguish between two classes [22]. The outcome is determined by the dichotomous variable. The logistic regression is the same as linear regression in which values can be calculated using the coefficients within each of the input variables [23]. The linear equation is $Y=b0+b1x$, where the $b0$ is constant and the slope is $b1$ that defines the steepness of the curve. The LR equation is

$$P = 1/(1+e-(b0+b1x)) \tag{14.1}$$

The logistic regression is responded by the variable y that is a binary variable that is autonomous factors [13,24].

14.4 Proposed Methodology

In this work, a heart disease dataset with 270 instances and 14 attributes was taken [11]. The implementation of the proposed method is done in Python Jupyter Notebook using the heart dataset (http://archive.ics.uci.edu/ml/datasets/statlog+(heart)).

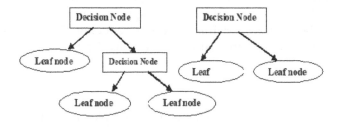

FIGURE 14.1
DT model.

1. Age of patient (years)
2. Sex – male=1, female=0
3. Chest pain type (CP)
4. Resting blood pressure in mmHg (restbps) (120/80)
5. Cholesterol (Chol) (170 mg/dL)
6. FBS (120 mg/dL, 100 mg/dL)
7. Restecg (electrocardiographic results in resting)
8. Maximum heart rate (MHR, Thalach)
9. Exang – exercise-induced angina
10. Oldpeak – exercise relative to ST depression
11. Slope for exercise ST segment
12. Ca-(fluoroscopy (number of major vessels 0–3))
13. Thal (normal=3, fixed defects=6, reversible defects=7)
14. Target (Tar) disease=0, disease=1.

In the first step, preprocessing of the data is done, which means cleaning the data so that the missing and noise data are removed. Then training and testing are performed on the given datasets using the ML algorithms, and finally, with the help of confusion matrix, it is checked whether a patient is suffering from heart disease or not. The proposed methodology is shown in Figure 14.2.

Figure 14.2 shows the attributes that are used to predict the heart disease, such as age, sex, and chest pain. If the target value is 0, heart disease is not present; if it is 1, it means

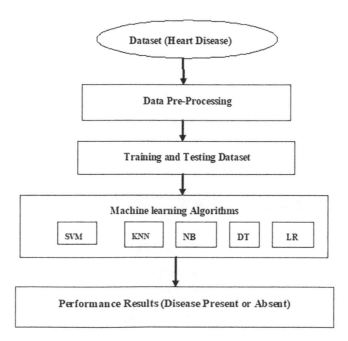

FIGURE 14.2
Proposed methodology.

heart disease is present; with the help of 13 attributes and ML algorithms, we can easily predict the disease with the target variable value.

14.4.1 Performance Evaluation Metrics

Classification accuracy is the rate of calculation of the correct classifications. It may be on some area of cross-validation or independent test set. It is used to evaluate the classification models. It is evaluated based on the predictions.

Classification Accuracy = Number of Correct Predictions/Total Number of Predictions * 100

In binary classification, it is calculated in terms of Pos and Neg as follows:

$$\text{Accuracy} = T\_Pos + T\_Neg + T\_Pos + T\_Neg + F\_Pos + F\_Neg \qquad (14.2)$$

The classification error is calculated as the percentage of incorrect predictions.

Classification Error = Incorrect Predictions/Total Number of Predictions * 100

In ML, each algorithm has different accuracy rates and error rates. It depends on their sample data and predictions [3].

14.5 Results and Discussion

By the following results using ML classifier, in existing related work. Figure 14.3 shows the results of accuracy of the proposed method used on the heart dataset. The results obtained using the proposed system in which SVM, KNN, NB, DT, and LR are used are reliable and significant.

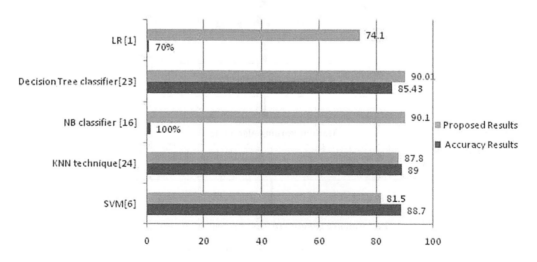

FIGURE 14.3
Accuracy results.

14.6 Conclusions

In this chapter, different ML types and their algorithms have been discussed. This chapter depicts heart disease dataset and compares proposed work to existing work in terms of accuracy. Different utilizations and numerous applications of ML are discussed with the help of the existing work. The existing work examines different ML methods proposed and used in various applications. In this chapter, an endeavor was made to audit the most habitually utilized ML techniques. This study used the Statlog dataset, and most of the researchers used different datasets and other classification techniques. Without approaching any technique, applying the training and testing on dataset gives better outcomes for the classifiers used in this study. This study shows how the ML plays a major role in recent technologies. In future, best algorithms could be implemented to get best results.

References

[1] P. Reddy, "Heart disease prediction using logistic regression algorithm using machine learning", *International Journal of Engineering and Advanced Technology (IJEAT)*, ISSN: 2249–8958, Vol. 8, Issue 3S, 659–662, February 2019.

[2] K. Das, R.N. Behera, "A survey on machine learning: concept, algorithms and applications", *International Journal of Innovative Research in Computer and Communication Engineering*, Vol. 5, 1301–1309, 2017.

[3] J. Qiu, Q. Wu, G. Ding, Y. Xu, S. Feng. "A survey of machine learning for big data processing", *EURASIP Journal on Advances in Signal Processing*, Vol. 2016, Issue 1, 2016. https://doi.org/10.1186/S13634-016-0355-X.

[4] A. Lakshmanarao, M. Shasha, "Survey on machine learning for cyber security", *International Journal of Scientific & Technology Research*, Vol. 9, Issue 01, 449–501, January 2020.

[5] S. Dargan, M. Kumar, M.R. Ayyagari, G. Kumar, "A survey of deep learning and its applications: a new paradigm to machine learning", *Architecture Computation Methods Engineering*, Vol. 27, 1071–1092, 2020. https://doi.org/10.1007/S11831-019-09344-W.

[6] S. Mohan, C. ThirumalaiAnd G. Srivastava, "Effective heart disease prediction using hybrid machine learning techniques", *IEEE Access*, Vol. 7, 81542–81554, 2019, https://doi.org/10.1109/ACCESS.2019.2923707.

[7] C. Beulah ChristalinLatha, S. CarolinJeeva, "Improving the accuracy of prediction of heart disease risk based on ensemble classification techniques", *Informatics in Medicine Unlocked*, Vol. 16, 100203, 2019.

[8] Ping-Feng Pai, Kuo-Chen Hung, Kuo-Ping Lin, "Tourism demand forecasting using novel hybrid system", *Expert Systems with Applications*, Vol. 41, 3691–3702, 2014.

[9] M.A. Jabbar, 2016, "Heart disease prediction system based on hidden naive Bayes classifier", *International Conference on Circuits, Controls, Communications and Computing (14C)*.

[10] S. Thaiparnit, S. Kritsanasung, and N. Chumuang, "A classification for patients with heart disease based on Hoeffding tree", *2019 16th International Joint Conference on Computer Science and Software Engineering (JCSSE)*, 352–357, 2019.

[11] M.A. Jabbar, B.L. Deekshatulu, P. Chandra. 2015. *Classification of Heart Disease Using K- Nearest Neighbor and Genetic Algorithm*. ArXiv, abs/1508.02061.

[12] Guang-Bin Huang, *An Insight into Extreme Learning Machines: Random Neurons, Random Features and Kernels*, Springer, 2014. 15.

[13] Taiwo Ayodele, "Types of Machine Learning Algorithms", 2010.

[14] S. Nashif, Md.R. Raihan, Md. R. Islam, M.H. Imam "Heart disease detection by using machine learning algorithms and a real-time cardiovascular health monitoring system", *World Journal of Engineering and Technology*, Vol. 6, 854–873, 2018. https://doi.org/10.4236/Wjet.2018.64057.

[15] Jason Brownlee, "A tour of machine learning algorithms", November 25, 2013; Jason Brownlee, "Machine learning tools", December 28, 2015.

[16] Aditi Gavhane, 2018. *Prediction of Heart Disease Using Machine Learning*, E, ISBN: 978-1-5386-0965-1.

[17] Xu Sun, Wangshu Sun, Jianzhou Wang, Yixin Zhang, Yining Gao, "Using a Greye Markov model optimized by cuckoo search algorithm to forecast the annual foreign tourist arrivals to China", *Tourism Management*, Vol. 52, 2016.

[18] http://archive.ics.uci.edu/ml/datasets/statlog+(heart).

[19] Alexis Fouilloy, Cyril Voyant, Gilles Notton, Fabrice Motte, Christophe Paoli, Marie-Laure Nivet, Emmanuel Guillot, Jeanlaurent Duchaud, "Solar irradiation prediction with machine learning: forecasting models selection method depending on weather variability", *Energy*, Vol. 165, 620–629, 2018.

[20] Yu Zhang, Yu Wang, Guoxu Zhou, Jing Jin, Bei Wang, Xingyu Wang, Andrzej Cichocki, "Multi-kernel extreme learning machine for EEG classification in brain-computer interfaces", *Expert Systems With Applications*, Vol. 96, 302–310, 2018.

[21] Yogesh Singh, Pradeep Kumar Bhatia Omprakash Sangwan "A review of studies in machine learning technique", *International Journal of Computer Science and Security*, Vol. 1, 70–84, 2007.

[22] Petersp, "The need for machine learning is everywhere" March 10, 2015.

[23] Spyros Makridakis, Evangelos Spiliotis, Vassilios Assimakopoulos, "Statistical and machine learning forecasting methods: concerns and ways forward", *Plos ONE*, Vol. 13, 2018.

[24] Teng Xiuyil, Gong Yuxia1, Research on application of machine learning in data mining, *IOP Conference Series: Materials Science and Engineering*, Vol. 392, 062202, 2018.

15

Breast Cancer Prognosis Using Machine Learning Approaches

Nadeem Yousuf Khanday and Shabir Ahmad Sofi

National Institute of Technology

CONTENTS

15.1 Introduction

In medical terms, cancer is an aberrant growth of cells which tend to propagate without stoppage and spread into surrounding tissues as well. It can involve any tissue, hence starts almost anywhere in the human body which contains trillions of cells. Mostly, the type of cell or organ where cancer originates gives the name to that type of cancer. In a healthy person, cells grow and divide to generate new cells when needed. Similarly, older cells or damaged cells die after a certain stage which is replaced by newly formed cells and the cycle repeats. However, this cycle breaks down when cancer develops. Abnormal cells continue to grow exponentially, damaged or older cells sustain when they should expire and new cells are formed when they are not needed. These extra cells further divide in an uncontrolled manner and may form aberrant growths called tumours which may result in masses of tissue.

DOI: 10.1201/9781003215981-15

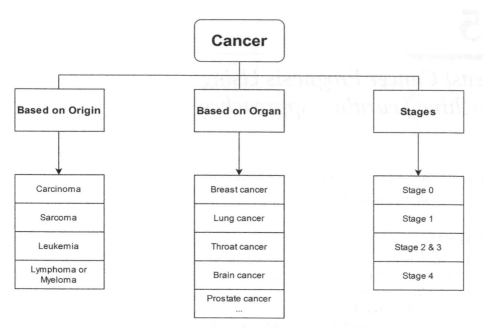

FIGURE 15.1
Classification of cancer.

Generally, cancer can be classified based on the organ in which they begin and the type of cell they are made of, even if they escalate to other parts of the body. General type of cancers with their clinical terms and stages are shown in Figure 15.1.

15.1.1 Breast Cancer

Cancer is a group of diseases and breast cancer is one of the leading cancer types in which cells in breast tissue change or reform abnormally and divides in an uncontrolled manner, typically emerged in a lump or mass [1]. Every year more than 2.7 million new cases for breast cancer are enrolled worldwide which is a primary cause of death in most cancer-affected women (one in eight women – 13% is having breast cancer in lifetime, However, breast cancer among men is rare, less than 1% suffers from breast cancer). As per GLOBOCAN statistics 2020 [2], breast cancer is the main cause of death among women followed by lung cancer (Figure 15.2). Around 14% of women expire due to cancer globally but 23% among them are cases of breast cancer. Lobules or the ducts that link these milk glands to the nipple are where mostly breast cancer starts. Breast cancer is contagious and has no symptoms when the tumour is small. Painless lump is the most common physical sign. Breast pain, swelling, thickening, nipple changes, etc. are other signs and symptoms of breast cancer. It gets worse if it spreads to underarm lymph nodes or other body parts.

Breast cancer is diagnosed during screening at early stages even when evidences have not matured or after a woman finds a lump. Different imaging tests to find breast cancer include mammograms, breast MRI, breast Ultrasound, digital breast tomosynthesis (3D mammography), molecular breast imaging, contrast-enhanced mammography, Positron emission mammography, optical imaging tests, breast-specific gamma Imaging, electrical impedance imaging and elastography.

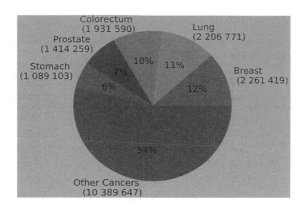

FIGURE 15.2
GLOBOCAN statistics of breast cancer 2020 [2], both sexes, all ages.

After imaging tests are done, biopsy is the only way to know the development of cancer. Although most breast lumps and masses on mammogram are not malignant (benign) but when suspected, needle biopsy or surgical biopsy plays a vital part in diagnosis (based on the size, location of the masses and other patient factors). Treatment options and prognosis are determined by the stage of cancer and its escalation at the time of diagnosis [3]. American Joint Committee on Cancer and Surveillance, Epidemiology, and End Results (SEER) are the two main staging systems used for clinical settings, statistical and descriptive analytics of tumour data. SEER summary stage system includes four stages which are mentioned below:

- Situ phase refers to just existence of aberrant cells but cancer has not yet developed.
- Local phase refers to cancer that is restrained to the breast only.
- Regional phase specifies to abnormal cancerous cells that have affected neighbouring lymph nodes or tissues also.
- Distant phase specifies to cancer when it has spread to other distant lymph nodes or organs also.

The two main variants of in situ breast cancer are lobular carcinoma in situ (LCIS) and Ductal carcinoma in situ (DCIS) [4]. However, LCIS also called as lobular neoplasia is mostly benign and not invasive, but DCIS is a precursor to invasive cancer (25%–53% progresses to breast cancer). However, 81% of breast cancers are invasive and grown into surrounding tissue. Based on shape, size, arrangement of breast cancer cells and through gene expression analysis, there exists different subtypes of breast cancer which are broadly categorized into two, namely **Histological** subtype and **Molecular** subtype.

Table 15.1 depicts that breast cancer occurrences and mortality rate increase with age. However, after the age of 80 years, it depicts but the reason may be non-screening. Median of 62 years of age was calculated to diagnose the breast cancer among women (Table 15.2).

15.2 Role of Machine Learning

Machine learning (ML) has a broad area of applications in medical sector, particularly those that rely on complex genomic and proteomic measurements. For cancer research,

TABLE 15.1

Shows the estimated DCIS and Invasive Breast Cancer Cases and Deaths among Women by Age, US, 2020 [4]

Age (Years)	DCIS Cases Number %		Invasive Cases Number %		Deaths Number %	
<40	1,170	2%	11,570	4%	1,270	3%
41–50	8,120	17%	37,350	14%	3,350	8%
51–60	12,630	26%	61,460	23%	7,560	18%
61–70	14,560	30%	74,520	28%	9,720	24%
71–80	8,670	18%	52,710	20%	8,710	21%
81+	2,750	6%	30,490	11%	11,250	27%
All ages	47,900		268,100		41,860	

TABLE 15.2

Based on Age, 10-year Probability of Breast Cancer Diagnosis or Mortality for Women in the United States [4]

Current Age	Diagnosed with Invasive Breast Cancer	Death Due to Breast Cancer
<20	(1 in 1,579) 0.1%	(1 in 18,403) <0.1%
21–30	(1 in 211) 0.5%	(1 in 2,026) <0.1%
31–40	(1 in 66) 1.5%	(1 in 635) 0.2%
41–50	(1 in 43) 2.4%	(1 in 312) 0.3%
51–60	(1 in 27) 3.5%	(1 in 195) 0.5%
61–70	(1 in 24) 4.1%	(1 in 133) 0.8%
71–80	(1 in 34) 3.0%	(1 in 103) 1.0%
Lifetime risk	(1 in 8) 12.8%	(1 in 39) 2.6%

Note: There is no previous record of any cancer disease among those included in Probability.

ML is not new. Over the past 20 years, the concepts of decision trees and artificial neural networks (ANNs) have been successfully used for the detection and diagnosis purposes. Nowadays, ML algorithms are successfully adopted in applications such as classification of tumours, segmentation of tumour parts from visual imagery, such as X-ray and CRT images, [5] and even from proteomic and genomic (micro array). Although breast cancer is the second major reason of death among women, researchers rose to all manners of challenges and working tirelessly to tackle this cancer by adopting the shreds of evidence of ML and artificial intelligence in alternate cancerous disease [6] to develop novel models, algorithm, methods, techniques and strategies. The new and ongoing developments of ML have shown satisfactory and stable results and undoubtedly improved the performance metrics for detection, screening, classification, segmentation, prediction, medication, treatment, etc. to decrease human intervention in biomedical practice [7]. ML methods improve 15%–25% accuracy of cancer susceptibility over simple statistical methods as per better designed and validated studies.

15.2.1 ML Methods

There are generally three variants of ML algorithms named as supervised learning, unsupervised learning and reinforcement learning. Supervised learning is the ML task in which models learn and get trained from the well "labelled" training data to predict better output. Actually, it learns a function that helps to map an input to the output based on sample input–output pairs. Student–teacher learning relationship is the best example of supervised learning. For regression and classification problems, supervised learning is the most suited.

Unsupervised learning, as the name suggests, it is a learning without any supervision. In unsupervised learning, training examples are given but labels are not assigned to them. It is the job of the learner or model to find the suitable hidden patterns or to discover the proper clusters or groups. Unsupervised learning is best suitable for clustering and association. It can be used for classification as well but not directly as in supervised learning. K-Nearest Neighbours (KNN), K-means clustering, self-organizing feature maps, principal component analysis, hierarchical clustering and anomaly detection are some prominent unsupervised learning algorithms.

In reinforcement learning, an agent or machine is allowed to learn its behaviour from its interactive environment by trial and error based on its feedback. For each and every action (good or bad), agent gets a reward (positive or negative) from the environment and uses this reward in training the model hence learns automatically without using any labelled data unlike supervised learning. Behaviours are learnt once and for all, or keep on adapting by experience as the time goes by because the ultimate goal is to improve the performance by getting maximum positive rewards.

15.2.2 ML Algorithms for Breast Cancer Prognosis

Medical and healthcare system is one of the primary application fields of ML where human intervention has been reduced drastically due to automatic detection, segmentation and classification of diseases particularly tumours. Most commonly used algorithms for breast cancer detection are briefly described in the following.

15.2.2.1 Naïve Bayes Classifier

Naïve Bayes classifier is simple in design and implementation and is a supervised ML classification algorithm [8]. It can be applied for both binary and multi-class classifications. It is based on the concept of Bayes theorem on probabilities (conditional probability). Training is fast because any trained Naïve Bayes model needs to calculate and store just a pair of probabilities, namely class probability and conditional probability. Class probability is for each class in training dataset, whereas conditional probability is for each input item given its class value. Mathematical representation of Bayes theorem can be shown as follows:

$$P(A|B) = \frac{P(A \cap B)}{P(B)} = \frac{P(A).\,P(B|A)}{P(B)} \tag{15.1}$$

where $P(A)$ is probability of A occurring, $P(A/B)$ is probability of A when B event is given, $P(B)$ is probability of happening of B, $P(B/A)$ is probability of B when A event has already occurred and $P(A \cap B)$ is probability of both A and B happening. Naïve Bayes can be easily extended to real-valued attributes by assuming Gaussian distribution as it supports continuous valued features.

$$P(x_i|y) = \frac{1}{\sqrt{2\pi\sigma^2}} \exp{-\frac{(x_i - \mu_y)^2}{2\sigma y^2}} \tag{15.2}$$

15.2.2.2 Decision Trees

Decision tree is a simple, supervised learning (non-parametric) and powerful predictive algorithm. Based on different conditions, it provides way to split the data. Tree structure is used for understanding and displaying decision trees in which leaf nodes hold a class label, internal nodes test on attributes and branches represent outcomes of the test [9]. Decision tree classifies the data by sorting it upside down the tree with root at its top. Output from decision tree is always TRUE or FALSE.

15.2.2.3 Support Vector Machine

Support vector machine (SVM) is a quite simple, persuasive, supervised learning algorithm and a commonly used classification approach in ML. Although it can be practiced both in classification and regression problems, it is most commonly adopted in classification problems with state-of-the-art results [10]. SVMs can handle multiple continuous and categorical variables. Hyperplane is created using support vectors which are extreme points of particular category. The objective of drawing hyperplane is to have maximum margin which provides maximum distance between extreme data points in each class. SVM can be linear if a single straight line classifies the data into two classes otherwise it is termed to be non-linear SVM classifier.

15.2.2.4 KNN

KNN stands for K-Nearest Neighbours algorithm which is simple in design, easy to implement and robust algorithm with more effective features when used for large datasets [11]. Although it can be practiced both in classification and regression problems, it is most commonly used in classification problems with high-performance metrics.

15.2.2.5 K-Means

In K-means, K is predefined non-overlapping clusters. It is an unsupervised learning algorithm which forms the clusters by grouping unlabelled dataset based on some criterion [12]. It assigns data points in such a way that it reduces the summation of distances between the data items and their respective cluster centroid.

15.2.2.6 Random Forest

Random forest is a simple, diverse and flexible supervised learning technique. It works on the concept of "ensemble learning" (bagging method). Random forest is an ensemble of decision trees which takes action on different subsets of the given dataset separately and finally merges them together by taking average to improve the predictive accuracy of that dataset [13]. Different decision trees are not only trained on different subsets of dataset but also use diverse features to make decisions.

15.2.2.7 Logistic Regression

Logistic model actually analyses the correlation between the number of independent variables and a categorical dependent variable, and fits data to a logistic curve after calculating the probability of occurrence of an event [14]. Logistic regression is based on logistic function also called as sigmoid function which is defined by the formula:

$$y = \frac{e^x}{1+e^x} = \frac{1}{1+e^{-x}} \tag{15.3}$$

The cost function for logistic regression function is:

$$\text{Cost}(h_\theta(x), y) = \begin{array}{ll} \text{Log}\,(h\theta(x)) & \text{if } y = 1 \\ \text{Log}\,(1 - h\theta(x)) & \text{if } y = 0 \end{array}$$

Cost function for logistic regression function is a non-convex function which makes sure of getting global optimum value and stable convergence as well.

Normally gradient descent algorithm is used to minimize the cost function. However, conjugate gradient, Broyden–Fletcher–Goldfarb–Shanno (BFGS) and limited memory BFGS are the most optimized algorithms used for minimization and convergence purpose which automatically adjusts the learning rate also. Logistic regression is used for binary classification and multi-class classification.

15.2.2.8 ANN

ANN is a computational model and is known as foundation of artificial intelligence. ANN is meant to mimic the behaviour of the human brain. ANNs are biologically inspired computer programs which provide self-learning capabilities to network and better results, provided they are fed with more data [15]. The basic types of ANNs are Feed-Forward neural network and Feed-Back neural network. Recurrent neural networks, convolutional and de-convolutional neural networks and modular neural networks are other advanced forms of ANNs.

Any ANN generally consists of three layers, namely input layer, output layer and hidden layer in between them. The structure of ANN provides flexibility, parallel processing capability, working with incomplete knowledge, robustness and fault tolerance. Aerospace, medical, military, time series prediction, electronics, telecommunication, speech and software are some application areas.

15.2.3 ML Approach for Breast Cancer Prognosis

Cancer is the extensive cause of death globally and is among the major concerns and threat to living world. As per the latest GLOBOCAN statistics for the year 2020 [2], breast cancer is the dominant cancer type followed by lung cancer [16] (Figure 15.1). Early detection of its symptoms and patterns can reduce the mortality rate and is more likely to respond to treatment [17]. The new and ongoing developments ML has shown satisfactory and stable results and undoubtedly improved the performance metrics for detection, screening, classification, segmentation, prediction, medication, treatment, etc. to decrease the human intervention in biomedical practice [7]. The process of cancer diagnosis can be performed in three stages (Figure 15.3). It includes clinical or physical examination which is the palpation of the breast that can give insights about the patterns or signs of appearance of cancer. After physical examination, medical imaging (mostly mammography, MRI and ultrasonography) is carried out for the detection of tumour masses. At this stage of ML methods, algorithms and techniques [18] play a vital role in automatic detection of tumour masses, and classify and segment them for further biopsy. Later, biopsy, aspiration or cytological

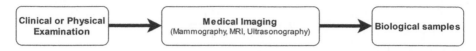

FIGURE 15.3
Chain of diagnosis process for breast cancer.

puncture and macrobiopsia are some techniques adopted to study the microscopic level of the lesions for proper diagnosis.

The whole process of diagnosis is divided internally into many steps. At each step, some techniques, methods and algorithms are adopted for better diagnosis. The pipeline of general ML approach for breast cancer prognosis is shown in Figure 15.4.

Step I: The first step is the selection of dataset which includes image acquisition (grey or RGB) and collection. Without detailed dataset, ML algorithm cannot be trained enough which results in overfitting. Data balancing is very important for better classification. Curated Breast Imaging subset of Digital Database of screening mammography (CBIS-DDSM)with 6,671 total visual imagery, Irvine Breast Cancer Wisconsin dataset, SEER dataset and PLCO dataset contributed by NCI, WBC original and diagnostic dataset are most prominent datasets used for training the learning models.

Step II: After getting the data, there is a demand for cleaning and pre-processing which adopts many techniques and methods based on the requirement. This step includes removing or at least reducing the noise using different filters (Gaussian filters, median filters, etc.) and also consistency of data has to be increased. Normalization is also carried out for feature scaling between its maximum and minimum values. Standard normal distribution is followed by rescaling the features which is called standardization of data. Both normalization and standardization helps to achieve better classification results. Augmentation can also be done to increase the number of data samples using rotation, flipping, cropping, translation, colour adjustments, etc. Adaptive contrast enhancement is often used with grey-scale images for better segmentation and visualisation results. Multiple imputation technique is used to substitute the missing observation to avoid inconsistency of data.

Step III: This step covers the heart of breast cancer prognosis system because the designing and core modelling of the system needs to be done here. If the data is not enough to train the model adequately, then the technique called "Transfer learning" can be used. In this we can use the structure of some pre-trained model (ResNet101, Inception v3, VGG 16, etc.) trained on some large dataset containing millions of images to be trained in our small dataset. If we have enough data, then we can skip transfer learning and find some suitable sampling strategy for efficient splitting of data into training, testing and validation set. Proper division of data helps to evaluate the classifier by finding its true error rate. Some primary sampling strategies include random sampling, K-fold cross-validation, holdout method and leave-one-out method. Training along with proper feature selection (size, age at diagnosis, stage, grade of tumour, etc.) is done to carry out the task of detection of tumour masses, their segmentation and classification for proper prognosis. Based on the results, model can make decision whether the subject is malignant or benign. After the computation of complex algorithms on trained data, there is demand to check the performance of the model using different strategies which include confusion matrix, sensitivity or recall, specificity and precision values.

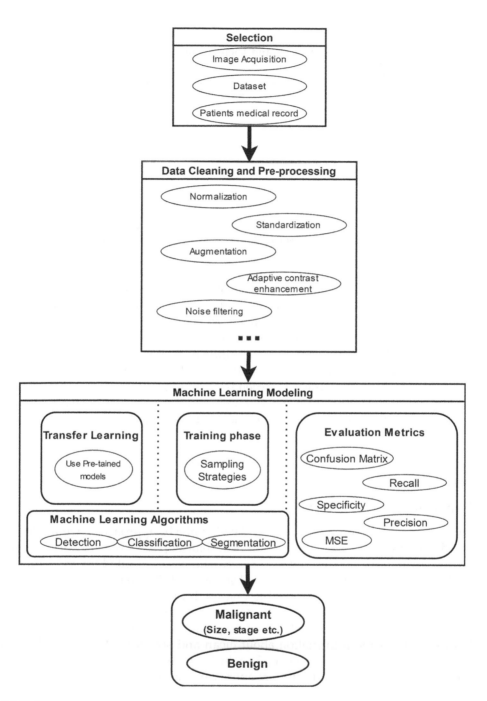

FIGURE 15.4
The pipeline of general ML approach for breast cancer prognosis.

TABLE 15.3

Performance Metrics Methods and Their Formulas Used for Evaluation

Evaluation Metric	Formula
Confusion matrix	$\dfrac{Tp+Tn}{Tp+Tn+Fp+Fn}$
Recall or sensitivity	$\dfrac{Tp}{Tp+Tn}$
Specificity	$\dfrac{Tn}{Tn+Fp}$
Precision	$\dfrac{Tp}{Tp+Fp}$

Tp, True positive; Fp, False positive; Tn, True negative; Fn, False negative.

Confusion matrix evaluates the performance of classifier by calculating its accuracy or inversely error rate (Table 15.3). Sensitivity or recall determines how many positive samples are correctly identified by a classifier. Specificity refers to how accurately classifier behaves while predicting the negative class. Proportion of the rightly predicted positive cases with respect to all predicted positive ones is determined by the precision value. Mean square error can also be used for measuring the accuracy of different prediction tasks which is determined by taking the difference between the original target value and the observed value while predicting. F-measure, Cohen's Kappa and Area Under Curve are some other metrics used to find the performance of the underlying ML model.

15.3 Experimental Summary

By following the above-mentioned general pipeline of ML approaches, we implemented different ML algorithms on Wisconsin diagnostic dataset [19] for breast cancer prognosis. Digitized image of a fine needle aspirate of a breast mass is adopted for the computation and selection of features. Overall, 569 data elements with 212 malignant and 357 benign elements are used for training and testing phase with portion of 70% and 30%, respectively. Features which are provided by the dataset include compactness, texture, smoothness, radius, area, perimeter, symmetry, concave points, concavity and fractal dimensions. Each feature contains the information about mean and standard deviation. The experimental results are summarized in Table 15.4 which contains information regarding accuracy, sensitivity and specificity of different approaches applied.

15.4 Challenges

Even though researchers are working tirelessly to improve the ongoing developments in the field of oncology, however, there exists some challenges which still needs to be addressed.

TABLE 15.4

Summarized Experimental Results of Different ML Approaches for Breast Cancer Prognosis

Parameter	GRU-SVM	Linear Regression	Multilayer Perceptron	L1-Nearest Neighbour	L2- Nearest Neighbour	Softmax Regression	Support Vector Machine	Random Forest
Accuracy	93.75%	96.093%	99.038%	93.567%	94.7368%	97.6785%	96.093%	96.37%
Data elements	385,000	385,000	512,998	175	175	385,000	385,000	569
Epochs	2,800	2,800	2,800	1	1	2800	2,800	1,000
False PR	16.66%	10.204%	1.267%	6.27%	9.385%	5.769%	6.3829%	NA
False NR	0	0	0.78615%	6.542%	2.8038%	0	2.47%	NA
Sensitivity	100%	100%	99.2138%	93.4589%	97.1962%	100%	97.53%	97.01%
Specificity	83.33%	89.795%	98.7329%	93.75%	90.625%	94.2307%	93.61%	97.01%

Some of these challenges can be lack of data which causes overfitting, large-scale datasets that are not only difficult to maintain but also lead to time complexity while training the model, data with high dimensions, data diversity, imbalanced datasets, choice of architecture, feature selection, interpretability or validation of approaches, computational costs to train the models and many more.

15.5 Conclusion

As discussed, breast cancer is the dominant and extensive type of cancer in the world as per GLOBOCAN statistics 2020. Mostly, it occurs in females although males suffer from this cancer. To reduce the death rate of breast cancer, its early detection and identification is necessary. Thanks to ML approaches which automate the process of detecting tumour masses with high-performance metrics and reduce human intervention. Deep insight of ML algorithms and their role in breast cancer prognosis has been explored. The pipeline of the general ML approach for breast cancer prognosis has also been exposed. Finally, some advanced challenges such as data scarcity, imbalanced datasets, dimensional-reduction and choice of architecture which need to be addressed for better results have also been explored.

References

[1] Harris, Jay R., Marc E. Lippman, Umberto Veronesi, and Walter Willett. "Breast cancer." *New England Journal of Medicine* 327, no. 5 (1992): 319–328.

[2] Global Cancer Observatory. 2021. Available at: <https://gco.iarc.fr/> (Accessed 28 July 2021).

[3] Key, Timothy J., Pia K. Verkasalo, and Emily Banks. "Epidemiology of breast cancer." *The Lancet Oncology* 2, no. 3 (2001): 133–140.

[4] Breast Cancer | Breast Cancer Information & Overview. [online] Cancer.org. Available at: <https://www.cancer.org/cancer/breast-cancer.html> (Accessed 30 June 2021).

[5] Abreu, Pedro Henriques, Miriam Seoane Santos, Miguel Henriques Abreu, Bruno Andrade, and Daniel Castro Silva. "Predicting breast cancer recurrence using machine learning techniques: a systematic review." *ACM Computing Surveys (CSUR)* 49, no. 3 (2016): 1–40.

[6] Khanday, Nadeem Yousuf, and Shabir Ahmad Sofi. "Deep insight: Convolutional neural network and its applications for COVID-19 prognosis." *Biomedical Signal Processing and Control* 69 (2021): 102814.

[7] Rezaei, Zahra. "A review on image-based approaches for breast cancer detection, segmentation, and classification." *Expert Systems with Applications* 182 (2021): 115204.

[8] Karabatak, Murat. "A new classifier for breast cancer detection based on Naïve Bayesian." *Measurement* 72 (2015): 32–36.

[9] Safavian, S. Rasoul, and David Landgrebe. "A survey of decision tree classifier methodology." *IEEE Transactions on Systems, Man, and Cybernetics* 21, no. 3 (1991): 660–674.

[10] Wang, Haifeng, Bichen Zheng, Sang Won Yoon, and Hoo Sang Ko. "A support vector machine-based ensemble algorithm for breast cancer diagnosis." *European Journal of Operational Research* 267, no. 2 (2018): 687–699.

[11] Medjahed, Seyyid Ahmed, Tamazouzt Ait Saadi, and Abdelkader Benyettou. "Breast cancer diagnosis by using k-nearest neighbor with different distances and classification rules." *International Journal of Computer Applications* 62, no. 1 (2013).

[12] Zheng, Bichen, San g Won Yoon, and Sarah S. Lam. "Breast cancer diagnosis based on feature extraction using a hybrid of K-means and support vector machine algorithms." *Expert Systems with Applications* 41, no. 4 (2014): 1476–1482.

[13] Wang, Sutong, Yuyan Wang, Dujuan Wang, Yunqiang Yin, Yanzhang Wang, and Yaochu Jin. "An improved random forest-based rule extraction method for breast cancer diagnosis." *Applied Soft Computing* 86 (2020): 105941.

[14] Ayer, Turgay, Jagpreet Chhatwal, Oguzhan Alagoz, Charles E. Kahn Jr, Ryan W. Woods, and Elizabeth S. Burnside. "Comparison of logistic regression and artificial neural network models in breast cancer risk estimation." *Radiographics* 30, no. 1 (2010): 13–22.

[15] Abiodun, Oludare Isaac, Aman Jantan, Abiodun Esther Omolara, Kemi Victoria Dada, Nachaat AbdElatif Mohamed, and Humaira Arshad. "State-of-the-art in artificial neural network applications: A survey." *Heliyon* 4, no. 11 (2018): e00938.

[16] Mushtaq Ahmad Shah, Nadeem Yousuf Khanday, Mridula Purohit, and M. H. Gulzar. "Enhancement and segmentation of lung ct images for efficient identification of cancerous cells." *International Journal of Electronics & Informatics* (2016), http://cennser.org/IJEI/eiV05N01/ei050102.pdf

[17] Elmore, Joann G., Katrina Armstrong, Constance D. Lehman, and Suzanne W. Fletcher. "Screening for breast cancer." *JAMA* 293, no. 10 (2005): 1245–1256.

[18] Khanday, Nadeem Yousuf, and Shabir Ahmad Sofi. "Taxonomy, state-of-the-art, challenges and applications of visual understanding: A review." *Computer Science Review* 40 (2021): 100374.

[19] Wolberg, William H., W. Nick Street, and Olvi L. Mangasarian. "Breast cancer wisconsin (diagnostic) data set [uci machine learning repository]." (1992).

16

Machine Learning-Based Active Contour Approach for the Recognition of Brain Tumor Progression

Amit Chopra
PEC-CCE

Dinesh C. Verma
Panipat Institute of Engineering & Technology

Rajneesh Gujral
M. M (Deemed to be) University

CONTENTS

16.1 Introduction

Disease recognition in medical imaging is quite complex and specialists are required to examine it accurately and improper observations may lead to an incorrect diagnosis. One of the most complex diseases is brain tumor. In this disease, brain cells may grow abnormally and it becomes very challenging to distinguish between healthy cells and affected cells and error-prone interpretation directly affects the treatment plan. There are numerous issues associated with the brain tumor detection process which are described below:

- **Disease Detection:** The tumor may grow over several years and its detection at early stages is a major challenge.
- **Parameter Identification:** In different patients, tumor attributes, such as its location, size, and growth interval, may vary. So its accurate detection is necessary for decision making.

DOI: 10.1201/9781003215981-16

- **Disease Categorization:** Tumor categorization is another major issue that may affect the diagnosis process.

The machine learning (ML) approach can be used for the automation of disease detection/-diagnosis process but the following are the limitations for the ML-based solutions:

- **Training Dataset:** A training dataset is required to build a training model that is used by ML schemes. It is prepared by a medical specialist but its sample collection accuracy depends on the knowledge and experience in the relevant domain.
- **Data Validation:** Validation of the collected knowledgebase is another major issue.
- **Lack of Standard Solutions:** For different diseases, there is a need to build training models and ML logic because there is no single remedy exists for all diseases.
- **Dataset Volume:** Training datasets may be quite large, so more it may increase the infrastructure/processing cost for the implementation of ML solutions.
- **Dataset Design:** Various researchers are engaged in ML research in medical imaging. There is a need to define some sort of standards to design the input datasets [1–5].

Brain tumor detection is a complex process and analysis of its growth over a certain period is very critical. To achieve this goal, this chapter introduces an ML method using active contour to analyze the tumor progression in sample input.

16.2 Literature Survey

The following sections describe the advancement in ML-based solutions in recent years.

16.2.1 Solutions for Automated Diagnosis

Badrigilan, Nabavi, Abin, Rostampour, Abedi and Shirvaniet al. [6] investigated the role of deep learning for the identification of various diseases (i.e. brain tumor and head/neck cancers). The study shows that classification, segmentation and grading of input can be used to improve the results.

Sharif, Li, Naz and Rashid [7] surveyed various deep learning approaches that can be used to detect different tumor types in the human body. The study found some common methods (classification/segmentation/feature extraction/neural network/support vector machine (SVM)) that are suitable for tumor detection. This study can be further utilized to develop more accurate diagnosis approaches.

Bagavathi [8] investigated the issues related to the analysis of medical image data related to brain diseases. It may be in the form of magnetic resonance imaging/functional magnetic resonance imaging/positron emission tomography, etc. These images contain the information of diseases and its manual interpretation is quite complex, and expert practitioners require 4d for its examination. Studies found that artificial intelligence (AI)–based processing of these image types can produce more accurate results and it can also boost the diagnosis process.

Kocher, Ruge, Galldiks and Lohmann [9] explored the role of automated diagnosis of brain tumor using ML methods. The study found some deficiencies in these schemes, i.e.

lack of standards for the methods to be used and the accuracy of all these also affected by the variations in medical imaging techniques.

16.2.2 Classification-Based solutions

Monteroa, V. esb, Nguyenc, Desbordesd and Macqd et al. [10] investigated the role of AI methods in the analysis of the medical domain. The study shows that ML can assist the diagnosis process and can also be used for the prediction/classification/decision making and diagnosis cost can be optimized. However, accurate input datasets are required for training model that directly affects the performance of AI-based solutions. The study data can be further utilized for the development of a medical expert system/automated clinical decision system for the healthcare industry.

Khan, Kader, Islam, Rahman, Kamal, UddinToha et al. [11] explored the role of machine/-deep learning for revealing various brain diseases (Parkinson/ epilepsy/tumor) and found that classification and feature extraction methods (principal component/correlation analysis/shearlet transformation/gaussian model/factorization) are very important for the processing of medical images. The study also found some other open issues associated with AI-based solutions, i.e. quality and availability of data, compatibility, data access, resource optimization, etc.

Kumar, Gupta, Arora and Raman [12] proposed a brain tumor classification method that uses an ML algorithm to recommend diagnosis instructions and it can also provide the estimation of residual lifespan of patients by calculating the grades of tumor. Analysis shows that it is more efficient as compared to traditional classification methods.

Kaplan, Kaya, Kuncan and MetinErtun [13] presented a scheme to classify brain tumor using feature extraction. It uses various parameters for classification, i.e. neighbor patterns, pixel attributes, intermediate distance and angle between them. Outcomes indicate that it can classify multiple types of brain tumor efficiently and can be utilized by practitioners in the real-time scenario.

Sharif, Amin, Raza, Almas Anjum, Afzal and Shad [14] proposed a method that performs automated segmentation with fuzzy logic to extract the features that are further processed by an ML method to produce output classification. For experiments, datasets of leaderboard-2013/MICCAI BraTS 2012–2015 were used and analysis shows that it offers higher accuracy in output and it can be further utilized with neural networks.

Swati, Zhaoc, Kabira, Alia, Alia, Ahmeda et al. [15] presented a brain tumor detection scheme by merging the classification and transfer learning algorithms. It uses the pre-trained models for precise tuning of extracted features followed by the validation process, and decision making is done based on the trial and error method. It can be further improved for multi-organ classification.

16.2.3 SVM-Based solutions

Chen, Zhang, Chen, Liang and Chen [16] proposed a scheme to detect brain tumor automatically using the combination of SVM and Kalman filter. Classification is performed to identify the region growth in a given cluster. Analysis shows that it outperforms in terms of specificity/accuracy/sensitivity as compared to traditional methods.

Shafi, Bayazid Rahman, Anwar, Halder and EmrulKays [17] developed a classifier/-prediction model using SVM. It extracts selective features and marks the region for classification followed by prediction process. Analysis shows that its performance is satisfactory and it also depends on the characteristics of the input dataset.

Khairandish, Sharma, Jain, Chatterjee and Jhanjhie [18] combined the Convolutional Neural Network (CNN) and SVM and performed segmentation over input data to detect/classify brain tumor. Analysis shows that it outperforms as compared to traditional classification methods.

Jalali and Kaur [19] explored various ML methods that can be used to detect brain tumor automatically. It includes SVM, K-nearest neighbor (KNN)/neural network/deep learning, etc. The study found that trained classifier, segmentation and feature extraction can improve the overall accuracy of automated detection schemes and this study can be utilized to develop selective classifier techniques for disease detection.

Akeret, Stumpo, Staartjes et al. [20] investigated the risks associated with the diagnosis of brain tumor and introduced a prediction scheme to analyze it using an ML approach. The analysis includes data related to topographic/histopathologic/demographic, etc. Results found that the generalized additive model is more accurate for prediction as compared to others (Random forest/Decision tree/generalized linear model/gradient boosting machine/radial kernel/neural network/SVM).

16.2.4 CNN-Based solutions

Woźniak, Siłka and Wieczorek [21] developed a correlation learning scheme using a CNN for the detection of brain tumors. It uses filters over layers to detect the presence of tumor regions. Analysis shows that its efficiency/accuracy is higher as compared to TensorFlow-based solution. Its performance can be further amended using biased filters.

Ramkumar, Prabu, Singh and Maheswaran [22] used Deep CNN Algorithm for brain tumor detection. It uses segmentation followed by classification over input data. Its output is further tuned using fuzzy logic. Investigational outcomes show that the hybrid solution is more efficient and precise as compared to traditional detection methods.

Hashemzehi, Mahdavi, Kheirabadi and Kame [23] developed a hybrid method that uses the combination of a CNN with a distributed estimation method to detect brain tumor. Classification is done using selective feature selection and a specific region is extracted. Analysis shows its performance in terms of higher detection accuracy and it can be extended for other medical imaging applications.

Mehrotra, Ansari, Agrawal and Anand [24] used pre-trained CNN models for the transfer learning and feature extraction of brain tumor. Finally, classification is performed by a Softmax classifier. For experiments, Cancer Imaging Archive dataset was used and results show that it outperforms in terms of higher accuracy as compared to existing schemes (i.e. SVM/KNN/genetic algorithm, etc.). However, it consumes more time during the training process, which is an open issue.

Siar and Teshnehlab [25] proposed a brain tumor identification scheme using neural networks with feature extraction. Interlinked layers are used with different classifiers (Softmax/decision tree/radial) and Softmax classifiers are more efficient and accurate than others, as illustrated by analysis.

Choudhury, Mahanty, Kumar and Mishra [26] proposed a brain tumor classification method. It uses a CNN to extract the features and later on, a classifier is applied over interlinked layers to generate output. Analysis indicates that it has optimal error rate/F-score/accuracy, etc.

Khan, Nazarian, Golilarz, Addeh, Li and Khan [27] presented a method to detect brain tumor using CNN. Tumor regions are marked through segmentation, and the outcome is directed to CNN for feature extraction. Selective feature strategy is adapted using SVM and the outcome is tuned using the black widow method. For experiments, BraTS 2015 dataset was used and analysis shows that it can be used for real-time diagnosis.

16.2.5 Active Contour–Based Solutions

Kumar, Panda and Agrawal [28] presented a method to recognize numerous types of brain tumors using an active contour approach. It finds the available regions based on their attributes. The largest one is highlighted as tumor region and the rest of all are excluded. Analysis shows that its detection accuracy varies with each tumor type and it is highest for Meningioma followed by the Pituitary type and average for Glioma type and its accuracy improvement is an open issue.

Badshah, Rabbani and Atta [29] developed an active contour-based scheme that marks the tumor region using Laplacian of Gaussian algorithm. Results show that it has average detection accuracy and cannot identify the presence of tumor in multiple regions and it is still an open issue.

Kot, Krawczyk, Siwek and Czwarnowski [30] developed a scheme to detect brain tumor using active contour. Analysis shows that it can efficiently identify the tumor and can also be used to produce 3D regions, and it outperforms as compared to existing schemes (Chan-Vese/ Contour Edge).

Soleymanifard and Hamghalam [31] merged the neural network with active contour to locate the presence of a tumor in the brain. A neural-network–based training model is used to mark regions and finally, contour segmentation extracts those regions. Analysis shows that marking of tumor region at local level produces more accurate/efficient outcomes as compared to existing schemes.

Thias, Al Mubarok, Handayani, Danudirdjo and Rajab [32] used an active contour approach to discover brain tumor. Outcomes display that using random shift, it has higher detection accuracy for meningioma, whereas it is average for others (glioma and pituitary).

Dake, Nguyen, Qi Yan and Kazi [33] introduced a scheme to track the tumor region using active contour. Using segmentation over input data, it can locate multiple regions and finally, active contour is used to detect the tumor inside the region. Analysis shows that it outperforms in terms of accuracy as compared to existing schemes.

16.2.6 Feature-Extraction–Based Solutions

Abbas, Khan, Ahmed and Song [34] developed a tumor detection method that uses ML-based segmentation for feature extraction/reduction. Projection-based classification is further used to reconstruct the regions to identify the exact location of tumor. Its performance was evaluated using various parameters (such as AUC–ROC/precise value/Dice and Jaccard Score). It can be further refined using different deep learning models.

Hemanth, Janardhan and Sujihelen [35] proposed a scheme to detect brain tumor at the primary phase using ML-based segmentation. First of all, it arranges the data for feature extraction and uses a classification approach to detect the tumor in input. Data mining is also performed to define the association between extracted features. The performance analysis indicates that it is more efficient and accurate in contrast to existing schemes (Neural Network/SVM/Random Field/Genetic Algorithm).

Rehman, Zia, Bojja, Yaqub, Jinchao and Arshid [36] proposed an ML-based brain tumor detection method that performs localization of tumor regions to extract their features/textures/-pixel information, etc. For analysis, MICCAI BraTS 2012 dataset was used and outcomes show that its performance depends on the training set used; however, it can detect the tumor regions efficiently. It can be further improved using the image classification approach.

Fatih and Sert [37] developed a brain tumor detection scheme using a fuzzy K-means algorithm and deployed it over the Raspberry platform. First of all, a training model is used at the initial stage followed by segmentation and finally, the distance between edges and pixels (boundary/ground truth) is calculated for decision making. Its performance was compared with the SVM using a metric (Figure of merid/Jaccard similarity coefficient/Dice index) and found satisfactory in terms of efficiency and accuracy.

Ucuzal, Yaşar and Çolak [38] developed a scheme for the classification of brain tumor categories. It performs feature extraction and classification at layer level and finally, optimization of output is done using the Bayesian algorithm. Its performance was compared using different parameters (G-mean/sensitivity/accuracy/precision/specificity/Matthew's Correlation Coefficient/F-Score) and analysis found that the values of these parameters vary w.r.t. tumor types.

Asodekar, Gore and Thakare [39] proposed a scheme to detect brain tumor using a selective feature extraction method over region attributes, and the classification of output is finalized using SVM and random forest algorithm. Analysis was done using MICCAI BraTS2015 dataset and results indicate that using random forest method, higher sensitivity/accuracy/ and specificity can be achieved in contrast to SVM.

Lathera and Singh [40] investigated various schemes to detect brain tumor. It includes deformable model/edge/region/threshold and a watershed scheme. The study indicates that its recognition is very complex and these schemes are less precise and experienced practitioners are required for decision making. This survey data can be used to refine existing methods.

16.3 ML-Based Active Contour Approach

Following are the steps of the proposed scheme (Figure 16.1):

Step 1: First of all, brain tumor progression data is obtained from The Cancer Imaging Archive (TCIA) [5] and arranged into a training dataset and a testing dataset (Figure 16.6).

Step 2: A decision-tree–based classification approach was used to identify the attributes from input samples (Figure 16.2)

Step 3: Figure 16.2 shows that input samples are categorized into pre-sample (taken at the initial stage) and post-sample (taken after some long interval) and then their features (region/location/size) are extracted w.r.t. each sample using Active Contour snake model that uses segmentation to mark the tumor area and finally, features are extracted in a given input. It can be derived through the following equation 16.1:

$$op = Lei(a_1, b_1) + Le_j |\nabla I(a_2, b_2)|^2 + \ldots + Le_n |\nabla I(a_n, b_n)| \tag{16.1}$$

where (a,b) are coordinates in 2D space, *Lei* is Line variable, *Lej* is Edge variable and *OP* is the output.

Variations in the values of *Lei* and *Lej* move the contour snake toward high-intensity areas in the image, and finally, the spline is used to mark the identified features (refer to equation 16.2):

$$V(s,t) = (a(s,t), b(s,t)) \tag{16.2}$$

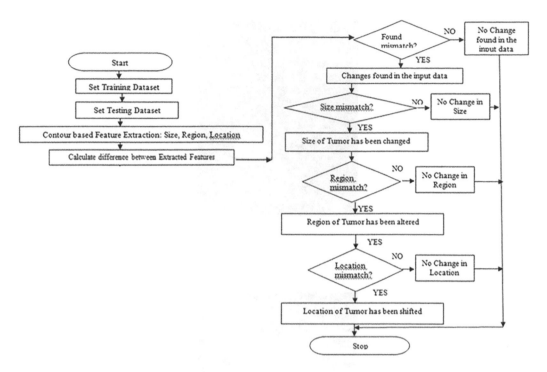

FIGURE 16.1
Decision-making about brain tumor progress.

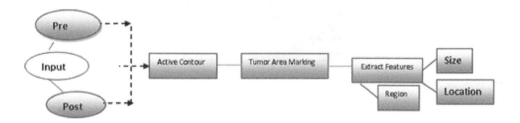

FIGURE 16.2
Decision tree for sample processing.

where v is Spline variable (0–1), S is linear variable (0–1) and T is interval

Outcomes of active contour snake include the following: (1) Tumor size in the brain that may vary and depend on its growth (Figure 16.3), (2) Tumor Region that may affect a particular area in the brain (Figure 16.4) and its location in the brain that may be anywhere in the brain (Figure 16.5).

Step 4: In this step, the difference between the previous samples and the new samples is calculated and if there is any difference then its progression is marked as 0 otherwise 1. Final decision-making is done by summing up these counts. Following Figure 16.6 shows a few samples used for training obtained from TCIA brain tumor progression dataset, and details are provided in Section 16.4.

FIGURE 16.3
Tumor size.

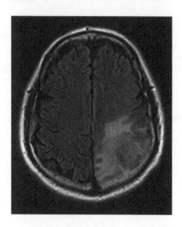

FIGURE 16.4
Tumor region.

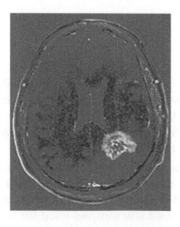

FIGURE 16.5
Location of tumor.

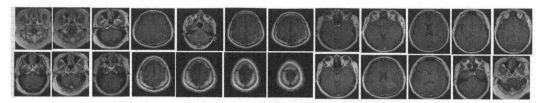

FIGURE 16.6
Sample brain tumor images used for training having 24 slices.

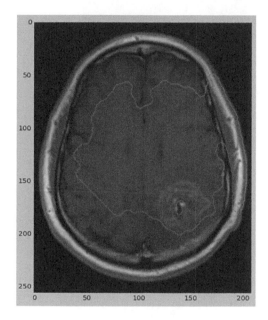

FIGURE 16.7
Active contour process-1.

16.4 Simulation and Performance Analysis

For experimental purposes, TCIA Brain Tumor Progression-2018 (3.2 GB) [5] was used for analysis purposes. It includes the 90-day study data of 20 glioblastoma patients (having surgery and concomitant chemoradiation/Chemotherapy) and 24 sample MRI images (DICOM format) per patient. Python and OpenCV-2 were used to interpret the MRI images over the Linux Platform. It includes two different scenarios for experiments as given below: **(1) ML-NAC:** Traditional ML (Without Active Contour method): In this scenario, a supervised learning approach was used and **(2) ML-WAC:** ML (With Active Contour method): In this scenario, a supervised learning approach with active contour was used.

Figures 16.7 and 16.8 show the active contour process over an input sample to mark the tumor area and Figure 16.9 shows the highlighted tumor region having 76.1 mm width and 116.8 mm height (in micrometer). The above process is repeated for all input samples to obtain the following data as shown in the tables given below. Table 16.1 shows various parameters, i.e. location coordinates, size and region of the tumor, and it also shows the

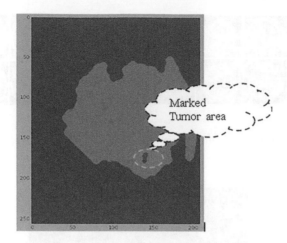

FIGURE 16.8
Active contour process-II.

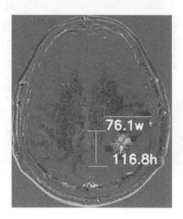

FIGURE 16.9
Highlighted tumor regions.

brief output for the decision making over brain tumor progression having 9 mismatched samples presented as 0 w.r.t. input and only 11 samples have no change presented as 1.

Figure 16.10 shows the brain tumor progression detection using the ML-NAC scheme. Analysis shows that there are fewer patients having tumor progression and Figure 16.11 shows the brain tumor progression detection using the ML-WAC scheme. Analysis shows that there are a higher number of patients having tumor progression.

Table 16.2 shows the brief output for the decision making over brain tumor progression having 16 mismatched samples w.r.t. input and only 4 samples have no change.

Table 16.2 displays the comparison of brain tumor progression over patients. ML-NAC successfully detected tumor progression (TPT) in 9 patients, whereas ML-WAC identified its growth in 16 patients. In the case of negative tumor growth (TPF), ML-NAC shows only 11 patients, whereas only 4 patients are considered by ML-WAC. Figure 16.12 shows the comparison of using different schemes (ML-NAC and ML-WAC). It shows that ML-WAC detected more patients having tumor progression in contrast to ML-NAC.

TABLE 16.1

Location Co-ordinates, Size, and Region of Brain Tumor in Samples

Input Sample	Co-ordinates (x, y)	Size (micrometer)	Region (micrometer)	ML-NAC	ML-WAC	Mutual Decision
		Brain Tumor		**Detected Brain Tumor Progression (YES: 0, NO: 1)**		
1	321.9264, 275.6726	30.1×79.8	2,401.98	0	0	Y
2	127.0144, 277.9853	37.3×139.5	5,203.35	1	1	Y
3	133.4899, 281.6856	46.8×102.3	4,787.64	0	0	Y
4	537.1902, 282.1482	42.3×99.7	4,217.31	1	0	N
5	241.8156, 281.6856	23.9×109.5	2,617.05	0	0	Y
6	347.3660, 277.5228	34.7×126.3	4,382.61	0	0	Y
7	355.2292, 270.1222	42.8×378.5	16,199.8	1	1	Y
8	362.1672, 263.1841	82.3×92.9	7,645.67	0	0	Y
9	383.0923, 258.5587	57.7×126.1	7,275.97	1	0	N
10	373.0923, 247.4578	49.2×68.2	3,355.44	1	1	Y
11	358.4669, 240.0572	33.5×78.6	2,633.1	1	0	N
12	323.8416, 236.3569	55.3×96.6	5,341.98	0	0	Y
13	350.6038, 229.8814	88.2×119.1	10,504.62	1	0	N
14	326.9035, 222.9433	97.4×221.9	21,613.06	0	0	Y
15	297.4868, 232.1941	79.1×227.4	17,987.34	1	0	N
16	262.3240, 237.7445	37.9×66.2	2,508.98	0	0	Y
17	147.4739, 172.8324	76.1×116.8	8,981.92	1	0	N
18	290.0113, 249.3080	80.7×79.5	6,415.65	1	1	Y
19	431.8615, 257.6337	48.3×88.2	4,260.06	1	0	N
20	297.4119, 267.8095	56.9×145.8	2,401.98	0	0	Y

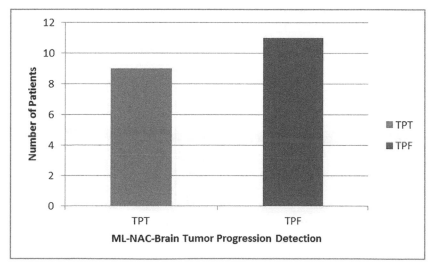

FIGURE 16.10

Brain tumor progression detection using ML-NAC.

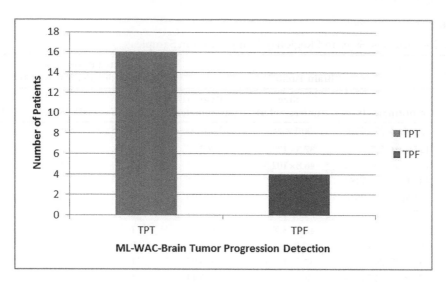

FIGURE 16.11
Brain tumor progression detection using ML-WAC.

TABLE 16.2

Comparison of Brain Tumor Progression Over Patients

Approaches	Tumor Progression: True (TPT)	Tumor Progression: False (TPF)
ML-NAC	9	11
ML-WAC	16	4

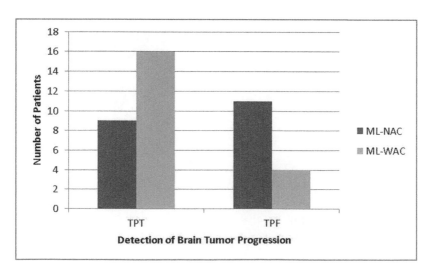

FIGURE 16.12
Brain Tumor progression comparisons.

TABLE 16.3

Detection Ratio

Scenarios	Detection Ratio
ML-NAC	45%
ML-WAC	80%

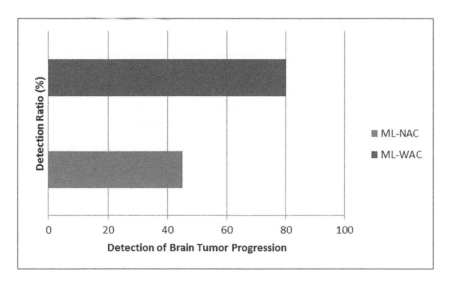

FIGURE 16.13
Detection ratio of brain tumor progression.

Table 16.3 shows the tumor detection ratio of ML-NAC and ML-WAC schemes. It shows that it is average for ML-NAC (45%), whereas it is 80% for ML-WAC (Figure 16.13).

As per Table 16.1, in case of a mutual decision, both schemes are agreed that there are nine patients having tumor progression where three patients have no tumor progression, and for eight patients, each scheme has its own decision.

Figure 16.14 shows that both schemes have higher value mutual decision (TPT-MD) for the progression of tumor w.r.t. input data. In case of no tumor progression, it is lowest (TPF-MD) and in some cases (TP-DD), both schemes have their own decision. The performance of ML-WAC was also compared to the relevant schemes developed by other authors (Table 16.4). It can be observed that ML-WAC and selective feature extraction offered by Asodekar, Gore and Thakare [39] outperform as compared to others.

16.5 Conclusion

Tracing the growth of a tumor in the brain is a quite complex process as it can appear in any location in the brain. Manual interpretation of the periodic MRI samples is a very time-consuming process and improper analysis of tumor growth may mislead the diagnosis process. In this chapter, this issue is highlighted and the contribution of ML for disease detection and diagnosis was explored and an ML-based approach was presented to keep

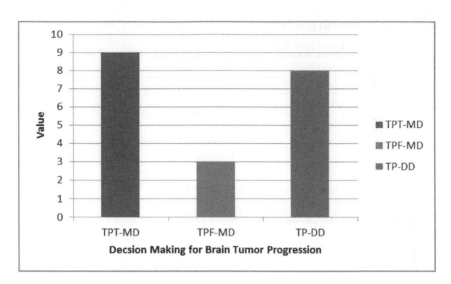

FIGURE 16.14
Mutual decisions over brain tumor progression.

TABLE 16.4

Comparison with Other Relevant Solutions

Authors	Accuracy (%)
S. B. Kumar, R. Panda and S. Agrawal [28]	56
A. H. Thias, A. F. Al Mubarok, A. Handayani, D. Danudirdjo and T. E. Rajab [32]	76.42
B. H. Asodekar, S. A. Gore and A. D. Thakare [39]	81.42
ML-WAC	80

the track of brain tumor growth in patients. It used the supervised learning method for training. Active contour was deployed for feature extraction and their matching was performed using decision trees.

The performance of ML-WAC was compared with the traditional ML-NAC method under the constraints of different parameters, i.e. detection ratio and decision making. Experiment results show that ML-WAC spotted more patients having tumor progression and delivered a higher detection ratio (80%) as compared to ML-NAC (45%) that just noticed the negative growth in tumor progression. In the case of decision making, both schemes are agreed in a few samples but also have different opinions in other cases. Both schemes have a higher value (9) for mutual decision over tumor progression and it is lowest for negative tumor growth (3).

The scope of this research work just considered the progression of a specific type of brain tumor. In the future, the analysis will be performed for other tumor types and it will be extended for other diseases such as liver and lung cancer.

References

[1] P. KaurChahal, S. Pandey and S. Goel, "A survey on brain tumor detection techniques for MR images" *Multimedia Tools and Applications* 79 (2020):21771–21814.

[2] F. Özyurt E. Sert, D. Avc, "An expert system for brain tumor detection: Fuzzy C-means with super resolution and convolutional neural network with extreme learning machine" *Medical Hypotheses* 134 (2020):1–8.

[3] G. SethuramRao and D. Vydeki, "Brain tumor detection approaches: A review" *International Conference on Smart Systems and Inventive Technology* (2018):479–488.

[4] T. Saba, "Recent advancement in cancer detection using machine learning: Systematic survey of decades, comparisons and challenges" *Journal of Infection and Public Health* 13 (9) (2020): 1274–1289.

[5] https://www.cancerimagingarchive.net

[6] S. Badrigilan, S. Nabavi, A. A. Abin, N. Rostampour, I. Abedi and A. Shirvani et al., *International Journal of Computer Assisted Radiology and Surgery* 16 (2021):529–542.

[7] M. I. Sharif, J. P. Li, J. Naz and I. Rashid, "A comprehensive review on multi-organs tumor detection based on machine learning" *Pattern Recognition Letters* 131 (2020):30–37.

[8] C. Bagavathi, "Machine learning for interpretation of brain images: A detailed analysis through survey" *International Conference on Computing, Communication and Intelligent Systems* (2021):48–53.

[9] M. Kocher, M. I. Ruge, N. Galldiks and P. Lohmann "Applications of radiomics and machine learning for radiotherapy of malignant brain tumors" *Strahlentherapie und Onkologie* 196 (2020):856–867.

[10] A. B. Monteroa, U. J., G. V. esb, D. Nguyenc, P. Desbordesd, B. Macqd et al., "Artificial intelligence and machine learning for medical imaging: A technology review" *PhysicaMedica* 83 (2021):242–256.

[11] P. Khan, M. F. Kader, S. M. R, Islam, A. B. Rahman, M. S. Kamal; M. UddinToha et al., "Machine learning and deep learning approaches for brain disease diagnosis: principles and recent advances" *IEEE Access* 9 (2021):37622–37655.

[12] R. Kumar, A. Gupta, H. S. Arora and B. Raman, "GRGE: Detection of gliomas using radiomics, ga features and extremely randomized trees" *International Conference on Information Networking* (2021):379–384.

[13] K. Kaplan, Y. Kaya, M. Kuncan and H. MetinErtun, "Brain tumor classification using modified local binary patterns (LBP) feature extraction methods" *Medical Hypotheses* 139 (2020):1–12.

[14] M. Sharif, J. Amin, M. Raza, M. Almas Anjum, H. Afzal and S. A. Shad, "Brain tumor detection based on extreme learning" *Neural Computing and Applications* 32 (2020):15975–15987.

[15] Z. N. K. Swati, Q. Zhaoc, M. Kabira, F. Alia, Z. Alia, S. Ahmeda et al., "Brain tumor classification for MR images using transfer learning and fine-tuning" *Computerized Medical Imaging and Graphics* 75 (2019):34–46.

[16] B. Chen, L. Zhang, H. Chen, K. Liang and X. Chen, "A novel extended kalman filter with support vector machine based method for the automatic diagnosis and segmentation of brain tumors" *Computer Methods and Programs in Biomedicine* 200 (2021):105797.

[17] A.S.M. Shafi, M. BayazidRahman, T. Anwar, R. S. Halder and H.M. EmrulKays, "Classification of brain tumors and auto-immune disease using ensemble learning" *Informatics in Medicine Unlocked* 24 (2021):1–8.

[18] M. O. Khairandish, M. Sharma, V. Jain, J. M. Chatterjee and N.Z. Jhanjhie, "A hybrid CNN-SVM threshold segmentation approach for tumor detection and classification of MRI Brain Images" *IRBM* (2021), https://doi.org/10.1016/j.irbm.2021.06.003

[19] V. Jalali and D. Kaur, "A study of classification and feature extraction techniques for brain tumor detection" *International Journal of Multimedia Information Retrieval* 9 (2020):271–290.

[20] K. Akeret, V. Stumpo, V. E. Staartjes et al., "Topographic brain tumor anatomy drives seizure risk and enables machine learning based prediction" *NeuroImage: Clinical* 28 (2020):1–16.

[21] M. Woźniak, J. Siłka and M. Wieczorek, "Deep neural network correlation learning mechanism for CT brain tumor detection" *Neural Computing and Applications* (2021):1–16.

[22] G. Ramkumar, R.T. Prabu, Ngangbam P. Singh and U.Maheswaran, "Experimental analysis of brain tumor detection system using Machine learning approach" *Materials Today: Proceeding* (2021), https://doi.org/10.1016/j.matpr.2021.01.246

[23] R. Hashemzehi, S. J. S. Mahdavi, M. Kheirabadi and S. R. Kame, "Detection of brain tumors from MRI images base on deep learning using hybrid model CNN and NADE" *Biocybernetics and Biomedical Engineering* 40 (3) (2020):1225–1232.

[24] R. Mehrotra, M.A. Ansari, R. Agrawal and R.S. Anand,"A Transfer Learning approach for AI-based classification of brain tumors" *Machine Learning with Applications* 2 (2020):1–12.

[25] M. Siar and M. Teshnehlab, "Brain tumor detection using deep neural network and machine learning algorithm" *International Conference on Computer and Knowledge Engineering* (2019):363–368.

[26] C. L. Choudhury, C. Mahanty, R. Kumar and B. K. Mishra, "Brain tumor detection and classification using convolutional neural network and deep neural network" *International Conference on Computer Science, Engineering and Applications* (2020):1–4.

[27] A. N. Khan, H. Nazarian, N. A. Golilarz, A. Addeh, J. P. Li and G. A. Khan, "Brain tumor classification using efficient deep features of MRI scans and support vector machine" *17th International Computer Conference on Wavelet Active Media Technology and Information Processing* (2020):314–318.

[28] S. B. Kumar, R. Panda and S. Agrawal, "Brain magnetic resonance image tumor detection and segmentation using edgeless active contour" *11th International Conference on Computing, Communication and Networking Technologies* (2020):1–7.

[29] N. Badshah, H. Rabbani and H. Atta, "On local active contour model for automatic detection of tumor inMRI and mammogram images" *Biomedical Signal Processing and Control* 60 (2020):1–20.

[30] E. Kot, Z. Krawczyk, K. Siwek and P. S. Czwarnowski, "U-Net and active contour methods for brain tumour segmentation and visualization" *International Joint Conference on Neural Networks* (2020):1–7.

[31] M. Soleymanifard and M. Hamghalam, "Segmentation of whole tumor using localized active contour and trained neural network in boundaries" *5th Conference on Knowledge Based Engineering and Innovation* (2019):739–744.

[32] A. H. Thias, A. F. Al Mubarok, A. Handayani, D. Danudirdjo and T. E. Rajab, "Brain tumor semi-automatic segmentation on MRI T1-weighted images using active contour models" *International Conference on Mechatronics, Robotics and Systems Engineering* (2019):217–221.

[33] S. S. Dake, M. Nguyen, W. Qi Yan and S. Kazi, "Human tumor detection using active contour and region growing segmentation" *4th International Conference and Workshops on Recent Advances and Innovations in Engineering* (2019): 1–5.

[34] K. Abbas, P. W. Khan, K. T. Ahmed and W. -C. Song, "Automatic brain tumor detection in medical imaging using machine learning" *International Conference on Information and Communication Technology Convergence* (2019):531–536.

[35] G. Hemanth, M. Janardhan and L. Sujihelen, "Design and implementing brain tumor detection using machine learning approach" *3rd International Conference on Trends in Electronics and Informatics* (2019) pp. 1289–1294.

[36] Z. U. Rehman, M. S. Zia, G. R. Bojja, M. Yaqub, F. Jinchao and K. Arshid,"Texture based localization of a brain tumor from MR-images by using a machine learning approach" *Medical Hypotheses* 141, (2020):1–12.

[37] Fatih S and E. Sert, "Brain tumor segmentation approach based on the extreme learning machine and significantly fast and robust Fuzzy C-Means clustering algorithms running on raspberry pi hardware" *Medical Hypotheses* 136 (2020):1–67.

[38] H. Ucuzal, Ş. YAŞAR and C. Çolak, "Classification of brain tumor types by deep learning with convolutional neural network on magnetic resonance images using a developed web-based interface" *3rd International Symposium on Multidisciplinary Studies and Innovative Technologies* (2019): 1–5.

[39] B. H. Asodekar, S. A. Gore and A. D. Thakare, "Brain tumor analysis based on shape features of mri using machine learning" *5th International Conference On Computing, Communication, Control And Automation* (2019): 1–5.

[40] M. Lathera, P. Singh "Investigating brain tumor segmentation and detection techniques" *Procedia Computer Science* 167 (2020):121–130.

17

A Deep Neural Networks-Based Cost-Effective Framework for Diabetic Retinopathy Detection

Pawan Kumar Upadhyay, Siddharth Batra, and Sunny Dhama
Jaypee Institute of Information Technology

CONTENTS

17.1 Introduction

Diabetes is increasing day by day and has spread vastly across the globe, especially in the urban areas and metropolitan cities. Diabetes is a severe disease that can affect the patient's life in endless ways. It creates a lot of stress for managing everyday tasks with all the precautions, managing blood glucose levels, having to control the food intake, type and quantity. On top of that, there has always been a worry of developing complications. This disease also generates a lot of monetary losses and draining a significant part of the savings on tests and medications. Although even if good care is not taken, this disease can develop major complications in various anatomical regions of the human body. One such artefact is Diabetic Retinopathy (DR), and it majorly affects the human vision. This demands an automation in the ocular disease prediction and wants to require a robust computer-aided diagnostic system which revolutionizes the disease detection in the eye region. In addition to this, the observatory symptoms are blocked blood vessels and damage to the light-sensitive tissues at the retina. In the initial phase of the disease, it does not show any symptoms or show only mild vision problems. As the stages increases, it causes complete blindness. Furthermore, it also evaluated with semi-stages and marked symptoms of vision loss, impaired colour, blurred, dark or empty spots in the vision.

Inertial Effects of DR: Type 1 and Type 2 diabetic patients are more likely to be prone to the DR or any ocular disorder. As the duration of diabetes increases, the amount of sugar proportionally increases to the likeness of getting this disease as discussed by Raju et al.

DOI: 10.1201/9781003215981-17

(2017). The high percentage of sugar in your blood vessels can be the cause of DR, and it blocks the tiny vessels in the retina and depletes the retina of fresh blood; as a result, the retina tries to grow new blood vessels which are comparatively weak and can leak as depicted by Khan et al. (2019). In addition to this, taxonomy describes **Severity of DR:** DR can also lead to several other eye disorders, out of them, one is *Diabetic Macular Oedema* that happens when blood vessels in the retina leak fluid, swelling of the macula and hence making the vision blurry (Wan et al., 2018; Chakrabarty, 2018). Moreover, most commonly found in India is *Neovascular glaucoma* that happens when blood vessels grow out of retina abnormally blocking any fluid to drain out of the eye (Sinthanayothin et al., 2002). Furthermore, a common abnormality in old-age persons is *Retinal Detachment* that happens when scars are formed in the back of retina, which pulls the retina away from the back of the eye creating dark spots in the vision. In addition to this, Mahendran and Dhanasekaran (2015) develop a framework for DR detection using recorded image samples and providing a complete solution of telemedicine.

Computer-aided screening systems recently utter a lot of importance, owing to their increase in the viability of DR detection. Various machine learning algorithms were developed and deployed for the detection of ocular abnormalities. In India, DR is only detected at a later stage, not due to lack of funds but lack of awareness. The other major reason would be the lack of facilities and resources available in the remote area. Keeping this idea, a new proposal for cross-platform mobile application has been developed for ocular disease (DR) detection at various stages. The novice framework, discussed in this chapter is fully automated, fast and accurate for DR detection.

The sections in the chapter are organized as follows. Section 17.2 draws the comparison of the proposed framework with existing systems. In addition to this, Section 17.3 describes the methodology of our framework. Moreover, Section 17.4 depicts the obtained results and evaluates the efficiency of the proposed framework. Furthermore, Section 17.5 discusses the remarks to conclude the article.

17.2 Related Work

Research and development in the field on computer-aided diagnosis (CAD) is apparently increasing in recent times, Sinthanayothin et al. (2002). The large-scale applications related to CAD are based on deep learning and computer vision, which has been developed to benefit the society. These are related to current technologies, which are continuously updated day by day and able to solve complex problems of the routine life, Khan et al. (2019). In healthcare system, these technologies have remarkably improved the non-invasive diagnosis methods and easing a lot of the actual work of medical experts (Jones and Edwards, 2010; Kahn and Milton, 1980).

Priya and Aruna (2013) have drawn a comparison of methods for detecting DR by various classifiers such as Bayes Classifier, Probabilistic Neural Network (PNN) and support vector machine (SVM). Out of them, the approach that provides high accuracies is PNN, attaining an accuracy of 89.6%, Bayes Classifier achieves an accuracy of 94.4% and SVM achieves an accuracy of 97.6%. They considered 350 images for system training; the use of less number of images in the dataset does not provide a substantial result and these accuracies can change when subject to more images. In addition to this, Colas et al. (2016)

proposed the solution, which helps them to statistically analyse the disease pattern and improvise the disease detection process. This work is based on similar dataset and obtained the sensitivity of 96.2% and specificity of 66.6% for identifying the referable DR. Their algorithm showed promising results on the dataset, but achieved a low sensitivity score; it also signifies that if the patient is referable or not.

Researchers have employed various deep learning techniques such as Convolutional Neural Network (CNN), Deep Neural Networks, Faster-Recurring CNN, Recurring CNN or Residual Neural Networks, depicted in the articles of Khan et al. (2019), Wan et al. (2018) and Dutta et al. (2018). They provide an empirical model and algorithms for detecting the DR. This development requires to connect the entitled patients with the doctor along with the disease prediction. Doshi et al. (2016) proposed the model for predicting DR using CNN. They showed promising results and achieved a kappa score of 0.3996. However, their dataset was not distributed evenly having 73.48% of images that showed negative results or not able to detect DR. This was due to uneven distribution of samples in the dataset, which were solely responsible for not obtaining the accurate predictions for positive DR. Moreover, Wan et al. (2018) in their work proposed a solution using CNNs and transfer learning. They compared different major models of DL such as AlexNet, VggNet, GoogleNet and ResNet and analysed their performance for DR detection. By tuning the hyperparameters of existing models using transfer learning, they were able to reach a classification accuracy of 95.68%. The obtained solution also does not indicate the use of the model in an application which can solve the problem of outreach and connecting remote patients. In addition to this, a related work of Dutta et al. (2018), proposed a comparison between different techniques of back propagation neural networks, deep neural networks and CNNs. This work majorly focused on identifying features such as blood vessels, fluid drip to classify different categories of exudates, haemorrhages and micro aneurysms. They further used C-means algorithm to identify the target class thresholds. Although, their work has the potential to identify the severity of the disease by taking into account different affected features and the obtained accuracy for back propagation neural network is 42%, in deep neural network, i.e. 86.3% and 78.3% for CNN. Furthermore, this solution does not involve its use as an application for solving the problem of outreach and connecting remote users.

Deep learning/Machine learning has been used for diagnostic applications, and detecting DR has been discussed by various researchers and scientists, but they did not advocate for the complete solution as a singleton framework, which are able to connect remote patients with appropriate doctors. The required applications completely fulfil the issues of funding from non-governmental organization (NGO) to different patients, if they required it for their treatment. Even though various solutions have been provided in the direction of DR detection, out of them, majority belongs to deep network models of Chakrabarty (2018), Rahim et al. (2016), Salamat et al. (2019), evaluated on a benchmark dataset of fundus images or any other modality of DR image dataset (Jitpakdee et al., 2012). Due to the lack of infrastructure or resources for disease diagnosis, including the availability of medical expert. In such situations, the best possible way to reach the remote sectors of society and identify this disease is by implementing a mobile application and connecting the doctors to the entitled patients. This demands a secure, efficient and cost-effective framework for connecting the patients, doctors and NGOs. All the requirements which are constraints in the existing approaches are achieved by our proposed framework, and ensuring the high participation of the patients due to better facilities and greater outreach. A detailed view of this proposal and an explanation of the complete procedure involved in our approach has been presented in the next section.

17.3 Methodology

The proposed framework for the DR detection is discussed in this section. This framework simplifies the DR diagnostic system non-invasively. It catered the services in user-friendly mode and kept their experience very seamlessly. The framework attributes and the developed blocks were well depicted in the subsequent section. The functionality of this framework is very interactive, which is remarkably explained in the following steps:

- The entitled user creates his/her account to participate in the application and its login registry information was updated in the database. Then, the registered user uploads the image samples from their end to the host server. The servers would then revert back with the response of exact prediction.

- The detection process consists of 24-layer deep model based on a CNN to detect the abnormalities in the input image sample and generate a report and referenced to the user for future diagnosis as well; there are other interactive attributes of this framework. The next subsection describes the complete system, as two of the modules of the framework; first, as a proposed computational CNN for processing and second, as an application interface.

- Another important feature is the appointment booking with the doctor. All the doctors are rated which are available to provide their services. In addition to this, there is a fund-raising solution for the economically weaker section by the method of crowdsourcing. All the records of the funds transferred are public preventing by the block chaining methods. In future, linking with various fund authorities such as NGOs and aided hospitals will help to support economically weaker section of the society.

17.3.1 Proposed Computational CNN

The proposed network is constructed in a way that it receives an input and predicts an output based on the class or grades of DR. The detection unit for DR is based on CNNs. These are the following steps to execute the model (Figure 17.1).

17.3.1.1 Preprocessing of Dataset

Image augmentation and number of image samples directly impact the results of computational network used in the framework. The images had to be re-scaled and kept in the similar colour model to get an evenly distributed dataset of images. These images are transformed to 256×256×3 taking RGB values into consideration.

Algorithm 1 Preprocessing

procedure CONVERT-IMAGE(*image*)
    image ← RESIZEIMAGE(*image*)
    image ← COLORCORRECTIMAGE(*image*)
    imageArray ← CONVERTTOARRAY(*image*)
    imageArray ← SCALEARRAY
    imageArray ← AUGMENTIMAGE(*image*)
    return *imageArray*

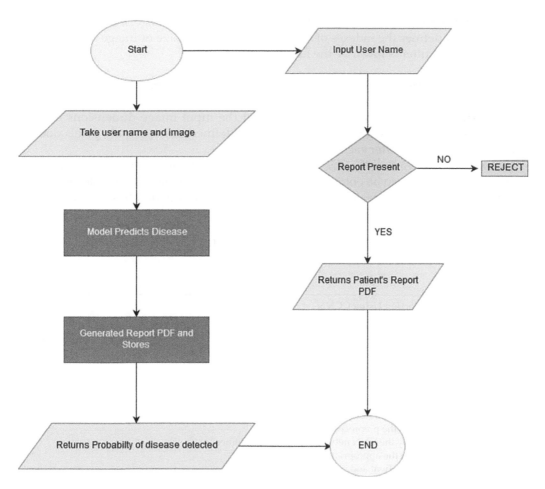

FIGURE 17.1
Flow diagram of framework.

17.3.1.2 Functionality of Proposed Convolutional Network

Detection of abnormalities from the images using CNN follows certain steps. These steps are defined below:

- Image consisting of pixels to generate features out of these pixels, various sizes of filters are used to extract the information as features vectors as edges, lines and curves. Detecting edges of the retina and haemorrhages in the retinal image allow us to better localise it and remove the unwanted clutter.

- Convolutional layer is responsible to extract the features by passing the image through high-pass filters where pixel change occurs very quickly with high intensity. Now to explain how features are extracted, we take a filter (kernel). We pass this kernel over different sectors of our image and obtain a matrix which is called the feature map of the image. This feature map(G) is calculated based on the following formula:

$$G[m,n] = (f*h)[m,n] = \sum_j \sum_k h[j,k][m-j,n-k]$$ (17.1)

where G defines the feature map matrix, f defines the input image, h defines the kernel matrix, m and n defines the indexes of the kernel matrix. The size of image after passing it through a layer of filter is given by the following formula:

$$\text{Size}(G) = \left(\text{Size}(f) - \text{Size}(h) + 2 \times \text{Padding}\right) \times \text{Stride} + 1 \tag{17.2}$$

where padding is the extra layer added such that the input image dimensions even out with the dimensions of the kernel matrix. Stride is defined as how many pixels does the kernel matrix is shifted after each computation.

The next step is to reduce the size of the image feature vector for better localization of abnormal region. This can be obtained using the max pooling method. In addition to this, to predict the class label of feature vector, RseLU activation function has been used in the network layer (Table 17.1).

$$ReLU(x) = \begin{array}{ll} x & \text{if} \quad x >= 0, \\ 0 & \text{if} \quad x < 0 \end{array} \tag{3}$$

Algorithm 2 Disease Detection Using CCNN

I-O

Input: *FundusImage*

Output *DR – Positive/Negative*

procedure Detection of DR(*image*)

1: Obtain the patient record as image samples.
2: From the base64 image obtained from the user, create the image.
3: Pass the image sample into the preprocessing Algorithm 1.
4: Feed the image obtained by the CNN network for the probabilities.
5: Match the probability with the appropriate class.
6: Generate the report of the patient and provide it back to them.

17.3.2 Framework User Interface

For the DR model, better representation has been developed as user-friendly interface to avail the services in a simplified way. The complete development of this framework is on "React Native" technology on an inter-operable platforms such as Android and iOS platform. The various attributes of the user interface (UI) are discussed below:

Instant Report: The user can easily select the image from the phone gallery and with just one click, it will get uploaded to our server which is hosted on Azure and within a matter of seconds he or she can get the report. We have selected a threshold value for a particular person, if the value is very low, then we mark him as negative and if it crosses the threshold, we mark him as positive. The user needs to record an image, and it has to be uploaded on the server, our model consider a recorded sample image as an input.

Interface with Doctors/Medical Experts: If our model predicts that a certain person has Retinopathic eye, he or she can directly book an appointment with a doctor with just one click. With the help of this feature, the user need not worry about the doctor availability, our framework provides the best available doctors around him/her vicinity. Finding a good doctor is a very crucial part and we simplify it for the user.

TABLE 17.1

Layered Structure of proposed CNN Model

Layer	Output Shape	Features
Conv2D	32×32	64
Conv2D	32×32	64
Conv2D	16×16	64
Conv2D	16×16	32
Conv2D	16×16	32
Normalisation layer	N/A	N/A
Max Pooling	8×8	32
Conv2D	8×8	32
Conv2D	8×8	32
MaxPooling	4×4	32
Conv2D	4×4	32
Conv2D	4×4	32
Conv2D	4×4	32
MaxPooling	2×2	32
Flatten	N/A	N/A
ReLu activation	N/A	N/A
Dense	N/A	N/A
Normalisation layer	N/A	N/A
ReLu activation	N/A	N/A
Dropout	N/A	1,024
Dense	N/A	1,024
ReLu activation	N/A	N/A
Dense	N/A	2
Softmax activation	Fully connected layer	

Fund-Raising: A person goes to the doctor, If he/she has not enough money to pay for it, then with the doctor's confirmation he/she can raise a request through this application to receive donations from people who want to donate. This feature is known as Crowdfunding. This is a very important feature, in which anyone can donate to the entitled patients and resultant log highlighted the contribution and also marked the number of time a single person benefitted or contributed.

Inculcation of Blockchain security (BS): In this chapter, Blockchain incorporated to make the donation process to make them secure, so that if someone donates money to a particular person through this platform, he/she will know that the entire money is going to the account of that person without any glitch, and that can be ensured by blockchain technology. For implementing the Blockchain, we used the Matic Framework. The role of secure transactions is well depicted in Figure 17.2.

As blockchain technology uses a public ledger, all transactions are shown publicly. Therefore, when a donor wants to help a patient, he/she can track the money donated. Every patient is assigned a hospital with a unique blockchain address, this is to verify that the funds transferred are completely secure. Every transaction gets stored as a blockchain hashed address in the database with encrypted metadata of patient details linked to it,

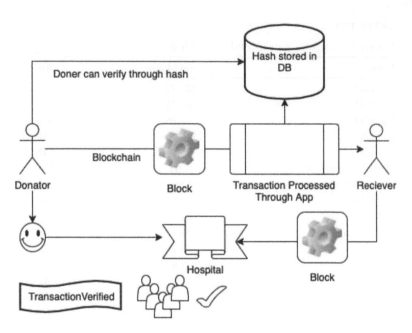

FIGURE 17.2
Use of blockchain in the novel framework.

so the donor may log into the framework and seamlessly track his/her fund. This makes the system robust and secure and develop the ample trust of entitled user as a donor. The main attributes of BS keep every transaction transparent and urge maximum trust of the donors, which in turn increases donor retention and recommendations to use this framework increases which may eventually lead to better usability of this platform.

Locate the Available Medical Experts: The authors have also given a feature to search for nearby doctors, suppose if someone tests positive, according to this framework, then he/she can select the nearby doctor for consultation. For this feature, author takes into account the location of the entitled user and after getting the location, the same can be displayed as results to the available doctors, as shown in Figures 17.3 and 17.4.

Mode of Interaction: These are implemented as a chatbot to ease the process of the request and providing the services. Another mode is voice or call to the doctor, this feature can only be used when the patient's report has crossed the minimum threshold value and even after consulting the doctor, with the help of this feature they can easily connect with the doctors in times of emergencies.

17.4 Results and Discussion

Every Image in the dataset has been classified into two different categories as positive and negative sample of DR. All the image samples are according to the international standards as denoted by Proposed Clinical DR. The positive/negative system considers the cases with no DR and mild DR. The primary step is preprocessing of images. The preprocessing method, minimizes the artefacts in the entitled image and concentrate only on the lesion

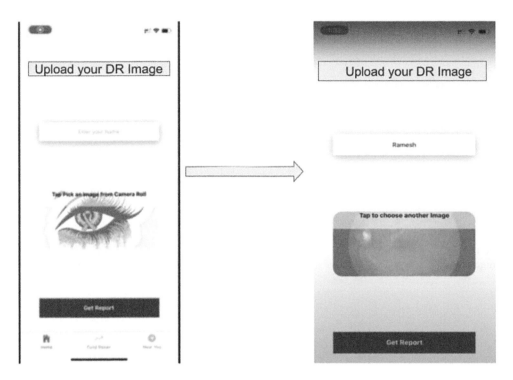

FIGURE 17.3
Framework UI for DR.

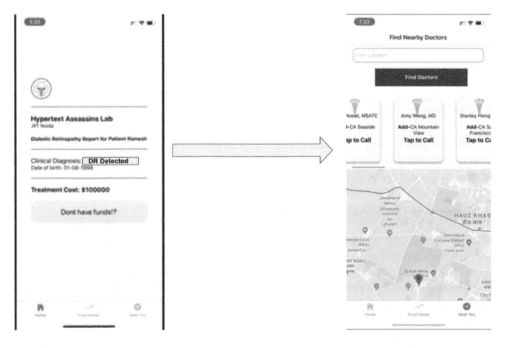

FIGURE 17.4
Framework features: Medical expert location and rating.

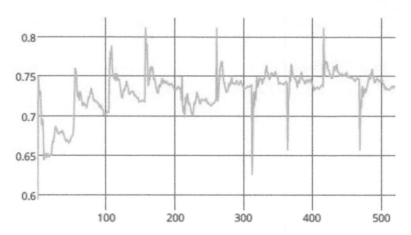

FIGURE 17.5
Training accuracy.

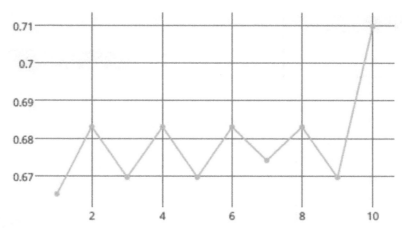

FIGURE 17.6
Validation accuracy.

region. The preprocessing included cropping of images and then resizing. The image was cropped to a size of 224 x 224 pixels after that background subtraction has been performed.

The processed datasets, further divided into Training and Validation sets. The training and validation sets were in the ratio of 80% and 20% of the total dataset size. Each of the training data was marked properly as per the grading. The obtained accuracy and loss depicted during training and validation are shown in Figures 17.5–17.8.

The model consisted of 24 layers. Images were augmented to increase the robustness in the obtained parameter as accuracy. The data augmentation includes rotation, scaling and shifting. This also led to a significant boost in the performance of the model in the classification of the images. Softmax activation function was used as the fully connected layer for defining the output of the model. Dropout layers were added to the model to overcome the overfitting obtained in the performance of the model.

The model was trained with a batch size of 32, epochs count is 15. The result obtained at learning rate of 0.001 and decay constant, adam optimiser was used to optimize the results by faster convergence of losses.

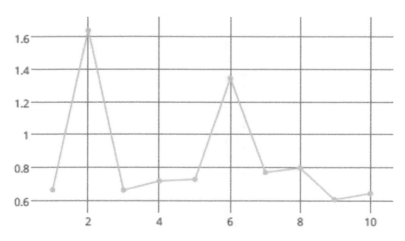

FIGURE 17.7
Validation loss.

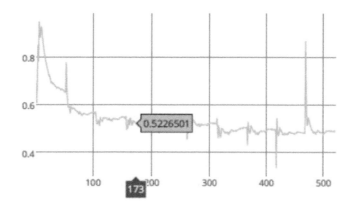

FIGURE 17.8
Training loss.

TABLE 17.2

Confusion Matrix for the Model

N=500	Predicted DR	Predicted Non-DR
Actual DR	315	30
Actual non-DR	25	130

Figure 17.9 shows the sample results based on the obtained probabilities after matching the entitled image samples with database samples and detect the DR having symptoms and non-DR as non-symptom image samples. In any of the case, the detection is not appropriate, it was considered to be misclassified sample or error. In addition to this, the confusion matrix shown in Table 17.2, signifies the obtained accuracy is 89% with other measures as sensitivity is 92.64% and specificity of 81.25%.

Label	Filename	predictions	probabilities
symptoms		nosymptoms	0.9835
nosymptoms		nosymptoms	0.7599
symptoms		nosymptoms	0.9737
nosymptoms		nosymptoms	0.9902
nosymptoms		nosymptoms	0.9723
nosymptoms		nosymptoms	0.9941
nosymptoms		nosymptoms	0.9836
nosymptoms		nosymptoms	0.9935
nosymptoms		nosymptoms	0.7949
nosymptoms		nosymptoms	0.7866

FIGURE 17.9
DR status report.

17.5 Conclusion

In this chapter, a cost-efficient CAD framework has been proposed for DR. The system model comprises computational model and elegant UI for handling two major issues. The first issue is based on efficient detects of DR and other is providing an easy interface to the end user. Out of the two, first achieved by the proposed computation network obtaining the results after data augmentation and remarkably manages the overfitting responses. The handling of overfitting is performed by the inculcation of the normalization layer with every response layer and obtained an accuracy of 89%. In addition to this, second issue requires better interface for entitled user. A client-server model is being developed for getting the information from the user and vice versa. Moreover, the other useful features induce in the framework are connecting the medical expert to the patient and rating them apparently on an interface. In addition to this, there is provision of crowdsourcing in concern of fund arrangements economically weaker category of patients.

References

Chakrabarty, N. (2018). A deep learning method for the detection of diabetic retinopathy. In *2018 5th IEEE Uttar Pradesh Section International Conference on Electrical, Electronics and Computer Engineering (UPCON)*, pp. 1–5. IEEE.

Colas, E., Besse, A., Orgogozo, A., Schmauch, B., Meric, N., and Besse, E. (2016). Deep learning approach for diabetic retinopathy screening. *Acta Ophthalmologica*, 94.

Doshi, D., Shenoy, A., Sidhpura, D., and Gharpure, P. (2016). Diabetic retinopathy detection using deep convolutional neural networks. In *2016 International Conference on Computing, Analytics and Security Trends (CAST)*, pp. 261–266. IEEE.

Dutta, S., Manideep, B., Basha, S. M., Caytiles, R. D., and Iyengar, N. (2018). Classification of diabetic retinopathy images by using deep learning models. *International Journal of Grid and Distributed Computing*, 11(1): 89–106.

Jitpakdee, P., Aimmanee, P., and Uyyanonvara, B. (2012). A survey on hemorrhage detection in diabetic retinopathy retinal images. In *2012 9th International Conference on Electrical Engineering/ Electronics, Computer, Telecommunications and Information Technology*, pp. 1–4. IEEE.

Jones, S. and Edwards, R. (2010). Diabetic retinopathy screening: a systematic review of the economic evidence. *Diabetic Medicine*, 27(3): 249–256.

Kahn, H. A. and Milton, R. C. (1980). Revised framingham eye study prevalence of glaucoma and diabetic retinopathy. *American Journal of Epidemiology*, 111(6): 769–776.

Khan, S. H., Abbas, Z., Rizvi, S. D., et al. (2019). Classification of diabetic retinopathy images based on customised cnn architecture. In *2019 Amity International Conference on Artificial Intelligence (AICAI)*, pp. 244–248. IEEE.

Mahendran, G. and Dhanasekaran, R. (2015). Investigation of the severity level of diabetic retinopathy using supervised classifier algorithms. *Computers & Electrical Engineering*, 45: 312–323.

Priya, R. and Aruna, P. (2013). Diagnosis of diabetic retinopathy using machine learning techniques. *ICTACT Journal on Soft Computing*, 3(4): 563–575.

Rahim, S. S., Palade, V., Shuttleworth, J., and Jayne, C. (2016). Automatic screening and classification of diabetic retinopathy and maculopathy using fuzzy image processing. *Brain Informatics*, 3(4): 249–267.

Raju, M., Pagidimarri, V., Barreto, R., Kadam, A., Kasivajjala, V., and Aswath, A. (2017). Development of a deep learning algorithm for automatic diagnosis of diabetic retinopathy. *MedInfo*, 245: 559–563.

Salamat, N., Missen, M. M. S., and Rashid, A. (2019). Diabetic retinopathy techniques in retinal images: A review. *Artificial Intelligence in Medicine*, 97: 168–188.

Sinthanayothin, C., Boyce, J. F., Williamson, T. H., Cook, H. L., Mensah, E., Lal, S., and Usher, D. (2002). Automated detection of diabetic retinopathy on digital fundus images. *Diabetic Medicine*, 19(2): 105–112.

Wan, S., Liang, Y., and Zhang, Y. (2018). Deep convolutional neural networks for diabetic retinopathy detection by image classification. *Computers & Electrical Engineering*, 72: 274–282.

Index

Printed and bound by CPI Group (UK) Ltd, Croydon, CR0 4YY

17/10/2024

01775700-0004